OUT OF THE DOLL'S HOUSE

Angela Holdsworth is a television journalist
and senior producer with the BBC. After working
for seven years in Current Affairs, she moved
to Documentary Features as a Producer on
Man Alive, and *All Our Working Lives*, and then
was Executive Producer of *Now the War Is
Over*. She conceived the BBC-2 series *Out of The
Doll's House* and has been Executive Producer
of the programmes. She is married to David
Neuberger, Q.C. and has three children.

Angela
Holdsworth

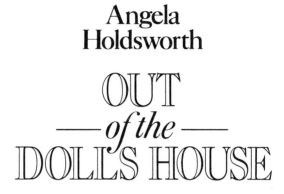

OUT
— *of the* —
DOLL'S HOUSE

The Story of Women in the
Twentieth Century

BBC BOOKS

For Jessica Neuberger

Published by BBC Books,
a division of BBC Enterprises Limited
Woodlands, 80 Wood Lane, London W12 0TT
First published 1988
Reprinted 1988 (three times)
Reprinted 1989 (four times)

ISBN 0 563 20631 4

Set in 10/12$\frac{1}{2}$ Photina
and printed and bound in Great Britain by Butler & Tanner Ltd
Frome and London
Jacket/cover printed by Fletchers of Norwich

Contents

Acknowledgments

I WOULD particularly like to thank all those who gave so much of their time to talk about their lives and so provided the basis for *Out of the Doll's House*. They are too many to mention here but without their memories the television series could not have been made and this book could not have been written. Many will find themselves quoted on the following pages; others, though not quoted, provided valuable background and research material.

I owe an enormous amount to the production team who conducted the interviews and worked with me on the television series over the last two years: producers Nikki Cheetham (who made three of the programmes), Olivia Lichtenstein and Deborah Perkin; Christine Whittaker who masterminded all the archive film; and our two assistants, Kate Macky and Sheila Johns. Their enthusiasm and hard work made this project the most rewarding I have worked on. Thank you also to those who joined us for part of the time to work on specific programmes: guest producers, Sally Doganis and Margaret Windham Heffernan; assistant producer, Betty McBride; researchers, Tracy Cook, Amanda Casson, Pennie Denton and Kerry Platman and to Mandy Temple, Louise Tillard, Kevin Hull and Catherine Colley.

The encouragement and support of Will Wyatt, Head of Documentary Features, has eased the making of the television series at every stage. I owe special thanks to Deborah Perkin for dreaming up the title, 'Out of the Doll's House', and for her help in compiling 'Milestones'. Sarah Colclough and Charlotte Gilbreath have in turn been excellent secretaries, Charlotte coping with the mounting frenzy in my office as both programmes and book approached their deadlines and still finding time to do much of the picture research. Thanks also to Peggy Bond for spending so many hours typing out transcripts of the interviews.

At BBC Books my editors, Susan Kennedy and Sarah Hoggett, have been unfailingly supportive and helpful throughout the writing of this book. Gill Shaw, the designer, has given careful thought to the appearance of the book and Paul Dowswell, the picture researcher, has enthusiastically contributed to the cartoons and pictures.

Outside the BBC, I am grateful to Angela Partington for her help and suggestions in the initial planning of the television series. Thank you, too, to Dr Carole Dyhouse of Sussex University, Lucy Bland of the North London Polytechnic, Dr Mary Evans of Kent University, Dr Penny Summerfield of Lancaster University, Dr Elizabeth Roberts of Lancaster University, David Doughan of the Fawcett Library, to Sue Sharpe and Mary Stott for their help with various of the programmes and particularly to Dr Jane Lewis of the London School of Economics for her advice and guidance both in the making of the series and the writing of this book. I am extremely grateful to Professor Harold Perkin and Joan Perkin for their careful reading of the manuscript and for all their thoughtful suggestions.

There seems to be no way of writing a book which does not intrude on family life. I owe my husband, David, and my children, Jessica, Nicholas and Max, a huge apology and also loving thanks to David for reading and correcting the manuscript and to the children for their eternal good humour and for not grumbling (well, not often) about the time this has taken up.

Foreword

'I WANT', said Bella Rokesmith, 'to be something so much worthier than the doll in the doll's house.' When Charles Dickens wrote those words in *Our Mutual Friend* in 1864, women had little chance of being anything else. As many manual and most professional jobs were closed to them, it was a struggle for single women to support themselves. All they could hope for was marriage to a good man and a lifetime of keeping his house and raising his children. Once married, women's property and income became their husband's by law. Circumstances forced them to depend on the goodwill of a father, husband or brother. Independence, a fulfilling career, even a decent job were not for them. Women were not allowed to vote, nor to stand for parliament, nor to hold any kind of public office. By necessity, their horizons were limited to their own private world at home.

Since that time, social and economic forces, combined with two world wars, have profoundly affected women's expectations and they have challenged the assumption that their proper place is in the home. Men, too, have seen their way of life change but the gradual transformation of the status of women has been one of the greatest social revolutions of modern times.

This book is based on the television series of the same name and looks at that uneven road to independence. The story of women this century is frequently one of frustration as they have had their hopes raised, only to have them dashed again and again. A concession won in one area has often been paid for by a setback in another. All of us researching the television series felt we owed a special debt to those pioneering women, often neglected by history, who continued undeterred by the strength of the opposition and whose work has eased the way for successive generations. Millicent Fawcett, Dorothea Beale, Marie Stopes, Eleanor Rathbone, to name only a few, stopped being simply names and took on a personality and importance of their own.

The circumstances of individual women varied enormously depending into which part of society they were born. The aristocracy made their own rules which were often different from the rest. Middle-class women progressed at a different rate and in different ways from working-class women. The span of living memory dictated we should start our story around the beginning of the century. Our research was drawn from the personal recollections of a wide variety of people, ranging in age from 18 to 102: from women bankers of today to munitions workers of yesterday; from 'anonymous' housewives in highrises to veterans of the suffragette movement. Midwives, models, maids, clippies, teachers, society hostesses and many others talked frankly about their lives. They tell touching tales of personal hardship, often seen as an inevitable part of 'the natural order of things'. There are those who reveal a bitter sense of frustration with what was seen as man's 'natural superiority' and those who happily accepted and enjoyed their 'proper role'. Together they provide a snapshot view of history, a picture of the past brought to life by reminiscences. Some we selected because they told the known history, others because their memories contributed something fresh. Some were found by targeting a specific town or village, some through their former or present work, some through schools, or health centres, or women's organisations. We interviewed 700 people, 255 of them on film, and a further 1250 wrote, describing their experiences.

The chapters of this book follow closely the themes of the television programmes. 'A Suitable Job for a Woman' shows how the nature and remuneration of women's work has traditionally been quite different from men's. As recently as the 1930s the scope for working women was limited to a narrow field of jobs and in most cases women were forced to leave work when they married. In wartime, however, or whenever the economy needed them, the old rules were relaxed and women undertook all sorts of work, undermining the argument that they were unsuitable or incapable of doing 'men's work'. In the second half of the century, automation has made muscle-power less important and brought new opportunities to women. Many have wanted to go out to work not just to help the family budget but because, better educated, less immersed in housework and with much smaller families than in the past, they felt unfulfilled at home. At the same time, as discussed in 'Mustn't Grumble', thanks to better health-care and an improved diet, women have become fitter and stronger. Arguably, the rapid spread of birth control this century has brought the most significant change of all, liberating women from years of childbearing and childrearing and removing a major obstacle to a full working life.

Women's clothes have reflected their newfound freedom. 'Mirror, Mirror' traces the sartorial revolution won by women, in the West at least, as they raised skirts above the ankle and even the knee, wore trousers when they pleased and defied the conformity of days gone by. Changes in fashion have, decade by decade, reflected the nuances of life: the impact of war and social change, snobbery and class consciousness, sexual modesty and permissiveness.

As women have got out and about more, their attitude to sex and marriage has also changed. In 'Thinking of England' women remember the days when couples had long courtships and sex was often looked on as duty as much as pleasure. They recall the influence of the two world wars which dislocated society and upset existing prejudices. Effective contraception and psychologists' theories about the dangers of repression have also contributed to a change in attitudes.

Women today play a fuller part in public life than ever before. 'Breaking Free' traces the battle women have fought for full citizenship. It took over fifty years and twenty-eight unsuccessful Bills from the first attempt to change the law until women over thirty were finally given the parliamentary vote in 1918, and a further ten years before that right was extended to all adult women. But many inequalities between the sexes remained and feminists continued their fight throughout the century. By 1975 most of the gates to a man's world had been opened. Yet women did not always take advantage of them. The new Women's Liberation Movement recognised that quite often women had only themselves to blame and they prescribed a radical programme of self-assertiveness. 'Just a Girl' shows that, for successive generations, the influences on girls growing up have tended to reinforce the idea that a woman's place is at home.

Traditional pulls are as strong as ever. Though families are smaller and take up much less time than in the past, motherhood still plays a dominant part in most women's lives. The changing fashions in mothering described in 'The Good Mother' explain the inadequacy many women have felt when bringing up their children. Motherhood has often stood in the way of women's jobs or careers as does the whole question of who manages the housekeeping. In 'Her Indoors' women recall the technical changes in housework over the last eighty years. Despite the improvement in household gadgets and the increased automation of housework, women still do a surprising amount at home while at the same time holding down jobs outside. The law no longer ties a woman to a man for life, but easier divorce has left many mothers bringing up their children alone.

Women have not entirely fought their way out of the doll's house. Certainly, they have opportunities undreamed of by their grandmothers. The variety of jobs open to them has never been wider. They can wear what they please. They can choose to limit the number of children they have. Most live longer and are physically fitter than ever before. Women can vote, run for parliament, they can even become Prime Minister, but home and family ties limit their freedom of choice to an extent few men would accept and there are still women who, like Bella Rokesmith, long for something more.

Milestones for Women

1839 The Infant Custody Act gave mothers the right of custody of their children under seven for the first time, but *only* if the Lord Chancellor agreed to it, and *only* if the mother was of good character.

1848 The Factory Act limited women's and children's working hours in textile mills to ten per day. (Women and children under 10 had been excluded from underground work by the 1842 Mines & Collieries Act.)

Queen's College for women was opened.

1849 Bedford College opened. Many of the pioneers of the Women's Movement attended both these colleges.

1857 The Matrimonial Causes Act allowed divorce through the law courts, instead of by the slow and expensive business of a Private Act of Parliament. The husband had only to prove his wife's adultery, but the wife had to prove her husband had committed not just adultery but also incest, bigamy, cruelty or desertion.

1866 The first Women's Suffrage Committee was formed by Barbara Bodichon.

1867 The first Parliamentary debate on Women's Suffrage was held. John Stuart Mill MP proposed an amendment to the Reform Bill, changing the word 'man' to 'person'. It failed, as did the first Woman's Suffrage Bill in 1870. Between 1870 and 1914 there were 28 unsuccessful Bills.

1869 The Municipal Franchise Act extended the vote to women rate-payers in local elections. The Bill passed into law with very little opposition.

1870 The Education Act allowed women not only to vote for the new School Boards, but also be elected to serve on them. Many pioneering feminists seized this first opportunity to do practical public work.

The first Married Women's Property Act, described by supporters of women's rights as a 'legislative abortion', was nonetheless the first recognition of a new principle: that married women should in certain circumstances own and control their own earnings, savings and legacies.

Girton College, the first women's college at Cambridge, opened but was not recognised by the University authorities.

1878 Women admitted to the University of London for the first time.

1881 Isle of Man granted the vote to women.

1882 The Second Married Women's Property Act embodied hitherto revolutionary principles: that married women should have the same rights over their property as unmarried women, and that husbands and wives should have separate interests in their property. Wives could also carry on trades and businesses using their property.

1886 The Married Women (Maintenance in Case of Desertion) Act enabled women to sue for maintenance without first going to the workhouse.

The Repeal of the Contagious Diseases Acts, which had allowed the forcible examination and imprisonment of any woman in an army garrison town or naval port thought to be a prostitute.

The Guardianship of Infants Act stipulated that the welfare of the child should be taken into consideration, thus undermining the father's assumed rights to custody of his children.

1894 New Zealand granted women the vote.

South Australia granted women the vote.

1897 The National Union of Women's Suffrage Societies, the first large national suffrage movement, was formed with Millicent Fawcett as President.

1903 The Women's Social and Political Union, the second national suffrage movement, was formed by the Pankhursts.

1905 First imprisonment of a suffragette (Christabel Pankhurst and Annie Kenney).

1906 A Suffrage Committee was formed by MPs.

1907 The Qualification of Women Act enabled women to stand for county and borough councils, and to be Chairman and Mayor. The first woman Mayor was Elizabeth Garrett Anderson, chosen by her home town Aldburgh in 1908.

1910 First woman chartered accountant and first woman banker.

1913 The first martyr in the suffrage cause, Emily Wilding Davidson, died after throwing herself under the King's horse in the Derby.

1918 The Representation of the People Act was passed before the end of the First World War. All men over 21 could vote, and for the first time, some women could vote. They had to be over 30, and a householder or the wife of a local government elector.

The Parliament (Qualification of Women) Act enabled women aged 21 and over to stand for Parliament. In December, seventeen women candidates stood in the post-war election. Only one, Constance Markiewicz, standing for Sinn Fein, was elected. She refused to take her seat in the British Parliament.

The Maternal and Child Welfare Act enabled local authorities to provide a wide range of services, including health visitors, infant welfare centres and day nurseries.

1919 The Sex Disqualification Removal Act made it unlawful to bar women from public office or civil or judicial posts.

Nancy Astor became the first woman MP to take her seat in the House of Commons.

1921 The first woman barrister – Helena Normanton.

1923 The Matrimonial Causes Act made the grounds for divorce the same for men as for women.

1925 The Widows, Orphans and Old Age Pensions Contributory Act introduced a 10-shilling weekly pension for widows.

The Guardianship of Infants Act finally gave fathers and mothers equal rights and claims over their children.

1928 The Equal Franchise Act ('Flappers' Vote') gave all women over 21 the vote.

1929 First woman Cabinet Minister – Margaret Bondfield.

1930 Welfare Centres allowed to give birth control advice to married women.

1937 The Matrimonial Causes Act extended grounds for divorce to cruelty, desertion and insanity.

1942 The TUC pledged itself to the principle of equal pay (first debated in 1888).

1943 Anne Loughlin became the first woman President of the TUC.

1945 The Family Allowance Act began a state system of child benefits to be paid directly to mothers, ending a 30-year campaign.

The first woman prison governor – Charity Taylor.

1946 The first woman British diplomat – Monica Milne.

1947 The University of Cambridge finally agreed to award full degrees to women – the last university to do so.

1948 The National Health Service began. Previously free health care had only been available to insured workers. Most women, therefore, were excluded.

1949 The first women KCs (English Bar) – Helena Normanton and Rose Heilbron.

1955 Equal pay agreed for teachers, civil servants and local government officers.

1958 Life peerages were created for men and women. Four women baronesses were created – Barbara Wootton, Stella, Marchioness of Reading, Dame Katherine Elliott and Baroness Ravensdale. Hereditary peeresses were not allowed to take their seats until 1963.

The first woman bank manager – Hilda Harding.

1962 The first woman ambassador – Dame Barbara Salt (Israel).

1964 The Married Women's Property Act enabled a divorced wife to keep half of anything she had saved from any allowance given by her husband.

1965 The first woman High Court judge – Dame Elizabeth Lane.

1967 The Abortion Act made abortion far easier as, in addition to medical reasons, social grounds were allowed.

The Matrimonial Homes Act gave both husband and wife the right of occupation of their home. Neither could be evicted during the marriage, except by a court order.

1969 The Divorce Reform Act (implemented in 1971) broadened grounds for divorce. Petitioners had to prove their marriage had irretrievably broken down.

1970 The Equal Pay Act stipulated that equal pay for men and women doing the same job had to be brought in within five years.

1973 Women were allowed to join the Stock Exchange.

1974 Contraceptives free for all women on the NHS.

1975 The first woman leader of a political party in Britain – Margaret Thatcher.

The Sex Discrimination Act banned sex discrimination in employment, education and advertising and set up the Equal Opportunities Commission to see that the new Act was observed.

The Employment Protection Act made it unlawful to dismiss a woman because she was pregnant and established the right to maternity leave and some maternity pay, as well as the right to return to her job within 29 weeks of giving birth.

1976 The Domestic Violence Act attempted to increase the Courts' protection of battered wives and gave police powers of arrest for breaching an injunction in cases of domestic violence.

1979 The first woman Prime Minister in Britain – Margaret Thatcher.

1981 The first woman Leader of the House of Lords – Baroness Young.

1983 The first woman Lord Mayor of London – Mary Donaldson.

1984 The Equal Value Amendment to the Equal Pay Act allowed women to claim equal pay to men doing similar, but different jobs if they were considered to be of equal value.

1987 Forty-one women MPs, the highest number ever, but still only 6% of the total.

CHAPTER ONE

Her Indoors
Women at Home

THERE is no argument about a woman's place in Easington, County Durham. Women belong where they have always belonged – indoors, seeing to the house and looking after the children. The profound social changes and upheavals of the last seventy-five years have barely touched the village. It is still dominated by the pithead, and a thick grey cloud hangs as ever over rows of identical Edwardian terraced houses, built by the coal company when the mine was first sunk. From each chimney a spiral of smoke billows upwards to join the cloud overhead. The smell of coal is everywhere.

Frances Graham has known little else: the hooter piercing through the village announcing the pit was working, the front steps that had to be cleaner than her neighbour's, the men returning from their different shifts demanding hot dinners at all hours. Her grandfather, father, husband, son and grandson have all been miners. Born in 1902, most of Frances's life has revolved around keeping her two-up and two-down in mint condition for her men. 'I've been a fool all me life. I've done all meself. If a woman's strong, she should do the housework. That's my way. I wouldn't let my husband do that, not when he's come from a pit, 'cos they're tired. They're worn out.' She has seldom needed to go beyond her own backyard: her children did the shopping while she cooked and cleaned and her men did not take her down to the pub with them. Holidays are rare and she has never been abroad. For all that she is content and proud of her achievements: sixty-three years of marriage, six children and eleven grandchildren.

There are two separate worlds in Easington – the men's, governed by pit and pub, and the women's, ruled by home and family. For generations it has been the custom for women to stay indoors, looking after their households while men go out to work. The historical and biological reasons which kept women protected from the rough and tumble of working life, producing and rearing large families, were idealised in the late eighteenth century. Women were thought to be the key to a better, more moral life. They had a vital role to play rearing the next generation and, to do it properly, they had to be protected from the polluting influences of the real world. In Victorian times, women were 'angels in the house', whose existence was defined only in relation to their men; central to family life but hidden from public view, looking after husbands, parents, children. They were 'doll's house women' – protected, idealised but confined.

At the turn of the century, when our story begins, this tradition was well established. Married working-class woman were inescapably tied to their homes by large families and the endless grind of domestic chores. Apart from areas where there was a tradition of married women working (for instance, in the cotton mills of the north-west), the small number who had to do paid work were pitied. Middle-class women, supervising staff and children, behind their Nottingham lace curtains, were equally entrenched. Their households varied in size from a general servant or skivvy at one extreme to a full set of butler, cook, nanny, lady's maid, kitchen maid and 'tweenie', at the other. An outing involved visiting a friend or relation. Household shopping was done in the privacy of their own home with local tradesmen calling to find out what deliveries were needed. They were born at home, married from home, nursed at home and died at home.

Myrtle Lane was born in 1899 into a family 'of comfortable means'. She lived with her parents and their three other children in a ten-bedroom house in Suffolk with five live-in servants and the 'outside lot' – two gardeners and a coachman. The maids worked non-stop from dawn until 8 p.m. and one remained on duty in case anyone from the family needed a hot drink later on. The family ate their way through three vast meals a day and still found room for scones with tea. Myrtle's mother was an early riser, banging on her ceiling at 6.15 if she could not hear the maids moving

Above: Pre-war advertisements show how much servants were an integral part of domestic life.
Below: The local fête, run by Myrtle Lane's mother (centre). She considered the whole village an extended part of her household.

in the rooms above her. Although she did no housework herself, she was constantly checking that the maids were doing their job properly. Her sense of responsibility extended beyond her own home to the whole village where she inspected the villagers' houses most afternoons.

The number of families who lived in such a grand manner in the early years of this century is probably exaggerated. Houses with one servant were far more common and the amount of work needed to keep the place clean and tend to the children was considerable, especially if one wanted to keep the same standards as neighbours with a bevy of servants. A country parson's wife had the worst of all worlds: the irritating example up the road of a household run perfectly by the richer squire's wife, with more servants, plus the burden of unpaid work in her husband's parish and a rambling house to manage on a shoestring. Frank Dash was born into such a family in 1900. He worshipped his mother who worked ceaselessly, without any apparent bitterness. Her tombstone, she told Frank, should have the following poem from Arnold Silcock's *Verse or Worse*:

Here lies a poor woman who always was tired.
She lived in a house where help was not hired.
Her last words on earth were, 'Dear friends, I am going
Where washing ain't done, nor sweeping, nor sewing
But everything there is exact to my wishes,
For where they don't eat there's no washing of dishes.
I will be where loud anthems will always be ringing
But having no voice I'll be clear of the singing.
Don't mourn for me now, don't mourn for me never.
I'm going to do nothing for ever and ever.'

The archfiend in Mrs Dash's life was Mr Dash, the vicar himself. King of his Castle, he had the best of everything: beautiful books, expensive delicacies to eat and the nicest room in the house as a study. 'Mother was in the back room – which was dark and dismal – preparing the cakes and so on, while father was enjoying himself in his study.' When the Reverend Dash saw his wife and children eating, he accused them of 'stuffing again'. Fathers frequently used their position as head of the household to hog the best food, aided and abetted by their wives who believed it their duty to see their husband well fed.

That was the nub of the problem. Father was, after all, the breadwinner and it was vital he kept fit for work. In poorer families he automatically had the pick of the best food. Edith Edwards's father, a shipyard worker in West Hartlepool, expected his wife to raise his children, to wash his clothes, to clean his house and to fetch his food *and* be grateful for the privilege. Woe betide her if he thought she had slipped up. After ten pints of beer (his daily dose) he did not always see things too clearly. One day Edith remembers he came in and, looking at his dinner, 'he said, "You haven't used all the meat; what about the other?" There was no other, he'd got the lot and he picked up the plate and let it fly at the back of the stove and mother never said a word. She cleared it all up and went to bed.' Edith's mother never went out although her husband was down at the pub every night. She never had a holiday and never complained about her lot. If she had reproached her husband she might have felt 'a touch of the old leather'. If she had left home she would have had nowhere to go, nothing to live on and no right to her children or house.

Until recent times, it was extremely difficult and rare for a woman to divorce her husband and, however bad his behaviour, her own reputation would be ruined if she did so. The law was unjust. A man could divorce his wife for adultery but she could not divorce him, however unfaithful he was, unless he committed an additional matrimonial offence such as incest or cruelty which were extremely difficult to prove. In families like Edith's, divorce was unheard of. Judicial separation would have been the best her mother could have hoped for, with little chance of forcing an unwilling husband to pay maintenance.

The legal view was that women were not merely dependent on their husbands, but had no separate legal identity of their own. In the eighteenth century, Sir William Blackstone had written in his *Commentaries on the Laws of England*, 'By marriage, the very being or legal existence of woman is suspended, or at least it is incorporated and consolidated into that of the husband, under whose wing protection and cover she performs everything, and she is therefore called in our law a feme-covert.'

It was not until the late nineteenth century that reformers began to challenge this view; and even then it proved slow progress unravelling and changing the laws and customs which left women with the legal status of children. For generations it had been accepted that men were superior to women mentally, physically and morally. Responsibility of any sort was thought to be more than women could cope with. They were expected to obey their men and, if they did not, an occasional beating did not seem unreasonable. It was not until 1878 that magistrates were given powers to grant separation orders to wives whose husbands were convicted of aggravated assault. Until 1882, a woman was not allowed to keep her own property after marriage. If her husband wished to sell all her possessions, they were his to do with as he pleased. And until 1891 he could in theory imprison his wife in her own home.

Feminists were becoming increasingly impatient. They were convinced that only when they had the parliamentary vote would they achieve true equality. In the years immediately before the First World War, their campaign intensified and grew militant. In London, Manchester and other big cities they hurled stones through windows, held angry meetings and did all they could to publicise their cause. But their calls for suffrage were scarcely heard in Easington where Frances Graham was growing up. What mattered there was that men held the purse strings. There was no work in mining villages for women, and Frances knew that, like her mother, she would have to marry to find someone to provide for her. Vote or no vote, she would have to earn her keep by doing the jobs indoors.

Frances was just twelve when war broke out in 1914, bringing change faster and more dramatically than anyone had imagined. The war had far more immediate impact on women at home than granting the vote would have a few years later and, for a while, the equilibrium between the sexes was thrown off balance. Many women gained their first taste of independence. They were forced to come out from behind their lace curtains to take over shops or small businesses vacated by their husbands who had left for the front or to work in munitions, drive trucks, dig fields and do many other jobs usually done by men. Some enrolled with the Voluntary Aid Detachments scheme as unregistered nurses, 'VADs'. Others joined the new Women's Institutes and preserved fruit, reared poultry and knitted for the war effort. It was not just that the war drew women away from their homes to do men's jobs but, with their husbands away, many women had control of the family purse for the first time. Wives of servicemen were paid a separation allowance of 12/6 per week and 2/- per child.

Above: The First World War forced many women out of the home and into the factory.

It was an important precedent. Feminists like Eleanor Rathbone were beginning to realise that the right to vote was not enough and that only through economic independence would women become equal partners in marriage or be in a position to leave a violent husband or stand up to one who squandered his pay packet on drink. In 1917 Eleanor Rathbone established the Family Endowment Council to lead a fight for family allowances. She called for a weekly payment of 12/6 for wives, plus 5/- for the first child and 3/6 for subsequent children to be paid direct to the wives, to ensure that the money went into the family purse and not to the local publican. Although her campaign did not bear fruit for nearly thirty years, it marked the beginning of a long battle to improve the financial position of women at home.

Middle-class women found their domestic lives in turmoil, too. Factory and munitions work lured their servants away. The pay was better, the hours shorter and their free time was their own. So women who had never dirtied their hands were forced to peer behind the green baize doors which had kept the world of servants separate from their own, and found they could not begin to keep their huge houses clean. Many who were abandoned by their staff at the first scent of warwork uprooted and moved to more manageable houses.

After the war, women were forced to give back their jobs to returning war heroes and go back to housework. They remained as much indoors as ever, and the sense of independence they had enjoyed during the war vanished as swiftly as it had come.

In Easington, things went on much as before. Frances Graham, setting up home with Jim in 1919, had as much cleaning, washing, baking and mending as her mother had ever had. Her house had no hot water tap, no bathroom and no electricity. Frances was well prepared for a lifetime of housework. Trained as a child in polishing and scrubbing, she could not relax until everything looked clean and tidy. 'I don't know what made us like this but when I was married, that day I swept the confetti out of the lobby meself.' All Frances's generation had been taught domestic skills at school, though their lessons added little to the thorough training they received at home. Usually, women rose at 6.30 and went to bed around 10.30, having spent about thirteen hours on their feet. Much of their work was exhausting: scrubbing floors, handwashing, carrying huge buckets of water for cooking and bathing. Some of it was repulsive, such as emptying and cleaning out chamber pots (commonly used until the 1950s to save nocturnal visits to a distant or outside lavatory) or soaking and washing sanitary towels.

In Easington, the housewife's main enemy was soot. An hour after an orgy of scrubbing and dusting, the surfaces were coated with a new deposit. Walls were distempered and re-papered annually (by the women) as they were black after a few months. In most cities bugs were a perpetual problem. In warm weather they invaded walls, bedding, upholstery; and all the scrubbing and disinfecting in the world would not budge them. All laundry was done by hand: clothes were first boiled, then thumped in a poss tub and laboriously mangled. One of the older miners remembers that at lunch-time the large pot for boiling water for clothes was taken from the range and replaced by another pot for cooking. The pudding was boiled below and potatoes and other vegetables steamed on top. Once lunch was over, the boiling tub was hauled back. Stooping, washing, lifting, wringing, hanging basketfuls of wet laundry was heavy work and made for a long day.

Most women had a weekly routine. Frances had what she called her easy day on Monday when she tidied up the house, sorted and soaked clothes for Tuesday's wash and did miscellaneous chores. 'I used to sew buttons and darn the pit stockings. On Sunday I did the same because I never got out. That was my best day, on the Sunday, getting the pit clothes out and patching them 'fore they started on the Monday and bits of jobs like that. Now Tuesday I washed. Ironed on the Wednesday because we had the lines up in the house them days and we had to wait till they dried, y'know. I'd do all me rooms through on Wednesday and Thursday. Friday was my baking day.' Cleaning the windows and any other outdoor jobs were usually done on Saturday.

If you consider housework as a job, and a skilled one too, these routines are not surprising. Women were not organised and regulated as they would be in a paid job so they devised their own rules and systems. It was also a question of pride. Doing housework to their own high standards and earning their husband's, neighbour's or even mother-in-law's approval was the only reward they could hope for.

Nobody in Easington had any mechanical slaves. Labour-saving gadgets developed only slowly in Britain between the wars, although Cecil Booth had invented a vacuum cleaning machine as early as 1901. Within a few years his company provided a cleaning service for the fashionable houses of London but had not spread much further. His large machines had to be parked outside a house and a team of uniformed men dragged hoses in through the windows to extract the dust. Portable vacuums were developed by Hoover before the First World War but did not become commonplace in Britain for another fifty years. In the 1920s, some middle-class homes ran to an electric washer. These were nothing like today's automatics but they saved women the chore of rubbing and wringing and were certainly kinder on the hands than washboards.

The slow development of household technology was partly because not many houses had electricity (only a third in 1930) but was also a consequence of women's lack of economic power. Housewives could not afford to buy a Hoover or an electric washer themselves. Many remember angrily that their husbands did not see the point of investing in a machine to do their wives' work for them. One housewife remembers the Hoover salesman calling with offers of a vacuum on 'the never-never'. But he needed her husband's signature on the hire purchase form. Her husband disapproved of such new-fangled contraptions. So she had to do without.

Life for middle and upper-class women, too, changed surprisingly little after the war. Despite the continuing trend to move to smaller, easier-to-run houses, with fewer servants than in the pre-war years, their world remained centred around the home. Rising unemployment forced some men and women back into domestic service. Diana McClure, born in 1914, never had to run a bath herself in her first sixteen years. She lived with her parents in a large London flat run by a parlour maid, housemaid, cook, under housemaid and occasionally a tweenie. 'My mother's routine was that the cook would come and see her in the morning and see what was happening: who was going to be in for lunch, what was happening in the evening and that was more or less that as far as my mother was concerned. Cook would do the ordering and the shopping and everything like that and my mother would get dressed and have her day,' consisting of a social round of bridge and golf with some charity work, which was usually fund-raising by arranging balls.

Women were encouraged to forget any new ideas they had entertained during the war about their place in the world. Women's magazines frowned on a professional life. They created their own idea of a successful woman. Quintessentially feminine, she busied herself around the house far more than her mother ever did. She dabbled in a little creative cooking, dainty

Above: Vacuum cleaner, 1910. Domestic technology developed slowly even after the war.

sewing, intelligent mothering and above all she ran a beautiful home.

Diana McClure, setting up her own establishment in the thirties, had servants to cater for nearly every whim. But her generation did not take their staff for granted and she was less of a *grande dame* than her mother. She lay awake at night rehearsing speeches before ticking off a servant. Unlike her mother, 'I didn't have cook into the bedroom, I used to go and see her in the mornings and we'd discuss things and then I would go and do my own shopping. I was very bad at it at first and didn't know what sort of joints to order. It was becoming much more the norm for people to do more than, certainly, my mother did.' The cult of housewifery was well aimed at the upper middle classes who were uncertain of their role in the new order. They were no longer presiding over large houses, a team of servants and a clutch of children like their grandmothers had been, yet many of them had domestic help and time lay heavily on their hands. Winifred Holtby in her book *Women, and a Changing Civilisation*, published in 1934, talked of women doing twice what was needed because of 'an unacknowledged fear lest, robbed of domestic work, they should find no real function in life.' For this reason she blamed women themselves for retarding the development of labour-saving gadgets. By 1939 two houses in three were wired for electricity and 68 per cent had electric or gas cookers. However, only 10 per cent had vacuum cleaners and fewer still had electric washers.

Above: A bridge tournament helps fill the day for ladies of leisure in 1922.

Most new houses built in the 1930s had bathrooms, indoor lavatories and running hot water, but a brand new house in the suburbs created a different kind of problem. Wives felt cut off during the day and missed the bustle and companionship of the town. Women who had had interesting professional jobs before marriage found it particularly hard to adjust to being a housewife. An ex-nurse explained, 'I resented it. There was something I couldn't put my finger on. I think I felt I'd lost my independence. But running a house was a pleasure. It's not boring unless you let it be. It's a grown-up version of a doll's house.' In nearly every professional job, and many manual ones, women were forced to resign when they married. Margaret Wheeler had to give up a good job in the Audit Department of Boots, Nottingham, when she married in 1933. Worse still, her husband's job necessitated a move to the country, miles from her family and friends. 'I was like most girls, I wanted to have a home, a husband, a family and I didn't realise what it was going to mean to be so isolated after I was first married. After being in a busy town, a big family, having lots of access to theatres and cinemas and art galleries and so on, I was sort of tucked away in the country not knowing anybody, isolated with not very much money, having to manage on housekeeping money instead of having my own money which I'd earned.'

An article in *The Lancet* in 1938 identified a new brand of female neurotic, 'Mrs Everyman is 28 or 30 years old. She and her dress are clean, but there is a slovenly look about it. She has given up the permanent wave she was proud of when she was engaged. Her clothes, always respectable and never as smart as those young ladies who work in the biscuit factory, are, like her furniture, getting a bit shabby. She is pale but not anaemic ...' The suggested cure for what was branded as 'surburban neurosis' was to give women new skills and interests but still keep them as homemakers. Dressmaking, keep-fit classes, involvement in the local nursery and canteen, or even a new baby, were all put forward as possible solutions. The diagnosis that many women needed an identity beyond family life was not articulated for another twenty-five years when its blinding obviousness swept another generation of women to militancy.

In the 1930s women were expected to be content at home. Apart from a trip to the shops or the cinema, there was little escape from domestic routine. Even then, Margaret Wheeler depended on her husband to take her everywhere. Diana McClure and a girlfriend made an ignominious exit from the Café Royal after the headwaiter explained he did not serve ladies on their own. Apparently women posed a threat in public places at night as it was assumed they were prostitutes unless they were escorted by a man. After all, what conceivable reason was there for a respectable lady to be away from home by herself in the evening?

The greatest constraint, as ever, was money. A trip to a matinée would have to be accounted for and explained to an often disapproving husband

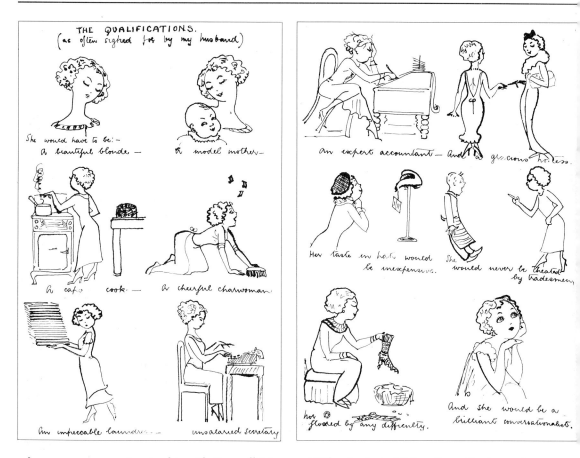

Above: The duties of a perfect wife, drawn by Margaret Wheeler in 1935.

who saw no reason to give his wife time off. Margaret Wheeler hated this dependence on her husband. All her circle were in the same position, banned from taking a job and obliged to beg handouts from their husbands, and not just for treats. She found a friend in tears one day: 'She'd had to ask her husband for sixpence for a packet of sanitary towels and she said she felt very humiliated and he'd ticked her off before because she'd spent all her 25 bob but she needed twopence ha'penny for a small white loaf.' Most women had to write everything they spent in an accounts book and submit it to their husbands. Even if they saved from their housekeeping, any money left over belonged to their husbands by law.

Most wives were given a weekly fixed sum for food and necessities and had no idea what their husbands earned. In Easington, the miners devised a way of syphoning some of their paypackets for themselves. Frances used to hear the men discussing it in hushed voices outside her door and suspected her husband was being less than frank about his earnings. 'They used to draw a combined wage for the team of men who were working. One man would draw the wage and distribute it round his workmates, but he knew how much he had to keep back for each individual one, y'see.

That's why it was called "keepyback".' The women did not mind except when the family had to do without meat and gravy for a week but, as Margaret Wheeler found, there was little they could do about it. 'You were not able to take a job if you were a married women, for a start. Then once you were married you were expected to get on with it and you had nowhere to go, no money and there was very heavy social pressure against leaving your husband.' If the house was in her husband's name, a woman had no share in it if she walked out. Starting a new life without his help was almost impossible. Margaret left her husband once, but, finding herself already pregnant, she soon went back. After that she began saving in secret. All she wanted was a nestegg of her own but she found that, as her husband would have to pay income tax on the interest, she was cheating the Inland Revenue, and so she confessed.

Above: Charles and Margaret Wheeler.

In the period between the wars, the position of married women remained one of almost total dependence. However, the legislative changes sought by feminists continued to bring gradual improvements. From 1923 a women was allowed to divorce a man for adultery alone, redressing the unjust system whereby adultery was acceptable for a man but not a woman. From 1925 a father was no longer considered the sole guardian of his children. In 1937 the divorce laws were broadened again. For the first time, cruelty and wilful desertion by the husband became grounds for divorce on their own. (Before that, a wife had to establish adultery as well.) Incurable insanity became a ground for divorce for the first time. The passing of the Act brought a record number of divorces – to 1.6 per cent of marriages (compared with over 30 per cent today).

The Second World War was far more of a turning-point for married women than the First. Margaret Wheeler, like many others, had her life knocked upside down but with an unexpectedly liberating effect. 'My husband went to India and I was left with five children including an evacuee and a four-week-old baby. I found that all the things that he used to do, I had to do. I had to take over and pay the bills; look after the rates and the rent and the gas and electricity bills; do the shopping and attend to all sorts of things that he'd done for me previously *and* manage the money. I had a sort of independence of action there, except, of course, taking five kids with you doesn't leave you very independent. But I was my own woman and could do, within those limits, what I wanted to do.'

Married women learned to be more assertive. The marriage bar, which had previously stopped married women from working, quietly disappeared once their labour was required for the war effort. So acute was the shortage of manpower that married women went out to work in unprecedented numbers. Once again, women did the jobs vacated by servicemen and took on civic responsibilities such as fire watching or driving ambulances. One million enrolled with the Women's Voluntary Service, which stepped in where local authorities were ill prepared, sorting out homes for bombed-out people, providing food for old people, running mobile canteens. Others joined the armed forces. It would be misleading to suggest that everyone enjoyed their independence. What with bombing and rationing, some thought they had as bad or worse a time of it at home as their husbands serving overseas. Families were broken up, not just by losing a husband to the front but by having children evacuated to the country or a bomb shattering their home.

Shortages of food, furniture, material and, above all, houses dogged housewives for long after the war. The nation yearned for a return to normal and normal meant family life: Mother at home with the children, Father at work. But for many this dream was suspended for a few years. Family life as often as not was a room with the mother-in-law. Eddie Reding lived with her mother until her elder child was four and a half. It was hardly the married life she had looked forward to. Like many others up and down the country, all she really wanted was a home of her own and when she finally had it, she was utterly content, 'I would never come out unless I was washed up and beds made and things like that. I'd be thinking about it all the time I was out, you know. I'd be thinking about the mess indoors, in case we had burglars, I suppose, leave it all nice for 'em!'

For many of the generation who married during or just after the war, the adventure into the world outside, the experience of a different, more independent way of living, receded into a distant memory. They settled happily into the new housing estates which sprang up in the postwar years and enjoyed security and prosperity when it came. Eddie has never paid a bill in her life and her husband, Fred, would not want her to. 'Fred calls me "Her Indoors" when he's talking about me. He means it nicely, you know.' Eddie is not in the least bit resentful of her dependence on the generous Fred. She is one of the lucky ones who has always got what she wanted.

According to Sir William Beveridge's Report, which laid down the frame-work for the Welfare State, happy homemakers were exactly what the country needed after the war.

Taken as a whole, the plan for Social Security puts a premium on marriage in place of penalizing it.... In the next thirty years housewives as mothers have vital work to do in ensuring the adequate continuance of the British race and of British ideals in the world.

The government endorsed Beveridge's view, and in 1946 family allow-ances were at last paid directly to women. (Though at five shillings for each child except the first, this was less, allowing for inflation, than Eleanor Rathbone had demanded in 1917.)

Domestic bliss continued to be the ideal for long after the war, with young girls rushing into marriage earlier than ever. The average bride was twenty-two, two years younger than she would have been before the war. In 1954 Frances Graham's son, John, married Mary, daughter of another Easington miner. Born in 1933, thirty-one years after her mother-in-law, their childhood memories are remarkably similar. Mary started scrubbing floors for her mother when she was three and as a child was expected to do many domestic chores. She grew up knowing nothing of the world outside Easington and had her first train-ride at twenty-one. Her domestic routine was almost identical to her mother-in-law's but with an important difference. Miners' wives were allowed to collect the weekly pay packet so there was no chance of John having any 'keepyback'.

A survey of a coal community in 1956, 'Coal is Our Life: An Analysis of a Yorkshire Mining Community', showed how little life had changed in mining villages since the turn of the century. Men's activities were in the outside world, women's were indoors providing 'a haven for a tired man when he returns from work; here he expects to find a meal prepared, a room clean and tidy, a seat comfortable and warm, and a wife ready to give him what he wants'. No short cuts were allowed. A bought meal like fish and chips, not prepared by her own fair hand, might be thrown on the fire. Anything beyond the normal household budget had to be agreed by her husband. While it was acceptable for him to have a night out with the boys, she was expected to stay in unless he felt like taking her out.

Yet some things were changing. When she first married, Mary was still using the same cleaning utensils that had been used by generations of

Above: The rapid spread of domestic gadgets in the 1950s did little to change attitudes about who did what around the house.

Easington housewives. By the late 1950s she had her own washing machine and used the latest detergents. In large towns up and down the country, Clean Air Acts reduced the amount of household grime by banning the burning of anything but smokeless fuel. Household technology was on the march. Television advertisements showed sponge mops, paper towels, plastic buckets and a wonderful new material called Crimplene that did not need ironing. Mary acquired a Hoover and got through her housework much faster. They were living through a time of growing prosperity and husbands could afford machines to liberate their wives from housework.

Women like Mary were now freer to fit in a part-time job, and the booming economy needed all the workers it could get. By the time Mary's children were at school, she was working full-time – but she still had to cope with the family and the house. 'I used to be up at 6.30, to get Alan and Anne-Marie ready for school. I used to take them to mother's and start work at 7.30 and when I came in on a night, I used to start straight away before anything with the dinner and I used to do all me housework, washing, if it was washing night. I used to do a little bit each night.'

Although the number of married women with jobs steadily increased during the fifties, they were still a minority. It was far more respectable to stay at home. 'My husband can afford to keep me,' a married doctor, continuing her own job, remembers a schoolfriend boasting. A romantic vision of marriage was spread by the fairytale wedding of Grace Kelly to the Prince of Monaco in 1955. It symbolised the height of feminine ambition in the fifties. To be a famous and beautiful film star and sacrifice that career to marry the Prince of your dreams was everything that a young girl dreamed of. At the age of eight, I remember thinking Grace Kelly was the luckiest woman alive.

Carole Steyne was married in 1958. Her wedding day was supposed to be the happiest day of her life. 'The white wedding was at the end of it all and that was it. You never looked beyond the wedding. I mean it was like the fairytale story, the Princess rode away on the white charger with the Prince.' Once Carole married she found living happily ever after was hard work. 'Your home had to look absolutely scrubbed and clean and wonderful. Your children, your pram, your own appearance, every hair was sort of ironed and manicured into order because the content wasn't important. It was only the appearance. So a woman wasn't supposed to have an opinion of her own. She wasn't allowed to. I mean if you had one, you'd better keep quiet about it. So everything was "Ideal Home". Whatever it was had to look nice. Everything was starched and ironed and the children had pure silk rompers. It wasn't all babycare and put into the machine. It was smocking and everything took ages to wash and iron.'

Young middle-class wives found the main problem was keeping up the standards of the previous generation without the advantage of even one general maid. As one housewife recalled, magazines and radio tried to fill the gap: 'Woman's Hour in those days was very different from what it is now. We used to be bombarded with household hints and recipes and how to do this and how to do that and we were always being sort of lectured. Housewives were always being told they must not become cabbages and bore their husbands either.'

The problem with preventing thinking, educated women from becoming frustrated at home was more acute in America where a higher percentage of girls went to college and then abandoned careers for marriage. In The Feminine Mystique (1963) Betty Friedan maintained that American business interests manipulated women through advertisements into cherishing their homes by encouraging them to clean, decorate and, above all, to buy for them. As early as 1945, market researchers recognised the possibility of a drift away from the home as automation not only made housework easier but also enabled women to do many jobs which had traditionally required a bit of masculine muscle. Besides, in a technical era, brains were needed and it did not make sense to educate half the population and then have them drop out of production once they married.

Perhaps this was the moment housework could have been professionalised with domestic cleaning agencies, laundry chains, improved take-away food services and properly staffed nurseries stepping in to liberate the housewife. Instead advertisers gave her a new image: 'The Balanced Homemaker'. This paragon took pride in doing all the housework herself the modern way, using the latest equipment, polishes and cleaning agents.

Wives fell into experimenting with different soap powders, trying a new polish, changing the washing-up bowl for a more exciting colour, saving for a new washing machine. It must rate as one of the more successful advertising campaigns this century.

In Britain the first generation to enjoy household technology *en masse* was also the first to have gone through full secondary education *en masse*. Like Carole Steyne, these women felt they had good brains going to rust. 'After a few years it was totally stultifying. I had the feeling, is this it? It was called "the problem which has no name". It was just unbelievably boring that one was having to spend the rest of one's life polishing the floor and the furniture.' ('The problem which has no name' had first been identified by Betty Friedan to explain the growing malaise among American housewives.)

Farsighted market researchers had already anticipated this. The solution, as they saw it, was to put skill back into housework. In the sixties, the modern housewife was encouraged to become a DIY expert. Her creativity was challenged by cookbooks sporting photos of mouthwatering dishes which took hours to prepare. Even washing machines were designed to provide more work than simple button pushing. Whites had to be treated one way, synthetics another, woollens entirely differently again. As washing was apparently easier, more clothes were thrown in the linen basket each day. Clothes that were slightly grubby couldn't be worn a second day. Sewing and gardening were promoted in women's magazines, department stores created 'bargains' to make shopping exciting. The housewife's days were filled. In an almost servantless world she was now gardener, cook, nanny, housekeeper and cleaner.

Yet there was something missing; perhaps it was the cut and thrust of professional life, or the office gossip or simply the fellowship of like-minded women who did not talk about their children teething or how long they had waited for the gas man to call. Maureen Nicol's sense of isolation intensified in 1960 when she moved to Cheshire with a small baby and a toddler. She knew no one and her husband was out at work all day. Reading *The Guardian* one day, she saw an article about dreary stay-at-home wives by Betty Jerman.

I blame the women: they stay home all day, they set the tone. Many look back with regret to the days when they worked in an office. Their work kept them alert. Home and childminding can have a blunting effect on a woman's mind. But only she can sharpen it.
The Guardian

Recognising herself, Maureen wrote suggesting interested women should band together to form a National Register. 'To my amazement I had several hundred letters and it was fairly obvious that the people who wrote wanted me to do something about it ... in fact to the stage where the postman staggered up the path and pushed letters through the door and the letterbox fell off.' Altogether, over two thousand women responded to Maureen's call. The National Housewives' Register was formed, publishing its own newsletter. Women used the Register to find other members who lived locally. Maureen made contact with half a dozen women within walking distance and from then on they babysat for each other, 'organised projects, painting, discussing, reading and getting much more out of life'. The Register grew until, in the 1970s, it topped 25 000 members. Today Maureen identifies her generation as the first in which a significant number failed to find fulfilment in home and family. 'We were reasonably well

"Here's a laugh, dear—'Provided his home is well run the average man is unaware if his wife is in or not.'"

educated. We'd all had reasonably satisfying jobs. We never ever considered – looking back, it's extraordinary how my daughter's generation
is so different – leaving the children and going back to work until they
were at school at least. But we needed more stimulation. We needed to
talk about things. There are so many more things in the world than just
in the confines of a home.'

In the early 1960s, these cries of discontent came mainly from graduate
wives but they were soon joined by another group who challenged the
conventional pattern of married life. Girls were increasingly sharing digs
or flats, wanting to get away from their parents or to live nearer work. In
the past there had been no staging post between their parents' home and
their husband's. Flat life showed an alternative way of doing things, where
shopping and domestic chores were shared. Diana McClure's daughter,
Liz, left a happy flat where everyone muddled in for a disciplinarian
husband who expected all the old-fashioned standards with no servants
and no input from him. The children were entirely Liz's responsibility, the
house had to look pristine, his suits be pressed immaculately and formal
dinner parties held on the dot of 8. Liz's anger at her husband's 'male
chauvinistic pig' attitudes finally erupted and contributed to the break-up
of her marriage.

A housewife admitted to us that she actually invented extra housework
partly to fill her days and partly because it was the only way she could
attract praise from her husband. 'I was the children's mother and I was
Gordon's wife,' she recalled bitterly. 'I mean that was how I was referred
to, you know, "the wife" or "Peter's Mam" or "Andrea's Mam" not
Olwyn.' 'Get out, find a job and a new dimension,' shouted the new
feminists: a more ambitious therapy than for suburban neurosis in the
1930s. Carole Steyne nervously asked her husband's permission to return
to college for a refresher course in sculpting. '*You* a sculptor,' he laughed.
'You're much too untidy.' When a few years later she told him she had
been offered her first exhibition, he just said, 'Hmph'. Carole left him.

In the 1970s it became increasingly common for married women to
work until, today, nearly two-thirds have some kind of paid work. Women
were needed in the expanding sectors of the economy such as the light
electrical and service industries, and they enjoyed the independence their
earning power brought. They were less dependent on their husbands
than they had ever been and demarcations within marriage were fading.
Legislation banished some of the old inequalities within marriage. The
1964 Married Women's Property Act allowed women to keep half the
money they saved from their housekeeping allowance and the 1967 Matrimonial Homes Act gave similar rights of occupation of the family home to
both husband and wife. After 1970 a wife's contribution to the upkeep of
the house and welfare of the family had to be taken into account when
dividing up the family assets. A woman no longer lost everything if she

left an unhappy marriage. Married couples could choose for a wife's earnings to be taxed separately and not added to her husband's.

However, despite their new jobs, many found it hard to abandon the domestic habits of a lifetime. They thought they should impress on all fronts, running a perfect job as well as a perfect house and rearing perfect children. Egged on by their husbands, angels in the house turned into superwomen. There are always a few efficient (usually rich) women who successfully juggle a variety of roles, but the pressures of pleasing everyone are daunting. As feminists pointed out, they were even more exploited than their mothers, taking on masculine responsibilities without shedding any feminine ones. What women should have been doing was challenging the whole structure of family life. Alluring clothes, cooking, cleaning, even mothering were branded as symbols of bondage. In a dual-earning family, why should the wife do all the domestic work? Marriages were put under a new strain. As one feminist put it, 'I was determined not to give an inch. I was not going to mend his socks or anything like that. So everything was this sort of fiercely fought battle which created so much tension that after a while it ate into the relationship.'

It was now much easier to get a divorce. After 1971 if the Court accepted that a marriage had irretrievably broken down, that was enough. As divorce became more common the number of single parents of both sexes rose, further undermining rigid gender demarcations at home. Eric Clark's wife walked out in 1971 leaving him with five children. He was astonished at how much work was involved and how little he knew about it. House-wifery, it seemed, was an acquired skill and he had no one to teach him. A neighbour came in to show him how to make pastry but her husband put a stop to her visits. 'There were mounting problems: how do you iron a dress properly? How do you iron nylon or cotton, you know, it's all different, which I didn't know.' He had to give up his job and manage on £12 a week social security. He did not know much about cooking and was terrified something might happen to one of his children when he was asleep. As a woman would understand only too well, he felt on duty twenty-four hours a day. When the social worker visited, he hid the washing and ironing because he was afraid he had not done them properly. He reckoned he deserved a wage for the hard work he was putting in. Luckily for Eric, he met Jan and gratefully let her take over his washing and ironing and eventually all the housework. Though Eric insists he gives her a hand, Jan just smiles, 'I don't like a man fussing around me. I'd hate to come home from work and see him doing the ironing or the washing machine going or anything like that. I'd rather do it myself.'

Eric Clark was speaking half in jest when he said he should have been paid a wage for his housework. The Campaign for Wages for Housework could not be more in earnest. Since 1972 it has collected useful figures demonstrating the extent of women's unpaid work at home and drawn

ON STRIKE

Gigi

Workers of the World, Unite

Left: Calls for strikes to support the campaign for wages for housework drew little support from housewives.

attention to the problems facing housewives today; but calls for a one-day strike in support of their claims have been largely ignored by British housewives. It is hard to put a value on work usually done for love. What counts as housework – shelf-fixing, changing bulbs, taking children to school? Who gets the money if the husband shares the work? Above all, where would the funds come from? In recent years, insurance companies have shrewdly spotted a new source of income. If the real value of a wife were clearly demonstrated, husbands might be persuaded to insure their wives under a sort of 'new for old' policy. Rosalind Hines's name rolled off the Legal and General's computer as Britain's average housewife, 1987. As a full-time wife and mother, working a 92-hour week, they estimated her labour to be worth £19,253 a year. In fact, Rosalind is totally dependent on her husband. 'You're not actually paid in pound notes and therefore you're not worth anything in society's eyes, which is a great shame – because one does give up treats, independence, money, clothes, to do this job.... I choose not to work to be here for the children – not the house – just the children. One is sort of insulted for it somehow by the term 'housewife' or 'average'.... I mean, to call yourself a housewife is the greatest conversation stopper of all time.'

In just twenty years 'housewife' has gone from a term of respect to one of disparagement. But the chores still have to be done and, more importantly, so does mothering. The amount of attention children supposedly need has increased dramatically since the war, while the amount they help around the house has dwindled. Modern children must be the most waited-upon in history. The best solution, if circumstances allow, is

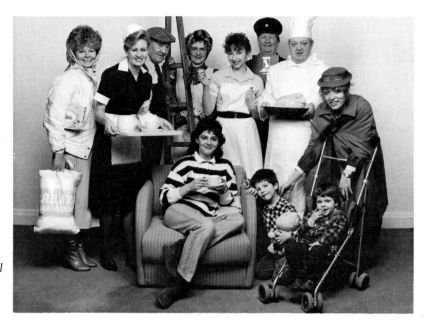

Right: Today's 'Average Housewife', Rosalind Hines, does all the work previously done by a team of professional servants.

to call in extra help or share the tasks. But common sense does not break tradition overnight. In Easington John Graham thought he should do his bit and volunteered to do the windows for Mary but he came in 'for a lot of stick from the men going past. They never used to bother with things like that. They never used to go shopping, it wasn't considered manly, you know, but things are changing now. We seem to see more men shopping down the street than what we did in our days. There's a shop just up the street here, just a few yards away and in all of my thirty-odd years in this house I was only in that shop about half a dozen times until recently and I'm in every day now with me shopping bag.'

The New Husband, caring, unmacho, sharing everything uncomplainingly, is a rare specimen. Although today it is more common to see men pushing prams, doing the shopping and washing dishes, in 1987 a BBC survey of one thousand randomly selected men and women showed that sharp divisions still exist. Women do the bulk of the shopping, cooking, tidying, laundry, sewing and cleaning whether they have a job or not. Men do most of the DIY and car maintenance. Only paying bills and gardening showed no clear divisions. Women complain that apparently willing husbands show two lines of resistance. The first is to prove that they are not really cut out for this kind of work. Determinedly Hopeless Husbands break glasses when washing-up, singe the ironing, burn saucepans and ask for instruction at every stage of cooking until their wives decide it is quicker and easier to do it themselves. The second is never to volunteer their services. These Passive Husbands protest they are willing to do anything and 'she's only got to ask'. As one frustrated housewife explained, 'this implies they are doing you a favour instead of sharing a joint responsibility. If I clean up the kitchen that is normal everyday life, if he does it everyone has to make a song and dance and say "thanks!"' Constant asking sounds suspiciously like nagging, so wanting to keep the peace, their wives just get on with it themselves.

There is a scale of acceptibility in what men are prepared to do. Taking children to school, cooking and shopping are permissible but cleaning lavatories, sewing on buttons and ironing are not. Full-time 'house-husbands' are few and far between. John Buck decided to give up work to look after his son as his partner, Sue, earned more than he did. He devotes most of the day to looking after Josh and then cooks the evening meal so that Sue can spend time with her son. He says they share the housework. Sue is not convinced. 'Even though I try to resist it, there are certain things that I feel are imposed on me because I'm a woman and because they're seen as my responsibility. One night I was sitting having a cup of tea and I looked up and noticed a cobweb and said to John, "Oh, there's a big cobweb in that corner," and he said, "Yes, that's where Bert lives." Now if *he* had said to me "there's a big cobweb," *I* would have rushed to get a duster and cleared it up.' The arrangement works well for them but John knows he is regarded as an oddity. 'Most men have better

Below: The duties of a perfect wife, drawn by Posy Simmonds in 1983.

earning power than women so even if a man wanted to stay at home, economically it would not be viable. Also I think men will probably want to resist that change anyway. I think they like to be the ones in the power situation, being the wage earner.'

Most women are still tied to the house when their children are young. Even if they return to work when they are older, they continue to do most of the cleaning, child-rearing and housekeeping and, unless women themselves change, they are likely to go on doing so. But there has been progress. Women are less their husband's servants than they were fifty years ago. Their contribution to the family purse coupled with the knowledge that they can, if need be, escape from an unhappy marriage has shifted the balance of power within the family. It is no longer assumed that married men are incapable of performing domestic chores any more than that their wives cannot extend their horizons beyond the house.

Frances Graham's grandson Alan, and his wife Christine, think they have a much easier life than she had. Alan is also a miner in Easington, but they have holidays abroad and a car to get about in and they can afford little luxuries that Frances never had. He helps a little around the house, but Christine has always done all their cooking and most of the housework even when she had a full-time job. 'Alan wouldn't know where to start with a vegetable, or dinners. No. I've always done it.' While her children are young she stays at home. 'Sometimes it's very boring.... Sometimes I wish I was working. I miss the company because I used to work in a shop, y'see, and you're meeting people coming in and out.' Like Frances fifty years ago, Christine has her routine: 'Monday's washing day, Tuesday I'll maybe iron, Wednesday I do the windows and inside. Thursday I do the bedrooms, and the bathroom out. So you're really going all the time. I'm always jobbing on. Simply it's because when you're on your own, you're just finding jobs to do.'

Christine's time-filling routines reflect the fact that today domesticity is far less encompassing than a hundred years ago when birth, illness and death were all dealt with at home, when grocers and doctors called and women had little need ever to venture outdoors. Many of the old 'domestic tyrannies' have disappeared. Shopping can be done less often and stored in fridges. Convenience food cuts out the continuous worry of preparing the next meal. Carpets and vacuum cleaners are easier than wooden floors, brushes and polish. Washing machines have liberated women from hours of physically punishing pounding and scrubbing. Modern plumbing saves endless fetching and carrying of tubfuls of water.

But although women have challenged the idea that it is their natural function to clean the house from top to bottom every day, there are always a dozen reasons why it's 'more convenient' for them to be the ones who stay at home, whether it is to nurse a sick child, or care for elderly relations, or clean out the lavatory or brush down the cobwebs or wait in for the gas man. Traditional values still hold strong, even in households which do not conform to them. In 1987, *British Social Attitudes* reported that in homes where mothers worked full-time, three-quarters of them thought that the mother of a child under five should stay at home and nearly as many believed mothers should not work at all. The gulf between what they say they want and what they actually do is enormous. The debate continues about whether it is nature or nurture that makes women feel their prime duty is to be home when the children come in from school or feel unfeminine if they are not a dab hand at pastry. However much women may wish to be different, most feel a certain amount of guilt about the time they spend away from home.

CHAPTER TWO

Just a Girl
Educating Daughters

FRANCES GRAHAM could not explain why she felt compelled to sweep up confetti at her own wedding. 'Just the way we was brought up,' she muttered. Whether women are obsessive house-wives, thrusting careerists or a guilty combination of the two, is largely a question of upbringing – both at school and at home. Despite the huge increase in women's responsibilities, the way they are prepared for woman-hood has not kept up with the pace of change. Past and present pupils from two schools talked to us about their childhoods and schooldays. Although their collective memories stretch back through the century, there were remarkable similarities. Today girls at Parklands Comprehensive in Lancashire and at Cheltenham Ladies' College in Gloucestershire look forward to a future far less certain than that of their grandmothers or great-grandmothers. Eighty years ago women assumed their vocation was marriage. Their main goal was to find a good man to keep them for the rest of their lives. Like them, modern girls have also been primed for marriage and motherhood but they are more sceptical of living happily ever after and they certainly do not expect to be kept for the rest of their lives. As a third former at Parklands explained; 'Girls shouldn't just leave school and chuck their education away, get married, be housewives and have babies. Suppose a girl doesn't get married, she'll have to find a job to support herself. Suppose a girl gets married, has kids and then gets a divorce, she'll have to find a job unless she'll live off child allowance – but that might not be enough. She'll still have to find a job.'

The ambition of most girls at Parklands is fairly limited. They want to find the sort of work that can be picked up at intervals to suit family life. The most popular jobs – nursery nursing, cooking, teaching, looking after the old – are exactly the choices their mothers might have made. They are all natural extensions of a housewife's duties and all involve helping others. Personal ambition does not figure in their calculations. What matters is fitting in and, as a last resort, being able to stand on their own two feet.

At Cheltenham Ladies' College they threw the whole question open to debate. The motion, 'Women always put other people first but men put themselves first', attracted seventy or so girls. Some bored, some absorbed, they listened as a speaker tried to persuade them that as women they would never have the single-minded determination to fight their way to

"IT MEANS MUCH TO BE A GOOD LISTENER."

Left: The main aim of nineteenth-century girls' schools was to prepare them to be good companions and helpmates to men.

the top. 'Mrs Thatcher proves it,' argued another. 'If the Prime Minister doesn't get round the question of women not getting to the top because of men, I don't know what does.' The majority agreed with her and the motion was overwhelmingly defeated.

Girls like these, well educated and from prosperous families, have benefited the most from changing ideas of what a woman's place should be. Their lives will be more exciting, with greater choices and fewer restraints than their grandmothers'. They will be doctors, lawyers and lecturers in greater numbers and with greater ease than the first Cheltenham ladies would ever have dreamed possible. Yet they have more in common with their predecessors than is immediately apparent. The motion of the debate was lost because these girls believe that if they do not become surgeons, judges and professors it will only be because they genuinely do not want to be and that the professional side of life means less to a woman than it does to a man. In other words they feel it will be their own choice, not male ego, that holds them back and keeps them content to play second fiddle. The Cheltenham girls did not question why this should be, they simply accepted it as feminine and natural.

The arguments they used echoed the principles on which their school, and for that matter modern education for girls, was begun in the middle of the last century. Cheltenham Ladies' College was founded in 1853 by a group of men (women were involved later on) who wanted a school which would stretch a girl's intellect sufficiently 'to fit her for the discharge of those responsible duties which devolve upon her as a wife, mother, mistress and friend, the natural companion and helpmeet for man.' They did not want to train her for any greater responsibility, nor in any way to undermine their own superior position. It was hardly a revolutionary proposal but teaching girls Greek, maths and literature along the same lines as their brothers was a breakthrough. Usually left to the mercy of governesses or teachers who, themselves, had no qualifications, girls grew up less informed than their brothers and husbands. After a small private boarding school a girl might have a sufficient smattering of foreign languages to drop a phrase into her conversation every now and then, some musical accomplishments, excellent deportment and, intriguingly, 'use of the globe'. This sort of education was an upper and middle-class affair. Working-class education was fairly haphazard until the elementary school system was established after 1870.

Few of the 'noblemen and gentlemen' whose daughters the new school at Cheltenham hoped to attract could see the point of teaching girls academic subjects. As they were destined for a life of drawing room chatter, children and charitable works, serious study seemed a waste of time. It is not surprising that, in its early years, Cheltenham Ladies' College was a flop. Dorothea Beale, its second principal, explained the early opposition in her history of the school.

Cheltenham was a very conservative place, and the very name 'College' frightened people. It was said, 'girls would be turned into boys, if they attended a College'. ... 'It is very well,' said a mother, who withdrew her daughter at the end of a quarter, 'for my daughter to read Shakespeare, but don't you think it is more important for her to be able to sit down at the piano and amuse her friends?'

In the mid-nineteenth century, Dorothea Beale must have been an extraordinary woman. As one of the few teachers of her day to have professional qualifications, she opposed the received wisdoms of the time with vigour and passion. Educating girls was thought to damage their health as adolescence was the time their reproductive organs were growing and so, the argument went, rest was essential. Schooling might damage this process by being too taxing. Experts predicted infertility or, at the very least, an inability to breastfeed – a strange view in a society which expected fourteen-year-old girls to undertake heavy domestic duties from dawn till well beyond dusk. Their mistresses, however, took resting most seriously. Here again, Dorothea Beale ran against the tide. 'I am quite certain,' she wrote, 'that there would be less illness amongst the upper classes if their brains were more regularly and systematically worked.'

She had a battle persuading Victorian fathers that their daughters

needed any education at all. Women were thought to have smaller brains and, it followed, less intellectual potential than men. It was also a common belief that women were behind men in evolution as their prime function, motherhood, kept them closer to nature. In short, they were inferior. An educated woman was a paradox and, if she showed she had brains, might frighten off potential husbands. So Miss Beale's girls were taught modesty, deportment and decorum along with science and mathematics.

Above: Cheltenham Ladies' College broke new ground by offering girls lessons in science and maths.

Apparently she found the right balance. Despite initial hostility, Cheltenham and its sister school, the North London Collegiate, became very popular. Educational pioneers like Emily Davies, who later founded Girton, the first women's college at Cambridge, were determined to bring girls' schooling up to the standard of boys'. Largely through the dogged insistence of Miss Davies, the Taunton Commission included girls' schools in its report on education in 1868. The conclusions were devastating. Inspectors were appalled by the teaching standards they found. It was a turning point. In the second half of the nineteenth century many more girls' schools were opened, both by the Girls Public Day School Trust and a number of independent bodies. Many were run by evangelical teachers, educated themselves at Cheltenham or the North London Collegiate. They turned out girls who could hold their own in national exams such as those set by the older universities. Public opinion on girls' schooling was changing. Women outnumbered men and fathers were beginning to see that teaching their daughters social accomplishments was not enough.

Above: Hockey at Cheltenham, 1906. Schools became more popular as they offered girls a far wider curriculum than a governess could at home.

Not all of them could look forward to marriage and a life of idleness. Some of them would need to keep themselves. Education improved their chances of a respectable position as a teacher or governess. Besides, schools offered girls a far wider curriculum than they could ever have at home. By the turn of the century, even those who would never need to work were often sent to school.

Once they left school, it was hoped that girls would marry. From early childhood, this assumption ensured they were treated differently from boys. Girls were given dolls to dress, little prams to push and miniature houses with furniture to arrange and curtains to pull while their brothers manoeuvred toy soldiers in military skirmishes around the nursery floor. Eileen Ivelaw Chapman was born in the last years of the nineteenth century. Her mother, a progressive women, tried to make no distinction between her children yet Eileen's younger brother was trained to take charge from an early age. When he was only four Eileen remembers being infuriated because her mother 'insisted he should hold the tram tickets because he was the boy and I thought he was a silly little object'.

The birth of a girl was looked upon as a disappointment as Victoria Wignall discovered. Born in Wigan in 1900, she was one of six daughters. 'I was the fourth down, you see, and as we grew a little older we would hear people saying, "what, all girls!" Couldn't believe it and they said it in such a way as though, really, poor father, poor mother, to have all girls and we just sort of got instilled in us this feeling of just being second best,

Left: Nursery toys encouraged girls to develop domestic interests.

of not coming up to scratch. We were girls, you see, and what use were girls anyway?'

Whatever their background, girls were expected to behave with decorum, modelling themselves on their mothers and lending a hand running the house. Seeing their brothers having a better time was a constant source of irritation. In 1909 twelve-year-old Sybil Canadine, daughter of the Chaplain to St Giles Hospital in Camberwell, helped her mother run a jumble sale every Saturday. While she and her mother were busy with their charitable works, she noticed boys wearing some sort of uniform, playing games on Peckham Rye. She found out they called themselves Scouts and, as it looked like fun, Sybil asked the Scoutmaster if girls could join in too. He told her, 'It is only for the boys, but if some of you girls like to get together, I can lend you the book *Scouting for Boys*. . . . You can follow the Scouts at a reasonable distance until you know where to go.'

The girls did not have to do much following. Their small group were soon tracking, stalking, knotting and waving the flag with the best of them. A few months later, they heard there was to be an international rally for Boy Scouts and were determined their troupe would be part of it. Delving into Sybil's mother's jumble cupboard, they made themselves

Above: Sybil Canadine was one of the first Girl Guides.

uniforms, dying scarves and making woggles from broken shoelaces. They walked six miles to Crystal Palace, nonchalantly marched through the turnstile, and tried to look as official as possible. All went well until Baden-Powell himself spotted them and challenged their patrol leader. ' "And what the dickens do you think you are doing here?" And she said, "We want to be Girl Scouts." "Oh," he said, "No, you can't be. It's only for the boys." Now that had been said to us all through the summer and we broke rank and gathered round him and somehow we got through because we said, "Please, please do something for the girls," and he paused and it seemed like the end of the world to us, we didn't think we had a hope. Then he said, "I'll think about it, I'll let you know." '

Three months later Baden-Powell gave the Girl Guide movement the green light. To begin with it was led by his austere sister, Agnes, described by Sybil as being rather like a maiden aunt. She insisted that the Guides must be markedly different from the Scouts, emphasising their feminine, caring abilities. They were taught first aid and various indoor skills for which they were awarded service badges, 'such as the little house emblem which meant you were able to do needlework, laundry, cooking and that kind of thing'. Camp fires were limited to a few weeks in the summer and tents to daytime use only. Sybil soon discovered that guiding was to be far less fun than scouting. 'The names of the patrols we were told were to be birds or flowers. We had called ourselves, of course, lions and bears and tigers, but we had to give those up. But that was no hardship because we were really on the same kind of syllabus as the Boy Scouts.'

In fact the syllabus was clearly different from the boys' but the girls had the illusion that they were enjoying the same opportunities. Few were searching for absolute equality between the sexes. Pioneers of girls' education such as Dorothea Beale of Cheltenham wanted her girls to stretch their minds as much as their brothers did but the similarity ended there. Though statues of patriotic women like Boadicea, Joan of Arc, Deborah, St Hilda and St Elizabeth adorned the walls of Cheltenham, the girls were not trained to be leaders themselves. While their brothers were prepared for command, they were brought up to be caring and selfless so they could 'perform that subordinate part in the world' to which Miss Beale believed they were called. Her girls were expected to give Miss Beale an account of everything they did in the holidays. She was delighted to hear reports of thoughtful deeds such as 'put baby to bed the day nurse was ill' but was deeply disappointed if they mentioned their own interests and pleasures.

Eileen Ivelaw Chapman went to Cheltenham in 1906, Miss Beale's last year. She was taught, above all, to be considerate to others. This was highlighted at mealtimes, when she was expected to look after her neighbours on either side almost to the point of not eating herself. Certainly it was not done to ask for anything. If Eileen wanted salt and no one spotted this she could mention the sugar instead. Directness was unfeminine.

Above: The new Girl Guide movement quickly established an identity of its own to distinguish it from the Scouts. The Little House emblem was awarded for domestic skills.

" Growing girls are very apt to slouch."

Above: Sketch from the instruction manual, Girl Guiding.

A girl could drop hints but never demand. Like her contemporaries, Eileen was being prepared for a future of service to others. 'Nine-tenths of the children went to live at home without professions and Miss Beale felt that they should all have an object in life. One of the first rules of the Guild of Old Girls that she founded was that the girls should be doing something useful, whether paid or unpaid; and you sent in a report each year on the work you were doing.'

Above: A classroom at Cheltenham, 1913. The College's influence was widespread as it turned out teachers and headmistresses for schools all over the British Empire.

Over a thousand pupils were crammed into Cheltenham's sombre Victorian Gothic buildings. A girl could go to the kindergarten aged three, stay throughout her schooling and finish with a teacher training course. Cheltenham turned out teachers and headmistresses for schools at home and abroad, spreading their own special brand of feminine chivalry throughout the Empire. They taught in private schools and also in the State system which expanded rapidly in the first decade of this century. Parklands Comprehensive started off as the Park School in 1907. Its second principal, Kathleen Reynolds, a former Cheltenham lady, believes the two schools were quite different as Cheltenham was made up of rich girls and the Park School was not. In almost every other detail, the schools were similar and were typical of the kind of secondary schooling available to girls in the first half of the century. Both were run by stern, crusading heads who believed in the dual goals of service and scholastic success. They boldly defended their pupils' right to education but they did not prepare girls to look beyond that. Both schools steered a safe course between academic and social priorities. Girls were expected to be ladylike at all times which meant having excellent deportment, good table manners and keeping their distance from boys. When Elsie Singleton started at the Park School in 1911, she was forbidden to talk to boys in public either in or out of school hours. 'You must not walk to school with your brothers.

Well, my brothers wouldn't have wanted to walk to school with me. I'm sure they wouldn't, but one girl stopped to speak to a boy after school and a mistress passed by, rang Miss Stoneman and told her and that girl was expelled for a week.'

Most girls at the Park School came from solid middle-class stock. They were daughters of bankers, doctors, businessmen and other local worthies who could afford the fees. However, as a maintained school, it was required by law after 1907 to keep a third of its places for scholarship children who paid no fees at all. This was the only way a working-class child could get a secondary education. Elsie Singleton came from a respectable Lancashire family, anxious to do their best for all their children. Her father, an overlooker at the local mill, allowed her to take up a scholarship to the Park School despite having four younger sons to educate. It was quite common for girls to have to forego a scholarship if the cost of uniform and books placed too much of a strain on the family purse. Not only were daughters more useful than sons around the house, but as boys were training for careers their education was considered more important. At sixteen, Elsie had to forget any hopes of going on to university because the boys' education still had to be paid for.

Such official thought as went into the education of working-class girls (and that does not appear to have been a great deal) concentrated on preparing them to be wives and mothers or taking work as domestic servants. As they could learn whatever was necessary at home or elementary school, secondary education did not seem relevant. In the early years of the century, however, the authorities were shaken by the high infant mortality rates and the alarming number of volunteers for the Boer War who proved physically unfit for active service. A report on 'Physical Deterioration' in 1904 blamed declining standards of housewifery and motherhood. The government decided the simplest solution was 'some great scheme of social education' to raise the standard of domestic competence among working-class women. This was certainly easier and cheaper than cracking the real problems of overcrowding, lack of medical care and malnutrition caused by poverty.

Cookery, hygiene, laundrywork and housewifery were all on the curriculum in elementary girls schools. These were now supplemented by 'infant care lessons' and the secondary schools expanded their domestic programmes too. Domesticity, already dominating girls' home lives, intruded into school too. Elsie Singleton had cooking lessons at Preston Park. 'You started in the second year for cookery and I liked that. We used to do it in the school kitchen where they made the meals and you had to write the recipe and I loved practising at home. You see mother let me practise. And we did an examination. You had to pick a paper out of a bag to choose what you were going to do. So you had to learn your recipes by heart. And I said to mother, "It's all right if I get little jam tarts, that's

easy. I hope I don't get lentil soup.'' My word, I got lentil soup. So I had to make that. But I enjoyed it.'

Schools that did not teach domestic science lost their municipal grant. The Board of Education wanted 'housecraft' on every secondary school-girl's curriculum. Even at Cheltenham, where academic learning was prized above all other, a domestic science house was added in 1906. Courses were offered in 'practical and high-class cooking, dressmaking, laundry (lace, blouses, woollens, feathers etc.) and housewifery'.

The First World War gave these budding helpmates and housewives their first real chance to challenge the assumption that this was all they could be. As they took on jobs they had never dreamed of doing, they demonstrated the scope of their ability to the world and also surprised themselves. A seed of feminine pride was sown and the argument that women were physically and mentally capable only of acting as helpmates to men was knocked firmly on the head. A new breed of single professional career women emerged from the war. There were many women who were forced by circumstances to be breadwinners not brides. Mary Gulland was the eldest of a family of six girls living in Sussex. Her father, a civil servant, brought them all up expecting they would have to earn their own living. Mary was at a grammar school during the war. They began each day with prayers for any brothers or fathers who had gone missing. 'It was rather sad growing up from that point of view. Every morning in school we had read out to us the list of those who had disappeared, as they did through

Above: In keeping with the educational demands of the time, Cheltenham offered lessons in 'practical and high-class cooking'.

*Above: Alice Stoneman,
Principal of the Park
School, Preston, from
1907 to 1930.*

the war. We had the spirits of the young, at the same time, we did have
this awful feeling of all our boy friends disappearing.... We had three
possibilities, nursing, secretarial or teaching, and as teaching involved
people that was my answer.'

For over forty years Mary taught first at Westonbirt and then at Cheltenham Ladies' College. She never married, although all her sisters did. A
remarkable number of successful career women from this period were
eldest daughters in families with no sons. Perhaps the lack of brotherly
competition made them more confident or maybe they absorbed parental
ambition that otherwise would have gone to the son.

Teaching had a special aura at that time. Apart from their own mothers
and their friends' mothers, teachers were the only women most girls came
to know well. Teaching promised a life of independence and respect.
Running an ancient car, having an influential voice in the community
and enjoying holidays on the continent, suggested that being a school-
ma'am had much to be said for it. In those days of single sex schools, there
was the added attraction of joining a charmed circle. Teachers still carried
some of the charisma of the pioneering generation. Most of them were
unmarried as convention and a marriage bar imposed by the schools kept
them single and able to dedicate their lives to their girls. It was a mark of
success at school if a teacher wanted a girl to follow in her footsteps.

Dorothy Marshall went to the Park School in 1914. She was a prize
pupil and, unlike her peers, felt no fear of the imposing principal, Alice
Stoneman. The rest brought flowers for the gym teacher, Dorothy took
them to the Head. 'Suddenly I was overcome with my emotion and my
love and my general affection and I think I more or less flung my arms
round her and I said, "Miss Stoneman, I do love you so very much," and
we looked at one another with horror and embarrassment. I don't know
which of us was the more embarrassed and I suppose she must have
decided even then that I was Girton material ... She was the most won-
derfully inspiring person and I kept up with her all my life.' Alice Stoneman
encouraged her best pupils to try for the academic plums and in 1918
Dorothy went to Cambridge where she found herself surrounded by an
exceptionally bright group of women. Joan Tredgold left Cheltenham for
Newnham in 1921 and found the academic standard was generally higher
among women than men at Cambridge. As she wryly pointed out, no
woman was there because she was good at rugger or rowing. Most of them
were ruled by a strong sense of vocation and, as Dorothy Marshall recalls,
most went on to become teachers. 'We took it for granted that we would
teach, though one or two in upper crust circles went on to Mrs Hosta's
Secretarial College.'

Yet these high achievers were less sure of themselves than they appeared.
Trail blazers they may have been, but they lacked social confidence.
Dorothy Marshall confessed that she felt very uncertain of herself when

she arrived at Girton and wondered if she could ever have real friends. 'I had no idea of how to cope with the situation and at first I was very lonely.' The sexes were kept apart as they grew up and so were uneasy with each other at the best of times. Even when chaperoning was no longer required, women undergraduates found it easier to be with their own sex. The men were uncertain how to treat them. They were not like the unassuming girls they met at parties and they could not have been more of a contrast with the idealised cinema heroines of the time, cowering in a corner at the sight of masculine strength, fainting into the hero's arms at the slightest opportunity. At a time when there was a shortage of men, women were expected to please. Feminine looks and charms were at a premium and those who appeared to renounce them for such masculine pursuits as higher education were seldom rated by their own or the opposite sex. Girls were dim but pretty, or clever and unattractive. Anything else was a paradox.

The universities did little to encourage women. At Oxford they were limited to 730 places and at Cambridge to 500 among thousands of men. Initially women were not allowed to take degrees. The male undergraduates resented any encroachment on their territory and in Joan Tredgold's first term at Newnham she remembers, 'they had another try at getting degrees for women and, as usual, it was turned down by the enormous preponderence of men. It was made the occasion for an undergraduate rag and the undergraduates came storming up and made a great deal of noise and attacked our wrought iron gates.' Apart from this Joan Tredgold remembers little outright hostility. They were simply ignored both by students and by lecturers. Sophie Baron, who went up a few years later, recalls that 'Until 1923 women had no right to attend lectures. It was by courtesy of each individual lecturer and he had to be asked. This particular one was a very good lecturer and they were anxious to send women and he refused several times. Well, at last they begged him to have these girls and finally he said very ungraciously, "Oh, all right, but put them where I can't see 'em." That was the feeling. That we were intruding.'

Above: Undergraduate, Dorothy Marshall, did not conform to the feminine ideal of the time, personified by film star Mary Pickford (right).

However, women were there to stay. Oxford allowed them to take degrees in 1920 although Cambridge held out until 1947.

The question of how girls should be educated, and for what purpose, continued to tax officials. The Board of Education published a report in 1923 on 'The Differentiation of the Curriculum for Boys and Girls respectively in Secondary Schools'. It was concerned that 'old and delicate graces had been lost and the individuality of womanhood had been sacrificed upon the austere altar of sex equality'. No wonder women graduates were made to feel deviant! Harking back to Victorian times it recommended various measures to 'protect' girls, such as letting them take their school certificates a year later and giving them less homework, 'especially in view of the fact that most girls were expected to do a certain amount of

household work in the home'. This report was aimed at secondary schools. Most girls never got that far.

Only elementary education up to the age of fourteen was compulsory though truancy was quite common. No one seemed to mind very much when a girl skipped school, particularly if she was 'helping mum'. Like many working-class girls growing up between the wars, Dorothy Capper had more than her fair share of housework and less schooling than she wanted. 'My mother died when I was nine and my sister was three and my brother was seven weeks old and me granny and grandad came to live with us and she was very, very strict, a very Victorian lady. So I ceased to be a child when I was nine years old actually because I was expected to scrub all the washing on Mondays and stand at the big table and scrub me grandfather's shirts and me father's shirts and overalls and then every Friday I had to scrub the kitchen floor before I went to school and I also had to take me brother and sister everywhere I went.'

On top of an exhausting domestic routine, Dorothy went daily to the Slyne Elementary School in Lancashire. She wanted to go to grammar school and then train to be a nurse, but her grandmother soon put a stop to that kind of dreaming. Dorothy was not even allowed to try for a school like the Park School. Like so many of her generation, she was unlucky. Her family needed her at home, so instead of reading books and writing essays she washed shirts and scrubbed floors. 'I don't think me granny believed in education for girls. All they needed to know was how to sew and scrub and wash and bake and patch and darn. You know, things like that. But I think she was probably preparing me for the time when she wasn't there in a way, because it was just taken for granted that I would take over from her. On the night she died me father said to me, "Well, it's up to you now." And that it was.'

Twenty-five years later when her own children could look after themselves, Dorothy finally started nursing. Dorothy got her second chance. Alice Horrocks never did. She, too, had ambitions to be a nurse and started at the local elementary school in 1925. Despite achieving the highest marks in her school, she was not allowed to take up her place at secondary school. Her brother was. 'He passed his exams to go as I did and I was over the moon but "you're going in the mill". It would have meant uniform and it would have meant money. Maybe it seems to you now in your day that that was awful but you accepted it because you'd got to. But I had that resentment. Not against mother or father but against not going.' All Alice could do was dream about the kind of schools she read about in *Schoolgirl's Weekly*. 'There was always a heroine wading through rivers and not getting drowned and maybe leading a few on.'

A mass of new schoolgirl fiction hit the bookshops and lending libraries between the wars. There were fewer tales of demure and dainty girls growing up to be rewarded by good husbands and more stories of daredevils

Left: Gymnastics at Cheltenham, 1933. Girls' schools between the wars became more like boys' schools, spartan in appearance and sporty in ethos.

of the Lower Fourth where tomboy heroines saved the day. Though these were immensely popular, they did not reflect real life.

Girls' boarding schools became more fashionable between the wars and many new ones were opened. Most were modelled closely on boys' public schools, spartan in appearance and sporty in ethos. It could be a confusing upbringing for girls; encouraged in term-time to bury their heads in books and, flattening their chests in gymslips, thrash the neighbouring school at hockey, then in the holidays to appear willing and winsome. At home girls continued to be treated differently from boys. 'My brothers would say, "You're just a girl," which was infuriating because I was just as good as they were,' remembers one girl, angry that her brothers were not only given more opportunities but dodged all the dreary household tasks as well. Another remembers having to put up with a cousin who was allowed to study whenever he wanted. 'We were told to do sewing and cooking, a bit of drawing and painting and perhaps play the piano a little and that was considered ladylike pursuits for us.... Girls were expected to be tidy and behave in all sorts of ways but boys, they just didn't pick up their own clothes or anything like that. You know, they had everything done for them – shoes polished, meals at the drop of a hat. You name it, they had it. When I come back I think I'm going to come back as a young man.'

The 1930s were a lean time for women. There were not enough jobs for men, let alone women, so they were encouraged to remain at home, firmly tied by their own apron strings. Schools reflected the opportunities in the outside world. Although some girls were going into professional life, mostly as teachers, the balance was shifting away from the sort of scholarship advocated by schools such as Preston Park. It was more important to be able to hold elegant conversations, based on a sound education, to play a useful voluntary role around the village, or to dish out low budget meals for the family and be sure never to put a foot wrong with the husband's boss. Like their mothers and grandmothers, they were trained to be adaptable seconds-in-command but the crusading zeal that had surrounded the early years of girls' schooling was missing.

Arguably, girls were receiving exactly the education their parents wanted. There were often clashes between teachers and parents about a girl's future. Sophie Baron's parents wanted her to go to finishing school abroad and were appalled when she announced her intention of going to Girton. After she won an exhibition they reluctantly allowed her to take it up. 'When my aunt heard of their decision she said, "I think it is very wrong. Your parents should never have allowed you to remain at school all these years." You see, eighteen was quite late. "Now it's your duty to stay at home and be a companion to your mother."'

Another reason for schools stagnating lay in the inordinate length of time a Headmistress stayed. When Kathleen Reynolds took over Preston Park School from Alice Stoneman in 1930 she found entrenched Victorian attitudes, not particularly surprising as Miss Stoneman, herself an eminent Victorian, had presided over the school since its beginning twenty-three years earlier. One of Miss Reynolds's first reforms was to abolish the practice of grading girls each week for everything they did and ordering detention for girls who did not come up to standard.

Grading dominated life at Cheltenham too but there was no change of direction. Berys Baynham, head of classics at Cheltenham today, was herself a pupil there in the 1940s and was struck by how competitive girls were forced to be. 'Whatever you did was being measured. I mean today it's gone to the opposite extreme where even competitive games are out of fashion because they make you compete. There's no doubt with us that we competed in everything. It was the nightmare of my life because I'm not particularly physically active, but every week you had to be tested for a gym jump and you were graded for gym. You were even graded on how you sat in college.' Not only did this give a disproportionate importance to deportment and gym but it encouraged a cult of conformity. Girls left school with a lingering need to fit in, anxious never to stand out from the crowd.

Fuller education with equal opportunity for all became a popular demand during the Second World War. As Britain evolved its own ideology to fight fascism, plans were laid for a welfare state. Out of this dream of a better postwar world came the 1944 Education Act, with free secondary education and the promise to raise the school leaving age to fifteen. The Park School, Preston, was officially categorised as a grammar school for girls with an entry exam for everyone at eleven. There were no fees and schoolbooks came free. In theory, at least, it was as accessible to working-class girls as to anyone else. The clever ones who passed their eleven plus had the chance of as good an education as their brothers. The rest, three-quarters of the country's children, 'failed' and, like Helen Gallagher, went to the local secondary modern. Helen had a limited choice of subjects and never had any homework. She was given no careers advice and no particular training except in domestic science. In her last year at school all the girls in her class were taken for a week to a make-believe house with its own kitchen, bedroom and sitting room. They were taught how to make a bed, sweep a floor, and iron a shirt.

Secondary moderns were frequently in antiquated school buildings, often the old elementary schools, where staff and parents complained of overcrowding and lack of facilities. Helen hardly has a good word for her school. 'We learned nothing. There was nothing to work for, no GCEs, nothing.' Most of her schoolfriends found work in shops or mills. She got a job in a florist's. Her sister, who passed her eleven plus, went to grammar school, did 'O' levels and at the end of it all got a far better paid job. Looking back Helen feels no anger at the system, only with herself for not coming up to scratch.

Above: After the war, housewifery enjoyed renewed popularity. Many schools provided furnished flats to give lessons an authentic flavour.

A flurry of reports in the late fifties and early sixties discussed whether the curriculum for girls should be different from that of boys. They were particularly concerned about girls leaving school in order to marry early. The postwar industrial boom needed women as workers as well as mothers. *Half our Future* reported on children between the ages of thirteen and sixteen 'of average or less than average' ability. Dame Kathleen Ollerenshaw, a member of the Committee, was appalled by the apathy of the girls she interviewed. By their mid-teens they had completely lost interest in school and were dreaming of wedding dresses, fitted kitchens and prams. Their urge to marry was fostered by romantic fiction in teenage comics. Heroines always ended up marrying and living happily ever after. Glossy advertisements for three-piece suites, frilly bedcovers, gleaming rotary grills and so much else seemed far more exciting than the classroom. 'The system is very much tied to age and age group. What the girl needs is a really honest to God second chance when she's in her middle twenties and then she can be tremendous. But it isn't always easy when you've got young children to get that second chance.'

Above: Advertisers encouraged girls to dream of getting married and to spend their money on their bottom drawer.

Above: The author, 1958. One of 'quantities of young, green ladies'.

Dame Kathleen's main criticism was that the education system had been designed by men for boys and did not suit girls who, in their teens, had strong nesting instincts. She wanted more training centres and colleges for adult women. They might well be eager to learn or train for a career once they had borne a few children, but at fifteen the average girl wanted to be in an office not a classroom and hoped that wedding bells would ring for her within a few years. Winklepickers, glossy make-up and coffee shops were more exciting than learning domestic science at school.

That fifties' teenage culture passed us by in Cheltenham Ladies' College. In 1958 I found myself clad in a green woollen suit, tie, felt hat, liberty bodice (it was still on the clothes list), two pairs of pants, white underneath and green on top, cotton gloves and 30 denier stockings, colour allure, though that was the last thing they would ever do. A visitor to Cheltenham once asked 'What's behind the walls?' and a local replied, 'quantities of young green ladies'. He was right.

While the winds of change blew outside and Britain tried to shed the past, Cheltenham Ladies' College did its best to live in it. The character of the College hardly changed from one generation to the next. We were still graded on how we jumped in gym, walked between classrooms and talked at table. Personal initiative was hardly encouraged. The whole day was mapped out for us in a relentless timetable: 7 a.m. bell, get out of bed, 7.05 strip bed, 7.10 wash, 7.20 dress. 7.30 silence in the dormitories for private prayer. 7.40 breakfast, 8.00 morning news. 8.10 make beds. By 8.30 we were supposed to be on the road to college. That was just the first 90 minutes.

No one stepped out of line. The most important thing was not to be singled out as bad. The common trait of my generation at Cheltenham – and possibly several before and after – was a desperate anxiety to please. Dorothea Beale's statues of heroines had vanished, probably removed to a place of safety during the war but, as no one knows the hiding place, lost to the school forever. The pioneering spirit they symbolised had also disappeared. Being there was enough. When Angela Partington's parents sent her to Cheltenham in 1958, they did not think beyond that. 'I was told that once you've been to Cheltenham, the world is your oyster, I'm not suggesting they thought that I'd become Chairman of the BBC or

ICI.... I mean, they felt that this would be a social ornament and I would be a very desirable catch. I would go to secretarial college and then I'd get a nice little job for a couple of years, then I'd marry well and have children. They weren't interested in further education. Neither of them had it themselves and I think they felt it was unfeminine.'

Even in the 1960s girls were still being schooled for a secondary role. But they were spending longer at school and far more of them had a chance of going to university too. Mary Ingham, born in 1947, had far more opportunities than her own mother who left school at fourteen. As a child, Mary's mother had to look after the house because of her own mother's ill health and was considered the dunce of her class in everything except domestic science. She grew up, married and had children. By the time Mary was doing 'O' levels at grammar school she was learning all sorts of things her mother had never been taught. 'I began to think of my mother as stupid and really sort of undervalue the kind of wisdom and skills which she was good at.... I was part of that part of my generation that looked around us at all that sort of stifling suburbia, all that kind of postwar "let's get back to the happy family", and thought "Help, get me out, I don't want to do this." I can remember when I was at university I used to ring up home and moan on about essays that I'd got to write and, oh dear, there were exams coming up and my mother would say, "Oh, give it all up, I know you just want to get married and have babies." So I suppose it was then I consciously thought, "No, no, that's the last thing I want." '

Around the corner, a more attractive life beckoned, where girls could share flats and earn enough money to be independent. Girls were far more likely to go to college than at any time previously. In 1962, 26 192 women were at university (though Oxford and Cambridge still clung to their all-male Colleges, with only 680 women at Cambridge among 7318 men, much the same position as in 1922). The prosperity and indulgence of the 1960s coincided with an expansion of university places. Thousands of girls seized the chance for reflection as well as qualification that three years at college offered. Many questioned the sense of settling down to have children after all those exams and hard work. Besides it seemed most unfair that even the dimmer men at university would have job opportunities that they would be denied.

While growing up, the sexes were more integrated than ever before. Single sex schools were going out of fashion. Co-education was thought to give children a more natural start. However, the changeover to co-education was not so much a deliberate policy as a by-product of replacing the old grammar and secondary moderns with comprehensive schools. Up and down the country the sexes were brought together under one roof as schools merged. The Park School, Preston, ceased to be a girls' grammar school and in 1976 became Parklands Comprehensive.

Ruth Seed, a former pupil, taught at Parklands before and after the merger, working closely with masters at the local boys' schools. Fifty years earlier, the headmistress of the Park School had been at great pains to keep her girls from talking to pupils from the boys' school in the street; now they shared classrooms. Having always taught girls, Ruth was looking forward to seeing some boys in her class but not many of them wanted to do English. It was 'a girl's subject'. She found it interesting to note the different approaches of the sexes. 'People say that boys are perhaps more quick and less hard-working than girls but that's very much a generalisation.... I think a lot of the girls that I taught were just as ambitious as the boys but perhaps there was the added incentive in the boys' case that they expected to have to make their own living whereas in the case of some girls there may have been in the background the feeling that, well, after all I may get married and perhaps it doesn't matter.'

The shift to co-education made both sexes more worldly wise but did little to boost any kind of feminine ambition or self-confidence apart from a crude sexual one. Often girls achieved less than under a single sex system. The debate continues about why boys are more assertive. Arguments range from explaining it by biological differences or girls' conditioning to blaming girls for shamming because they think boys would not like them if they appeared brainy. For whatever reason, while generally ahead of boys at eleven, girls do progressively less well from then onwards. In 1985 they outshone boys in 'O' level grades, but did fractionally less well at 'A' level. They made up 42 per cent of undergraduates and 37 per cent of postgraduates. Only 15 per cent of lecturers and a mere 3 per cent of

Right: Reading books for young children were attacked by feminists for narrowing girls' horizons by this kind of stereotyping.

Here we are at home, says Daddy.

Peter helps Daddy with the car, and Jane helps Mummy get the tea.

Good girl, says Mummy to Jane.

You are a good girl to help me like this.

Good good girl

"Well, at least let me make a doll's house, then."

professors are women – supposedly ideal jobs for a mother with school-age children. Even in those professions where women are joining in numbers equal to men, few aspire to the top jobs.

Feminists recognise that school is only one of many formative influences and to get girls out of their traditional grooves they need to change those customs which reinforce their passive role. Nursery stories, advertisements, history and everyday language have all come under scrutiny. Picture books depicting mothers in aprons and daughters pouring tea into toy tea sets or Jane watching Peter climbing a tree, history lessons which concentrate only on kings and soldiers have all been attacked and are becoming less common. Words which wrongly imply masculine exclusivity such as 'chairman' now stick in the throat when applied to a woman. Though often ridiculed, feminists stood their ground and slowly the climate is changing. But confident girls, like the sixth formers at Cheltenham, are still a minority and, though ambitious, they too look set to curb their professional ambitions if wifely duties call.

Despite public awareness and various programmes such as WISE (Women into Science and Engineering), most girls still have limited horizons. The pupils at Parklands Comprehensive differ little from those described in *Half our Future* twenty-five years earlier. The law requires both sexes to be given the chance of doing any subject on the curriculum but there are still 'girls' subjects' and 'boys' subjects'. Maths and physics are unpopular with girls who are convinced they are bad at them. Only one boy is doing cookery (he wants to be a chef); all the rest of the class are girls who say it will be useful at home. Faced with a limited choice of jobs, they are not very ambitious. They recognise the need to work but only to supplement the family income or support their children if ever the need arises.

At Cheltenham 85 per cent of the girls go on to university. The school will probably produce more satisfied women than in the past but fewer remarkable ones. Increasingly, over the century, girls have ceased to find inspiration from that breed of fine spinster teachers who developed a cult of feminine superiority in the past. Berys Baynham, who has taught at Cheltenham for over twenty years, echoes much the same sentiments as women undergraduates sixty-five years ago. Despite her formidable academic achievements, she self-deprecatingly feels her particular brand of authority is hardly relevant any more. 'I mean I'm dull compared with the young member of staff who's got a husband and the breadth of contacts, the variety of interests that the more modern teacher has. These girls go to far more foreign places and are at home in far more strange societies and different societies than I've ever been in my life. They're far in advance of me, many girls here. It's a different tradition certainly. I would have thought I'm at the end of that line.'

A modern woman is expected to tag professional success on to domestic bliss. Ever anxious to please, she is determined to give equal weight to both. The sort of single-mindedness that makes for excellence remains largely a male prerogative and, if the Cheltenham sixth formers are anything to go by, another generation of girls accepts this as a fact of life.

CHAPTER THREE

A Suitable Job for a Woman
Women at Work

CATHERINE INMAN has broken the mould. At eighteen, she is an apprentice engineer at Vickers Shipyard in Barrow-in-Furness – as much a man's world as the pit at Easington. All the women in Catherine's family have worked in Barrow: her mother, Maureen, as a secretary, her grandmother, Gladys O'Flynn, as a shop assistant and her great-grandmother, Rose Ashton, as a domestic servant. Catherine is a source of mingled pride and puzzlement to the rest of the family. They are not quite sure what to make of her. None of them would have worked in the shipyard even if they had been given the chance. Certainly Maureen never expected any daughter of hers would leave home in overalls every morning. Catherine thinks she is the luckiest of them all. 'I had lots more opportunity than me Mum had and specially me Nanna and me great

Above: A woman in a coal mine, 1842.

Left: The different jobs held by four generations of one family reflect the changing nature of women's work. Left to right: Catherine Inman, shipyard engineer; Maureen Inman, typist; Gladys O'Flynn, shop assistant; Rose Ashton, domestic servant.

Nanna. They just went into a job, anything. Me Mum did have a little bit of a choice but she got pushed into being a secretary, which maybe nowadays she wouldn't quite have wanted to do.'

The four women make a lively and garrulous quartet, each a head taller than her mother, arguing frequently but affectionately. The older three present a formidable united front, clashing with Catherine about many issues, particularly those to do with working women. Their views reflect their own experiences. Rose and Gladys gave up work on marriage, Maureen when she had her first child. Catherine plans to keep her job going through marriage and children. The others think she will be ducking her real duty. 'A woman should stop at home and look after her family,' says Rose. 'You can't expect a husband to work all day and then come home and do so much at night time,' agrees Gladys. They confidently predict that Catherine will feel differently once she has children of her own.

The passions aroused by the idea of working women, and working mothers in particular, have their roots in the industrial revolution which forced men, women and children away from farming or domestic manufacturing and into factories. Working life became more squalid and exhausting, especially for women and children who were badly paid and often had the nastiest jobs. Children old enough to work were treated badly and younger ones at home were neglected while their mothers went to the factory or down the pit where they worked 'chained, belted, harnessed, like dogs in a go-cart'. But there were no family arguments about whether it was better for these women to stay at home and look after their children. They had to work or they starved.

When reforming middle-class Victorians realised how the masses lived and worked, they were shocked. The dignity of women and the future of the family itself were at stake: two of their most firmly held beliefs were threatened by a third – freedom in the marketplace. In those days businesses were left alone by government. Bosses were not expected to conform to standards which might undermine their control and lower the productivity of their employees, so a compromise was reached. Women were legally classified, as 'non-adults' so that they and their children could be protected from the worst industrial hazards. Their working hours were limited by law in the hope of improving family life; and to safeguard their 'morals' women were not allowed to work night shifts. Their husbands, on the other hand, went on as before, so drawing a distinction between the sexes. There was work which was suitable for women and work which was not.

It is still common today for people to separate men's work and women's work, despite recent legislation banning such categories. At ninety-four, Rose Ashton is too old to change her views. The Prime Minister should be a man because that is the way it has always been. (Rose regards Mrs Thatcher as some kind of temporary freak.) Dirty work or physically punishing work is for men. 'You can't expect a woman to go out and build a house or go out with machines to dig the road, it wouldn't do her metabolism any good.' Another legacy from the bad old days is the assumption that working women neglect their families. 'It's all different once a woman has kiddies,' explains Rose. 'Her place is at home with them as my mother was with us and before that her mother was with her children.' The need to encourage women to make family life their priority has influenced attitudes from Victorian times to the present.

At the beginning of the century, only 29 per cent of the workforce were women and only 10 per cent of married women worked. Men lost face if they could not support their wives. Middle-class women did not work and respectable working-class women tried hard to do the same. Their unmarried daughters expected to stay at home, kept by father, until their wedding day. Few women worked for the love of it. Financial necessity forced the less fortunate into a limited range of jobs, usually the sort they could be taught by their mothers. They became domestic servants, shop assistants, seamstresses, laundresses and, in some areas, factory workers. Ninety per cent of them stopped work when they married and hoped they would never have to earn another penny in their lives. If disaster struck, leaving them either widows or with an invalid husband to support, they were ill-equipped to cope. There were few enough opportunities for single women, let alone a widow with dependent children.

Ethel Dean's father died in 1896 when she was four months old. Her mother had three other children under five and no obvious way of supporting them. 'They wanted her to take us to the workhouse, but she wouldn't. My mother was born in Upminster and she knew all the houses and things round there so she rented a house and took in lodgers to keep us. They paid 14 shillings a week each for lodgings and that's the only way she kept us on.' Deprived of her own husband, Ethel's mother could 'do' for other gentlemen. It was her only skill. Like childminding or domestic service, taking in lodgers was a way of earning without upsetting the strongly held view that a woman's place was at home. Some women took

Above: As this cartoon shows, ideas about suitable work for women are deeply ingrained.

Above: It was often much easier for women to do work at home than find a job outside, but they had no industrial clout and wages were shockingly low.

in sewing or washing, 1s. 6d. for a pile of washing could keep a family in food for two days. Women were grateful for small manufacturing jobs in the 'sweated trades' such as covering tennis balls, pulling fur or making match boxes which they could do at home; but as a scattered, dependent workforce they were always paid the lowest rates.

If single girls could not find suitable work near their parents' house, they looked for live-in jobs as domestic servants or shop assistants. No respectable unmarried girl took lodgings on her own. In residential work there was little opportunity to stray from the straight and narrow as long hours and strict rules kept the girls in their place. Shop assistants remember being fined not only for mistakes at work but also for misbehaviour out of hours. Evidence given by the Union of Shop Assistants and Clerks to a House of Commons Inquiry in 1908 revealed the severity of these fines. Smoking on the landing or in the bedroom or sleeping out without permission might carry a fine of 2s. 6d. Wrongly addressing parcels cost them 6d. A mistake in adding up a bill, a wrong date on a receipt or addressing a customer as 'Miss' instead of 'Madam' often carried a penalty too. On a weekly wage between 8s. and 10s. 6d. these fines cut cruelly into earnings.

Domestic service also involved long hours and little independence, but in 1905 it was Rose Ashton's only hope of work. Then aged thirteen, she was sent by her parents to the local hiring fair at Ulverston. Rose remembers the local farmers inspecting the girls rather like cattle at a market. If they liked what they saw, they made an offer. ' "We'll give you six pound for six month." We would say no. We would move on, try and get the biggest [bid] – about seven pound for the six month." The fair ended at noon, by which time Rose had to accept whatever was on offer. 'This farmer came up to us, he said, "Is thee for hiring, lass?" He says, "I'll give you six pound ten." "Righto." And he gives us a shilling. Now that silver shilling bound us, if we took that silver shilling we had to go to the farm, their house, and stop there six month or else our parents would have to pay that six pound ten back to that farmer.'

Rose's parents could never have afforded to repay such a sum, so for six months she was virtually a slave in her employer's house, working even on Christmas day. 'We had had a nice Christmas dinner and I washed all up and she come out to me and she said, "Have you finished, Rose?" And I said, "Yes, madam." She said, "Well, there's a bowl of string there and there's a big needle, and there's a heap of papers," she said, "I want you to go down the paddock." Now the paddock was their toilet ... and I had to sit there and tear these papers into pieces like you have a toilet roll and then I used to thread them and hang them on the back of the toilet. Well, I think I shed a bucket full o'tears. That was my Christmas day.'

It was a far cry from the congenial surroundings conjured up in nostalgic novels about life below stairs. More often than not, servants worked alone. In 1909 Ethel Dean left her mother's lodging house to find a job. She was only thirteen but it was time to earn her own living. She found work as a general maid in a small house where she worked on her own, consumed with loneliness. 'I had no one to talk to and I had to have meals on my own. I sat in the kitchen. I had half a day a week off.' Her mother soon found her another job as a 'between maid' in a doctor's house with three other servants. At least she had someone to talk to but she worked nonstop for fourteen hours a day, starting at 6 a.m. when she took a cup of tea to Cook and ending at 10 p.m. if she was lucky.

However miserable, domestic service was considered more respectable than industry. Factory girls were thought of as the lowest of the low, except in a few regional pockets where there was a tradition of women's work (in textiles in Lancashire, pottery in Staffordshire and flax and jute in Dundee). Bella Keyzer, a Dundee weaver, remembers Dundee before the war. 'The men in Dundee dialect were called kettle boilers, meaning that they had the kettle boiling for tea when the wife came home from work because it was an impossibility for men to get a job.... They were taken on at fourteen and paid off at nineteen. Men were just not employed. It was a woman's town. Everything was women. And that was why women in Dundee became very industrialised, very militant.'

Unlike other parts of the country, it was common for married women in these areas to work. Elizabeth Bullock, a pottery worker born in 1894, had thirteen children and worked until she went into labour with each one of them. 'I had a good mother as used to look after me children, that's how I used to go to work. We couldn't do without because one man's money wouldn't keep y' and we couldn't get any social money. . . . I used to go to work at six o'clock in the morning and come home at breakfast time and get 'em up – take 'em up in their nighties to me mother across the way.' Elizabeth started work at the age of thirteen, cutting transfers for decoration. It was heavy work for a young girl, carrying loads of unglazed pots, then 'rubbing transfer prints onto the ware and washing off the paper in tubs of water. My fingers used to be red raw and bleeding from the roughness of the biscuit ware.' Although Elizabeth's trade consisted largely of women, none of them ever became supervisors, There was always a man in charge, often years younger and less experienced than the women but they never challenged his right to be boss. 'Women hadn't reached that stage when they wanted to be anything, y'know. You were sort of subservient always.'

It was an accepted fact of life that working women were treated as dependants, being paid half or, if they were lucky, two-thirds the wage of a man. Nellie Boulton was one of the best pottery decorators in her firm in the early decades of the century. Her supervisor once told her she worked as well as a man which she proudly claims, without irony, was the greatest compliment she was ever paid. However, Nellie never expected a man's pay. 'He got a tremendous amount of money more than us. Ours was just coppers and shillings where he would have a home, wouldn't he? And he'd want full responsibility, want a full wage. I couldn't see a man ever doing the job for the wage we got!'

Trade unions dominated working life, though women played little part in them. Nellie was one of a handful of women active in the Ceramic and Allied Trades Union. Most unions excluded women altogether. As they could be employed for less money than men, they were seen as a threat, particularly when new technology made it possible to learn some skilled jobs without long apprenticeships and reduced the muscle power needed in others. Through complex codes of restrictive practices, men kept women and other unskilled workers out of favoured jobs, sustaining the idea that men's work and women's work must necessarily be different. A factory inspector at the turn of the century reported:

Women will never become engineers, mechanics, stonemasons, builders, miners and so on and men are not likely to become operatives, dressmakers, milliners or launderers.

Middle-class women also had great difficulty breaking into male territory. Irene Angell's father, a general merchant, had eight children to bring up. By the time Irene was born in 1896, the shortage of marriageable men was acute. Boys were less likely to survive infancy and the Empire enticed thousands of men to leave the country every year. It was a subject frequently discussed around the Angell family table. Mr Angell was determined his daughters would have some way of earning their own living in case they were left on the shelf but there was little choice for them. They could become teachers, governesses or nurses but not much else. Most professional jobs were closed to them. However, feminists had begun to demand entry into the professions and had achieved some successes. The medical profession had, albeit reluctantly, opened its doors to a few women, and in 1900 there were two hundred women doctors. So, too, had accountants' firms and some banks. Mr Angell had noticed that women were beginning to work in offices and were particularly adept on the new typewriters. In 1912 he sent Irene to learn shorthand and typing at a college in Lavender Hill and, when she qualified, found her a job in his own office. Not surprisingly male clerks were worried about the number of women coming into their line of work, particularly as they were doing the job for a smaller wage.

These intrepid 'typewriter pounders', instead of being allowed to gloat over love novels or do fancy crocheting during the time they are not 'pounding' should fill in their spare time washing out the offices and dusting same, which you will no doubt agree is more suited to their sex and maybe would give them a little practice and insight into the work they will be called upon to do should they so far demean themselves as to marry one of the poor male clerks whose living they are doing their utmost to take out of his hands at the present time. (Letter from a male clerk to *The Liverpool Echo*, 1911)

In fact, Irene never came across such outright hostility. As women found themselves doing the menial chores, such as tea-making and stamping letters, the men felt they had achieved a promotion of sorts and congratulated themselves on being no longer general dogsbodies at the bottom of the office hierarchy.

It was the First World War which really turned the idea of a woman's place upside down. Patriotic fervour swept through the country as everyone rushed to play a part in the war effort, transforming traditional attitudes to work. While the men were at the Front, women replaced them in jobs that would never have been thought suitable before. As well as volunteering for nursing, middle-class women drove ambulances, joined the civil service or Land Army, worked in businesses, banks and insurance companies. They even formed a small Women's Police Force. Working-class women became stokers, tool setters, painters, carpenters, bus conductors and did many other jobs previously only done by men. Such radical change was not achieved without a fight. Intransigent trades unionists opposed women joining the workforce with every argument they could muster, from the inadequacy of the lavatories in factories and shipyards to women's physical unsuitability for heavy work. All the unions' carefully constructed safeguards to protect men's jobs appeared under threat from this new source of unskilled, cheap labour. The government persuaded them to relax their rules to allow women to do semi-skilled work or assist

Above: During the First World War, trades unions agreed to let women do men's jobs, but for the duration of war only. As the board in the window makes clear: 'When the boys come we are not going to keep you any longer – girls'.

men in skilled jobs but promised this would only be for the duration of the war. Managers were delighted. Not only was a woman cheaper but, as a manager of a munitions factory observed, she adapted instantly to the new assembly lines.

On mass production she will come first every time ... we were never able to get the men to cope with it.... Men will not stand the monotony of a fast repetition job like women, they will not stand by a machine pressing buttons all their lives, but a woman will.

Four hundred thousand domestic servants left their jobs for the more popular factory work, including Ethel Dean. Landing a job on munitions at Woolwich Arsenal was the break she had been waiting for. She was thankful not to become one of the 'canary girls' working with TNT which had serious side effects and turned the workers yellow. Her own job was hazardous enough. Surrounded by barrels of gunpowder it took little to set off an explosion so every morning Ethel had to strip off her clothes and wear regulation overalls, a special hat and shoes. 'You wasn't allowed to wear any hairpins in your hair, no hooks and eyes in your clothes, nothing metal whatever on you, even linen buttons with metal rings.' Many of the girls working on shell-filling with Ethel suffered from abdominal pains and nausea.

Despite its drawbacks, Ethel found life in a munitions factory far more fun than domestic service had ever been. The pay was better too although,

even where they were doing identical jobs, women were paid less than men. The first strike for equal pay was by women tram workers over war bonuses. They won. Working on the buses became one of the most popular wartime jobs. Annie Fry applied to join the Southampton trams when she was only sixteen. To qualify as a conductor she needed to pass a test. First she had to add up a few numbers to show she would not lose the bus company any money when selling tickets and then she had to explain how she would handle a drunken passenger. Her answer that she would call the driver so he could put him off the bus satisfied the inspector and she got the job. No one had realised the difficulty of running up and down stairs in long skirts so the bus company designed a uniform for Annie and the other girls. 'They decided we'd have puttees and knickers and then they thought that was disgusting, so then they decided to have short skirts. But boots. We had our own boots.'

Many an eyebrow was raised at their new hemlines, though by today's standards they were hardly revealing. The mother of one of Annie's colleagues, Violet Pattinson, was so shocked by the length of her daughter's skirt that she refused to let Violet out of the house without a long overcoat to hide her black stockinged ankles from the sight of passers-by.

The TUC lobbied hard to make sure all tram conductresses' licences would be revoked when the war was over. Violet and Annie were resigned to leaving the trams in 1918 but, when the war was over, begged for other work with the company. 'We asked if they could find us a job in the house, you know, where the buses were parked, or cleaning them. Anything. But no, it had to be men. It was for the men – well that was natural, wasn't it?'

Women's ideas about work were as fixed as men's. They felt they had no right to take a job from a man who had a family to support and that the changes in their lives belonged to the mad world of war. Once it was over, most returned without fuss to their 'proper place' – the home. But others were less satisfied; the war had given them a taste of a different life and putting the clock back proved difficult. The last thing Ethel Dean wanted when she was no longer needed on munitions was her old job as a maid-of-all-work. 'When you were in service you couldn't go out when you liked. When you work in the factories you've got your own time, haven't you? You just go home of a night, wherever you live, and you can go out when you like.'

Women's war work helped politicians see the nonsense in denying them the vote which was given to women over thirty in 1918. They were also allowed to stand for Parliament and, after the Sex Disqualification (Removal) Act of 1919, in theory at least, to 'assume or carry on any civil profession or vocation'. However, many spheres, from the synods of the Church of England to the floor of the stock exchange, were not covered by the Act, and in the civil service women soon discovered that, despite the Act, women were kept out of the more exciting jobs such as overseas postings in the Foreign Office. All the same, professional women had far more chance of a career than before the war.

Working-class girls, on the other hand, had the same choice of jobs as ever. As agreed with the trades unions, their wartime jobs had gone. Once again their best chance of finding work was as a domestic servant. Although an unpopular job, in many parts of the country it was all there was. Daisy Noakes and her sisters, living in Brighton, had all been trained for domestic service by their mother since they were young children. Daisy's father, a gentleman's gentleman, considered factory work beneath him and his family but his children had to find jobs once they were fourteen as there was no question of him supporting them. One day, without warning, Daisy was taken out of school by her mother and told to take off her gymslip as she had to go for an interview. When she went up to her bedroom she found her mother's suit laid out on her bed. Reluctantly she put on this voluminous outfit which reached her ankles, assuming her mother would soon see how ridiculous she looked. Instead her mother added a few accessories to complete the picture. 'She took her own hat,

Far left: Violet Pattinson's mother was so shocked by her daughter's tram conductor's uniform that she made her wear a coat over it to hide her ankles.
Left: at the end of the war, women tram workers were given a farewell certificate but no jobs.

LADIES' MAIDS AND MAIDS.

LADY HOUSEKEEPERS, HOUSEKEEPERS, AND COOKS.

PARLOURMAIDS AND HOUSE-PARLOUR-MAIDS.

DOMESTIC.

GOVERNESSES, HELPS, LADY NURSES, AND NURSES.

which was black beaver, and by turning down the leather lining and folding paper inside by trial and error kept putting it on my head to see if it fitted. When it eventually fitted every bit of hair was pushed out of place and she stood back and thought "not quite right" and she put her big fox fur round my shoulders. It was one complete fox fur with the head biting the tail. And that is how I looked.'

Happy that her daughter at last looked the part, Daisy's mother dragged her along to a grand house to see if she passed as good servant material. They were interviewed by Daisy's prospective employer, a gaunt and imposing woman. 'She said, "Sit down, girl." "That's it, girl." Every time I was addressed it would be "girl" and she addressed everything to my mother. Am I clean? Have I got regular habits? Was I an early riser? Had I been schooled into all these sort of chores? And my mother was saying, "Yes, Ma'am. Yes, Ma'am." She said, "Stand up, girl. How old are you?" I said, "I shall be fourteen next month, Ma'am." She said "I think you'll look a bit older when you get a longer dress on," and this skirt was to my ankles and I thought whatever should I do, I should fall over if I had a longer dress.'

So Daisy found herself before her fourteenth birthday living away from home for the first time, rather frightened and lonely in a strange household. Life as a single maid in a house with no other servants was as miserable for Daisy in 1922 as it had been for Ethel Dean before the war. Like Ethel, Daisy sought to improve her status by applying for better work after a year

Top left: In the 1920s the best chance of work for women was once again in domestic service, as before the war.
Above: Daisy Noakes, aged 13, dressed in her mother's clothes for her first interview.

or two. At one interview she was asked what her name was. ' "Daisy," I said. "Daisy," she said, "haven't you any other name?" she said. "Well, my other parlour maid was called Dorothy. Have you any objection to being called Dorothy?"'

Whatever she was called, Daisy was grateful for work. There were fewer women in paid employment than before the war. Retraining schemes were mostly in cooking, housecraft or dressmaking. Half those who had left domestic service were forced to return though many still resisted. Rose Ashton was determined that her daughter, Gladys, would not be a servant as she had been herself; though in Barrow, as Gladys remembers, 'there was only shopwork or service.... Most of my friends went into shops.' And so did Gladys, working first in deliveries and then in a tobacconist's, considered by the family to be a definite improvement on her mother's job as a farmer's servant.

By contrast, there were some exciting new opportunities for middle-class women. In 1920 Theodora Llewelyn Davies became one of the first women to apply to read for the Bar. She immediately found that the Bar was quite unprepared for women. All the documentation assumed barristers were men. On her application form each 'his' was scratched out by hand and replaced with 'her'. Two years later when she started practising, she discovered there were no ladies' rooms in the Courts or Chambers. But at least the professions were opening their doors, even if only a crack, and it was becoming possible for a resolute spinster to have a career. It was still almost impossible for her to get to the top, however. There were estimated to be around two million more women than men during the 1920s, who would therefore remain unmarried, but only a handful of them rose to positions of authority. Married women could not contemplate careers. Women had won the right to work in the professions but they lost it as soon as they married. A marriage bar prevented them from keeping most jobs beyond their wedding day. Theodora Llewelyn Davies abandoned her wig and gown on marriage. 'I decided that I'd rather devote my time and interest to joining my husband and the work he was doing. In those days it wasn't very customary for married women to work apart from their domestic duties and it didn't really occur to me that it would be possible to combine the two.'

Above: Daisy Noakes in her maid's uniform. Her employer preferred to call her 'Dorothy'.

The BBC, publishing houses and other new organisations, unhampered by traditional work practices, appeared to offer unparalleled opportunities to women. The BBC, in its early years, had a reputation for being an enlightened employer with a clear policy of treating men and women identically.

An internal memo in 1928 stated:

The principle of women working with equal status is accepted. The principle of married women so working is equally accepted. (November 1928, Assistant Controller to Director General.)

In 1932, only four years after this policy was declared, the BBC decided to dismiss women on marriage, justifying its change of direction on the grounds that married women were taking jobs from single women who had no other means of support.

Many spinsters did, indeed, have a hard time. Jobs were scarce and one woman in three had to support herself. The cost of living had doubled since before the First World War and most women's work was as badly paid as ever. Finding affordable board and lodging was such a problem that many women were still forced to find a live-in job. This was hardly the future Sue Quinell had dreamed of when she broke the family tradition of domestic service. She had imagined herself a brave pioneer in a new, progressive era, earning enough to rent a small flat of her own. She ended up grateful for a residential job as a shop assistant at Bon Marche in Gravesend. 'The living-in part was wonderful but we had rigid discipline, long hours, very little money. That's the basic three I could moan about. It was shocking. I remember ten o'clock closing. It was very hard.' Sue's ambition was to become a secretary, but neither she nor her family ever had enough money for the basic course in shorthand. Instead she stayed at Bon Marche for twenty-five years. When she lost her job in the 1950s she had no pension and no home.

As women were not expected to spend a lifetime in paid employment (it was assumed they would have a husband to provide for them), the needs of older, single women were often overlooked. Aging spinsters found it hard to keep their jobs and harder still to find new ones. They were particularly bitter that widows could draw pensions while they worked for years often with no hope of a pension at the end of it all. It was not unusual for women to be excluded from state assistance altogether. Domestic service, for instance, was not covered by unemployment benefit yet most

Below: Married women were banned from working in many jobs. Janet Robson never told anyone she was married. When circumstances changed, she wed her husband openly, no one knowing they were already married.

19_35_.	Marriage solemnized at *The Church of Saint Faith* of *Saint Faith, Great Crosby*				in the *C*

No.	When Married	Name and Surname	Age	Condition	Rank or Profession	Residence
44	December 15 1935	Stewart Young	25	Bachelor	Marine Engineer	3 Lan
		Janet Hamilton Robson	27	Spinster	—	3

Married in the *Parish Church* according to the Rites and Ceremonies of the *Church*

This Marriage was solemnized between us, *Stewart Young* / *Janet Hamilton Robson* | in the Presence of us, | *Mildred Jst* / *James B* of the posts women were offered at the Labour Exchange were as servants. If a woman refused a job her benefit was stopped but if she took a domestic servant's job she sacrificed her future unemployment claims.

As jobs grew scarcer during the depression, hostility towards working women hardened. An article in the *News Chronicle* in January 1934, making a case for better wages for women secretaries, provoked an angry letter the next day: 'Better pay and smarter clothes for women: unemployment and patched clothes for men.' Extremists argued there should be no women workers at all. Sir Herbert Austin, who employed thousands of women in his car factories, expressed himself vehemently:

I don't think a woman's place is in industry. If we were to take women out of industry I believe we could absorb all the unemployment. I think the men ought to be doing the work instead of the women.
(*The Times*, 25 September 1933)

Most of the bitterness was saved for 'pin-money wives', though with an effective marriage bar these were hardly in threatening numbers. In most cases, once a woman married she automatically lost her job. Faced with a drastic cut in income, there was temptation to deceive. A surprising number of women confessed to us that they had kept their marriages a secret. Many a tangled web they wove. A secretary told us she had to pretend that her husband was her brother-in-law. Janet Young, one of the first women to work in the Bank of England, secretly married a ship's engineer and continued working as he could not afford to keep both of them. Four years later when her husband's pay was better, Janet went through a second wedding service, never whispering a word to her family about the first. A nurse, desperate to stay in work, pretended for some years she was single. She was never discovered but came perilously close to it a few times. 'I dared not go to hospital with the ring on, so I took it off and put it into a little tiny purse that it had been sold in and put it in my handbag. One day I had a shock because one of the nurses was looking through my handbag and she said "What's this?" and picked out this little pigskin bag. And I said "Oh, that's nothing to do with you." And I took it off her because I was terrified she was going to open it, 'cause she might have been thinking I was having an illicit honeymoon somewhere. Actually I was married.'

These secret marriages became far more complicated and traumatic if children were involved. Margaret Willett was the only child of an out-of-work actor and a school teacher. The whole family depended on her mother's salary so, not wanting to lose her job, the marriage and Margaret's birth were a closely guarded secret. In Margaret's early years her mother found the only way she could manage was by paying for her daughter to be looked after in the country. 'It broke her heart and my father once told me she used to sit in the evenings, rock herself backward and forward and say "Oh I wish I had my baby, how I would love to have my baby."'

When she was older Margaret returned to her family but her mother continued to keep both her marriage and her daughter a secret. They lived in constant fear that somebody from the school would find out. When they bumped into her mother's headmistress at Victoria Station, they thought the day of reckoning was upon them. 'My father gripped me by the arm and said "Now remember, don't say Mummy." And my mother introduced my father as "my friend, Mr Willett, with his little daughter" and I clenched my teeth and hoped I wouldn't be asked to say anything in case I said the wrong thing.' This unacknowledged relationship has haunted Margaret ever since. Years later, when her mother was terminally ill and unable to collect her pension, Margaret Willett was not allowed to take over her affairs. As far as the bank manager and officials at the Ministry of Education were concerned, her mother had never had a daughter.

The marriage bar was a weapon of convenience, used unashamedly to limit the number of working women. But even during the Depression, it did not apply to unpopular jobs which were traditionally women's, like cleaning. In the BBC, lavatory attendants, charladies and wardrobe women were exempted from this bar because it was 'normal custom' for 'women of this class' to have outside employment.

In March 1934 women's organisations arranged a mass rally to argue the right of married women to paid work but Nancy Seear, at the time personnel manager of C. J. Clark's, insists there was little grassroots support for this or for equal pay. 'It was very largely a professional women's middle-class thing for a very long time. When I was in industry for ten years in the shoe trade, which was 50 per cent women, I don't remember any of our women ever raising the issue of equal pay. There was the general view that the man was the breadwinner and that it was therefore reasonable that he should have more money than a woman.'

Twenty years after the First World War, it was as much a man's world as ever. Women were looked on as cheap, second-class labour, useful in the expanding car and electrical industries where their 'nimble fingers' were needed on assembly lines. There were more professional jobs for single women than a generation earlier, but many were still closed to them. A London stockbroker said there was not the slightest chance of women being allowed on the floor of the exchange as it was not a 'suitable job for a woman'. The BBC, which had begun so promisingly with women in various senior positions, was by 1939 as much a male stronghold as other large institutions. A BBC executive explained to a Political and Economic Planning Researcher, 'Take a regular management meeting – every Monday morning say. It's a closely knit little circle of men meeting. It knows its own mores, language – and then suddenly a species with entirely different reactions is introduced into it. . . . They don't like it.' (PEP, *Women in Top Jobs*, Allen & Unwin, 1971).

The place for this different species was at home not in the Board Room, nor even the office. Mary Stott was working on the *Leicester Mail* during the 1930s. 'Some of the staff had to go and I was an obvious candidate. My mother had died recently so I was a clear choice for redundancy. After all, I wouldn't be out of a job. It seemed quite reasonable to the editor to expect me to stay at home and look after my father.'

Once again it took war to cut through established prejudice. Mobilisation for the Second World War quickly absorbed unemployed men, and women were the next reserve. Girls were less enthusiastic about leaving shops and offices for munitions factories than their mothers had been to leave domestic service. However, some married women like Annie Fry who had not worked since the previous war were keen to get back their old jobs. She sent off an application to rejoin her old tram company and was disappointed not to get a reply. She later discovered that her husband had never posted the letter because he thought she should stay at home with her children.

In the black days of 1941, the government decided it could no longer wait for women to come forward voluntarily. All women between the ages of nineteen and forty (later raised to fifty) were obliged to register for war work. Only the elderly and those with young children and husbands at home were exempt from war work. Once again unions were persuaded to relax working practices during wartime. The government could direct a worker to any job to fit in with national needs. Bella Keyzer, a Dundee weaver, was delighted when she was sent into shipbuilding and trained in welding. She had never enjoyed a job so much in her life and was entranced by the shipyard. 'Out of this place full of rough raw men, they built a thing of beauty, a ship, a wonderful thing ... the skill, the knowledge, to me it was beautiful. I saw everything as beautiful.' Welding was the most

Left: 'The average woman takes to welding as readily as she takes to knitting once she has overcome any initial nervousness due to sparks.' Ministry of Labour leaflet.

exciting and creative work Bella had ever done. She was completely content.

A wartime Ministry of Labour leaflet for the shipbuilding industry encouragingly explained:

The average women takes to welding as readily as she takes to knitting once she has overcome any initial nervousness due to sparks. Indeed the two occupations have much in common, since they both require a small, fairly complex manipulative movement which is repeated many times combined with a kind of subconscious concentration at which women excel.

The men Bella worked with were quite friendly. They did not consider her serious competition as they knew she was only a temporary and besides they earned three times more money than she did. It took Bella ninety-two hours' work to take home the same money as the men did in a week with no overtime. The only women who received equal pay were those who worked on trams or buses. All the same, compared with the wages women were used to, their war work was well paid.

As married women made up the main labour reserve, even those with young children were targeted as potential workers. They were never actually forced to work, as it was feared it would damage morale since a man serving his country overseas liked to feel that his wife was at home, looking after his house and children. A job nearby, however, did not appear too threatening. Specially commissioned surveys revealed that married women were prepared to do part-time work near home and pinpointed housewives' main worries as childcare, shopping, housework and husbands. From the vantage point of the 1980s these findings hardly sound surprising but they were one of the first clear indications that working mothers required not only a more flexible approach to work but new attitudes to domestic routines. Propaganda films gave the impression that a great deal was being done to make working women's lives easier, but in fact this did not amount to a great deal. Fifteen hundred nurseries were opened, a few managers tried to fit work shifts around school and nursery hours and others gave women time off for shopping. One factory even issued cosmetic rations to all their women employees on Saturdays to encourage them not to skip work. Works canteens were opened, more schools provided lunches and two thousand British Restaurants opened, providing inexpensive meals. In theory, at least, women were saved the worry of midday cooking.

During the war two million women learnt to combine their work at home with work outside. Married women emerged as steady workers, often favourably compared with single girls. They were more reliable and were praised for bringing housewifely pride to their jobs as in this Ministry of labour leaflet:

A healthy, and not too heavy, sensible woman who has to run a home is marvellously adaptable, and will turn her hand to anything with good will.

In 1945, her praises no longer sung, her skills no longer needed, the sensible housewife was expected to down tools and return to her knitting. Months before the war ended, the shipyards informed Bella Keyzer she was no longer wanted. 'There were about twelve women welders in the yard at that time and we were sent for one morning and the personnel officer sat there at his desk. He lifted his head and he said one word "redundant". That was a new word to our vocabulary. We really didn't know exactly what it meant. There was no reason given. There was no explanation. There was plenty of work in the yard.'

As women returned to full-time housework, it looked as if there would be a repetition of the back-to-normal routine that had followed the First World War but, in the post-war economic boom, this was not to be. The need for married women to work during the war had ended the marriage bar, and attitudes had shifted sufficiently to make it difficult to bring it back. The trend away from domestic service towards employing women in the new engineering and electrical industries accelerated in the 1940s and 50s. Modern industry no longer demanded the brute strength of the old manufacturing sector and women were thought to be ideal employees: cheap labour, prepared to take on mindless, repetitive work.

Below: At the end of the war, women were expected to be happy to become housewives once more.

Your "after-the-war" dream . . .

is coming true . . . war duties ended . . . Dad finished with night shifts . . . family reunions. Peacetime gives you new interests and new cares.

Now yours will be the responsibility of looking after the family's health. Wartime experience has shown you the value of ' Milk of Magnesia,' so you won't forget to keep this always in the medicine cabinet as a stand-by against minor upsets of the system.

'MILK OF MAGNESIA'

' Milk of Magnesia ' is the trade mark of Phillips' preparation of magnesia

Part-time work continued to be popular both with women and their employers after the war. Women liked it because they had a chance to supplement the family income while leaving time for housework. Bosses liked it because it was cheap, flexible labour in a period of full employment. By 1951 22 per cent of married women had jobs, compared with 10 per cent before the war. Yet despite a shortage of labour, many jobs were still closed to women. Bella Keyzer could not get back into welding. 'This was the job that suited my personality. It was an individual job to me and I started a little game. Every time I saw welder jobs being advertised I would apply, but I would only put my initials on the paper. I never put "Mr" or "Mrs". And back would come a reply addressed to "Mr" and I would be granted an interview and off I'd go for the interview and when I was introduced they would say "Oh my goodness, you've got the best qualifications that we've had that's applied for the job, but you are a woman." As if I didn't know that, you know. "But you are a woman, and I wonder what the boys would say if I employed a woman." ' Bella never gave up but it took her thirty years to get back the job she had in the war.

High-powered jobs were just as elusive. Mary Stott, by now working for the *Manchester Evening News*, was in line for promotion. Every Saturday she acted as deputy editor when suddenly, for no apparent reason, she was dropped. 'So I went to the editor and I said, "Why am I not to go on doing this deputy job?" he said, "Oh Mary, it's nothing wrong with your work, but we have to safeguard the succession and the successor has to be a man." End message. How can you go on doing something knowing there is no promotion, knowing that young men whom you have helped to train will inevitably jump over you?'

Women were regarded as fleeting figures dropping in and out of the labour market to suit their circumstances. They were not expected to stick at a job for twenty years or more, so they were not given the same consideration as a man who might well devote all his working life to one firm. Besides, it was argued, women only worked for extras in the house, while men had to pay for the house itself. Until women could show they were a permanent part of the workforce, they would never be treated as equals. They would not have the same chance of promotion or be paid the same wage.

A 1946 Royal Commission on Equal Pay had opposed equal pay except for some categories of civil servants, although three of the four women on the Commission had dissented. Fed up with nothing being done, women in teaching, local government and the civil service started a four-year campaign for equal pay in 1951. The government claimed it accepted the principle but protested that the country could not afford it. So campaigners lobbied MPs, designed 'Equal Pay: When?' badges, led deputations, held protest meetings and organised petitions. In 1955 they won a limited victory when the professional branches of all three areas were granted

"LADIES, THE GOVERNMENT AGREES IN PRINCIPLE, BUT DOES NOT THINK THE TIME OPPORTUNE etc, etc ..."

Right: The cartoonist in 1954 clearly thought equal pay was still a long way off.

THINGS TO COME – MARCH 9. 1994.

phased payments bringing women's wages up to men's. Manual grades and those which were seen as purely women's work (like nursing) were excluded.

The number of women dividing their time between work and home continued to increase in the 1950s. As service industries such as catering, hairdressing and office work grew, women were in particular demand yet the prevailing wisdom dictated that mothers should stay home with their children. Rose Hagan, a widow, had to work to support her son. She had a good job in the car industry, working at Fords, and was lucky enough to have a mother who came in to look after her son when school finished. Even so, she ran into trouble with officialdom. 'I came home one night and my Mum was crying and I said to her, "What's the matter with you?" "Well, I've had a lady down here," she said, "an inspector," she said, "and she thinks you should be at home when Terry comes in from school. She's coming back to see you." At the time I was doing overtime and I think it was about 6 o'clock when I got in and she was there and I said to her, "What did you make me Mum cry for?" So she said, "Your job should be here when your son comes home from school." So I said, "But he's never on his own. My Mum's here. He never comes into an empty house, she's here." I said, "But then again, if you'd pay me the money and up my pension, I'll stop at home and look after him but otherwise I'll go to work."'

It was hard for mothers to know where their duty lay. The baby boom needed mothers as much as the industrial boom needed workers. Single women, however, were expected to work. Whatever their background, once they left school they went out to work and enjoyed a standard of living far higher than their mothers had ever known. There were plenty

*Left: Dolly bird
secretaries were
popular, but this pet
name kept them firmly
in their place as little
more than office
decoration.*

of jobs; assembly lines cried out for workers, offices for typists, hotels for
receptionists. In the Swinging Sixties the height of many a young girl's
ambition was to do a little modelling or work in a boutique. Whatever the
job, there was usually enough money at the end of the week to buy the
latest off-the-peg fashions but seldom much hope of promotion. The pet
name 'dolly bird' kept girls in their place, as useful adornments, easy on
the eye but definitely not to be taken seriously.

Catherine Inman's mother, Maureen, worked as a secretary in Barrow-
in-Furness. There were only three girls in a department of three hundred
men. She basked in all the attention she was paid – having doors opened
for her, appreciative glances as she walked through an office and willing
hands to carry any load of files. Eventually she married someone she met
at work and left at her husband's insistence when she had their first child.
'It was more important to him than to me but I cannot say I have regretted
it.' With her daughter Catherine and two younger children, she was kept
busy enough at home.

Women in industry became more assertive as their numbers swelled. In
1968 Rose Hagan led women machinists at Fords to strike for recognition
as skilled workers. A new grading system placed them on a level with
unskilled men who, unlike Rose and her group, had never taken a pro-
ficiency test. 'We were skilled. We were made to do a test before we could
work at Fords. Nobody wanted equal pay. We wanted our grading. If we
had got equal pay we thought we would have to do shift work and none

of the girls wanted that.' Within days the whole plant was forced to close down. After three and a half weeks Barbara Castle, Minister for Employment and Productivity, visited the Fords women and promised them more money and equal pay legislation though not the higher grade they were after. Union officials were delighted and pushed the women into accepting the deal against their better judgement. They had lost the grading dispute but at least, after years of campaigning, the practice of setting women's rates and men's rates was to be abolished. But it took a committed woman politician to reach a position of power to push it through.

The more cynical say the main reason for the timing of the 1970 Equal Pay Act was to bring British laws in line with Europe's as Britain looked likely to sign the Treaty of Rome, after which equal pay would be obligatory anyway. The 1970 Act applied only to 'men and women employed on work rated as equivalent' but because many women worked in jobs done only by women, the Act did not cover them. There were really two labour markets, one for men and one for women, and the Act only covered the small areas where they overlapped. There were plenty of dodges too. The content of work could be changed and jobs further segregated to make comparisons difficult.

Further legislation was needed to improve the position. The Sex Discrimination Act of 1975 was piloted through the House of Lords by Nancy Seear, author of *The Position of Women in Industry* and a keen campaigner for women's rights: again the right woman was in the right place at the right time. The Act banned the practice of refusing a job to an applicant

If God had intended women to think he'd have given them better jobs

Left: Thirty years after losing her job at the end of the war, the 1975 Sex Discrimination Act finally enabled Bella Keyzer to be a welder again. Her pay rose from £27 to £73 a week.

on the grounds of sex. Even sixty years after women had clearly demonstrated that they were capable of taking over their husbands' and brothers' jobs, it needed the full weight of the Law before they got a fair deal. As soon as the Act was passed, Bella Keyzer went straight down to the shipyard and demanded a welding job. 'It was the climax to the game I had played these thirty years about asking for jobs. Because when I went back in everybody was expecting this young dolly bird, woman's liberator, to come walking in, and who walks in but this grey-haired, 54-year-old woman ... My wage had been £27 and when I went into the shipyard it went up to £73. That is what equality did for me.'

The Sex Discrimination Act also extended the horizons of many young girls leaving school. Catherine Inman had a far wider choice of jobs in Barrow when she left school than any woman in her family had ever had. The only job her great-grandmother, Rose, could hope for in 1905 was as a servant. Catherine's grandmother, Gladys, had a choice of domestic service or being a shop assistant. Things were looking up by her mother's time. Maureen Inman had a choice between a variety of jobs in the 1960s: nursing, secretarial or shop work or the assembly line. Catherine, by taking an engineering job in the Barrow shipyard, joined what used to be a man's world. Though her own family thought it odd, Catherine says boys of her own age saw nothing strange in a girl working in a shipyard. 'Most of them are fairly broadminded. They've been brought up with the idea that women are tending to go into engineering.' However, the older men in the shipyard found it hard to treat her as one of them. 'Quite a lot of the men tend to coddle you and tell you "Don't carry that toolbag, I'll carry it, it's a bit heavy for you. You won't manage it going up that ladder." Or they'll say "Oh, I'll take that over, you can't get it quite tight enough." It really annoys me that sort of thing, 'cos I can, y'know, and if I can't I'll make sure I can. Sometimes they say "You sit down there, have a rest, you've climbed a lot of ladders," but even if I was tired, I wouldn't let on.'

Employment laws were changed to give women paid maternity leave and the right to return to a job after pregnancy. These changes made an enormous difference to the attitude to working mothers. I remember when I had my first child in the mid-1970s it was still unusual for women to return to work while their babies were small. A long career break was far more common. Four years later when I had my third child it was automatically assumed that I would be back at my desk after a few months. The BBC learned to allow for 8 per cent of its female production staff to be off on maternity leave at any one time.

The third important piece of legislation for women workers came in 1984 when, after being taken to the European Court, the government was made to amend the Equal Pay Act so that women could get equal pay for work of equal value. This Act was supposed to sort out the problem of the separate labour markets for men and women. After the Amendment a low-paid secretary, previously not helped by the Act as she had no point of comparison, could claim her work was of the same value to the company as, say, a junior executive and get her salary brought up to his. On average women now get 74 per cent the pay of men. As it is still being tested in the Courts, it is not yet clear whether the Equal Pay Amendment will really help the majority of women who work in almost exclusively female jobs.

It is particularly difficult to help the five million women in part-time jobs. They often receive no state or fringe benefits and do jobs no one else will do: fluffers who scrape the dirt from the underground tracks from 1.15 to 4.30 in the morning, cleaners who sweep through offices before everyone else's day begins. Echoing the custom at the start of the century, there are still women who take in work at home. An Asian housewife in Leicester, for instance, sews gussets in knickers for only a penny a pair. At the same time she looks after nine relations who all need meals at odd times of the day and night as they come in from shiftwork and school. One of her children is handicapped so she can never leave the house. She manages about six hundred pairs of pants a day and working every spare moment brings in £30 a week. While it is true that since the war job opportunities have opened up for women, married women find it difficult to take advantage of the market because of their domestic ties. They still measure the suitability of a job by how well it can be fitted in.

The general trend is for mothers to stay at home until their youngest child is of school age, then to work part-time until that child is around eleven, after which they return to full-time work. Clearly part-time work has been a godsend to millions of women, enabling them to work and spend time with their children. On the other hand, it frequently leaves them in a rut. In her study of women's career prospects in banking, Nancy Seear found that French women reached a higher level in banking than women in England. 'French trade unions set their face against part-time work and I think from the women's point of view this is probably one of the reasons why they have done as well as they have. If you're working part-time you can just manage at a low level. If you're working full-time you can't and, therefore, you have to make proper child care arrangements.' In France nurseries are widespread even in the smallest communities and schools stay open to fit in with working hours.

Today nearly two-thirds of married women have jobs. When we asked women why they worked, money and companionship were far more common answers than ambition or personal satisfaction. Women's earnings have raised family expectations and a second income is often essential to pay the mortgage or weekly shopping bills. Professional women are far more likely to say they work because they find their jobs rewarding. A high ranking civil servant in the Department of Trade and Industry had her first child in 1980. She assumed she would resume her career after a few months but wanted to work part-time. Traditionally women at her level had left altogether when they had children. She did not want to abandon a promising career but she did not think she had 'the emotional stamina to work full-time with a husband in a high pressure job too. One of us had to have a reserve of energy to deal with children, schools and the house.' The civil service was forced to adopt a more flexible approach. Its annual intake of graduates contained an increasingly high percentage of women and it could not afford to lose them all a few years later. To begin with the part-timers were not taken seriously – one of them remembers her boss pondering aloud whether it was worth bothering to write her annual report – but they are now making their way up the hierarchy, although at a rather slower pace than those who work full-time.

It is still unusual for women to reach the top in any of the professions although they are entering them in ever-increasing numbers. Since 1975 the number of women becoming chartered accountants has gone up from 7 per cent to 23 per cent of all entrants, becoming bankers from 4 per cent to 21 per cent and qualifying as solicitors from 19 per cent to 54 per cent. Yet hardly any women reach the top of the professions. Women, themselves, often bow out of the race. They are more likely to consider whether a promotion will threaten their family life. A woman journalist admitted she preferred the flexibility of being features writer to the responsibilities of being editor and having to work a fifteen-hour day and six-day week. Optimists hope that this kind of 'feminine approach' will influence work patterns, that men too will refuse to be governed solely by corporate demands. The real test will come in the next decade when the surge of women who joined the professions in the seventies reach the age for command.

Confronted with jobs designed for men, the first generation of women have simply tried to prove they are no different from the men they work with. Elizabeth Sullivan, one of a small number of women to reach the floor of the stock exchange before the 'Big Bang', is convinced she would never have made it with domestic ties. 'The pressure can be too much. I mean, you have to be in so early and you'd have no time to take your children to school and then by the time you leave you haven't got time to pick them up. I think a normal working-class woman would find it difficult to bring up children and to cope with it.... I think it suits a single woman more than anything else because you're not committed to anything or anybody, and you haven't got to rely on people to sort of stand in for you.'

Above: Nancy Seear, a successful politician. As she says, it has helped being single.

A woman who has made it to the top today has usually done so by proving she was the 'best man for the job'. This is not difficult while she has the same flexibility as a man but once she has children it is far harder for her to compete. Unless there are changes in the rigid patterns which govern most senior posts or a transformation of domestic routine, there will continue to be a scarcity of women at the top. Unlike their grandmothers, they have the chance of getting there but too often, as Nancy Seear, now a leading politician in the House of Lords, observes, at the expense of family life. 'Let me put it like this, I'm a single woman. There is no doubt that it is very, very much easier if you are single than if you are married. I think myself there's more difference in terms of opportunity, between a single woman and a married woman than there is between a single woman and a man.'

With every decade this century the skills which marked work 'for men only' have counted for less. Jobs requiring muscle have declined along with the old heavy industries or been replaced by automation. It is hard to argue that women are not suitable for modern jobs which need deft fingers or brainpower. The nature of work has changed and so too has the capacity of women to hold down a job. Physically, women have never been in such good shape. Medical developments have helped everyone to live a longer and healthier life; but for women, being able to control when and how many children they have has been arguably the greatest advance of all.

CHAPTER FOUR

Mustn't Grumble
Women's Health

NEVER before has so much attention been paid to women's health. In October 1986 the government announced that a Minister in the Department of Health would have special reponsibility for women's problems. The following year the Labour Party published a special paper on *Women and Health* attacking the government's record, saying:

In recent years there has been mounting evidence that women – young and old, in work or at home, black or white – are at risk of ill health in specific ways and that the National Health Service alone cannot respond adequately.

In the Liverpool suburb of Sefton, a red double-decker bus has been turned into a mobile health centre, providing an informal meeting place for any woman who wants a check-up, advice or simply a cup of tea among friendly faces. The bus travels to shopping centres, housing estates and schools – all the sort of places where women congregate. Children are looked after in a creche downstairs, leaving their mothers free to talk over their problems with one of the health team or chat to other women on the top deck. The Sefton Health Bus is run by enthusiastic staff who try to give the kind of support they feel is not offered anywhere else. Nearly half the regional health authorities have set up Well Woman Clinics or neighbourhood health schemes as part of a new approach to healthcare. It is no coincidence that this policy has come at a time when women are playing a more critical role in the economy and becoming more vocal about their particular problems.

In the past, when women were simply wives and mothers, they neither demanded nor received much professional attention. The rich could afford the best treatment money could buy – private nursing, anaesthetics, a doctor on call. The poor could not. Few of the older women who talked to us were ever well off. They remember their mothers, some with as many as ten children, coping with miscarriages, difficult childbirth, untreated gynaecological disorders, painful varicose veins and constant tiredness (probably caused by anaemia). They never saw a woman doctor. In 1900 there were only two hundred women doctors in the whole country and the medical profession often appeared unsympathetic when faced with feminine ailments. Women had no alternative but to soldier on. Besides, one explained, 'women were expected to be frail, it was thought ladylike'.

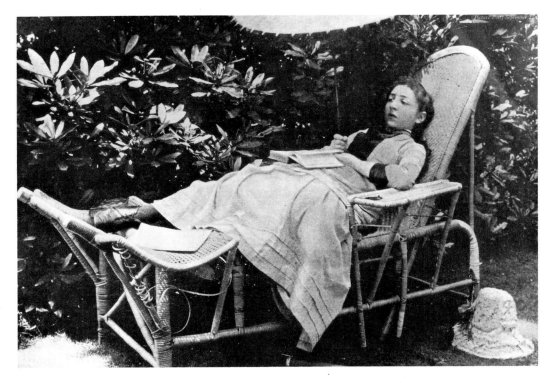

Above: 'Women were expected to be frail. It was thought ladylike.'

So they suffered in silence. Victoria Wignall's experiences were commonplace. She was born in 1900. Everything went well in her first twenty years: she had a happy marriage, a home of her own and good health but the birth of her daughter changed everything. Labour was a long, drawn out affair, quite normal, she was assured, but it left her tired, weak and in constant pain. Victoria's doctor put it down to nerves and told her she would soon snap out of it. 'I was ashamed of what I thought was my lack of character and tried to do all in my power to overcome my pain and weakness. I struggled for many months as do many mothers, washing, scrubbing, cooking and nursing with too many trials and disappointments to describe.'

After the birth of her second child the pain became acute. Victoria survived another seven years living in 'a kind of faint' until a new doctor sent her to a specialist who immediately found extensive internal injuries caused by the instruments used in her first labour. An operation was arranged and Victoria restored to normal. Just as important as the cure was the knowledge that she had a genuine complaint. She had been told for so long not to fuss or grumble and that all she had to do was pull herself together that she had come to believe there was nothing physically wrong with her. 'I had such a feeling of relief, I felt so happy I felt I could tell the world. It was something with a name. It wasn't me. Somebody had believed me at last.'

In the 1920s, medical know-how could put Victoria right; but earlier in the century women had no alternative but to put up with such problems. They accepted that a level of mild ill health was normal, putting it down to 'being a woman' in much the same way as the elderly dismiss their aches and pains as a sign of 'getting on'. Birth, death and illness were all managed at home, with little outside help.

When state health care was created, it was largely for working men. The 1911 National Health Insurance Act entitled insured workers (those in regular employment earning less than £160 per annum) to choose a doctor from the 'panel' of those who agreed to take part in the scheme. They received free medical treatment but had to pay part of the cost (on a means test) if they went to hospital. Their wives and children were not covered at all. Apart from a small number of women in insurable jobs, women had to pay the doctor or, more often, do without.

Gynaecological problems, in particular, were likely to go untreated. The medical profession had been slow to recognise obstetrics and gynaecology as a legitimate branch of medicine so, as Victoria Wignall discovered to her cost, doctors lacked experience. (Respectability did not come until 1929 with the foundation of the British College of Obstetricians and

Women's ailments were not openly discussed but middle-class women could buy manuals like this 1913 Wife's Handbook.

Gynaecologists, now the Royal College.) Edwardian women were shy of talking about their bodies. Some of their embarrassment rubbed off on their children and grandchildren, extending a veil of silence on feminine matters well into the second half of the century. Alma Rosser, a direct, very unprudish community health officer, understood implicitly as a child that there were forbidden topics. 'Anything from the waist down was absolutely taboo. And I suppose my grandparents would be afraid to go to the doctor. They preferred to go to someone they trusted and knew had these marvellous remedies. And my mother was inclined to carry on in this way although she did go to the doctor about various things. But I don't think she liked doing it at all. There was a certain amount of embarrassment and shame about women's illnesses.' Alma, born in Wales in 1923, observed this diffidence all through her early years. Often it brought unnecessary illness or worse. Alma's mother-in-law died at the age of thirty-two from septicaemia brought on by infected piles about which she was too shy to confide in a doctor. Pregnancy, women's most natural function, shamed them into hiding their shape. No matter how much joy attended a birth, no one was supposed to know it was imminent. Pregnant women stayed indoors or wore voluminous clothes to camouflage their condition. As late as the 1940s, women remember wearing coats on hot summer days to conceal a bulge.

Few women were covered by medical insurance. Most depended on home remedies or concoctions from the local chemist.

As Alma Rosser recalled, women habitually looked after themselves and had their own special treatments. Before the First World War a network of handywomen, midwives, chemists and herbalists tended most of their needs. Home remedies were handed down from one generation to another: brimstone and treacle to clear the bowels and purify the blood, tobacco for toothache, a burning tomato to lance a verruca. Everyone had her favourites. Kathleen Dayus lived in a slum terrace in Birmingham. At sixpence a visit, her parents seldom took her to the doctor. 'Headaches, we had vinegar and brown paper; for whooping cough we had camphorated oil rubbed on our chests or goose fat. For mumps we had stockings round our throats and measles we had tea stewed in the teapot by the fire – all different kinds of home cures. They thought they were better than going to the doctor's. Well, they couldn't afford the doctor because looking at sixpence in those days was like looking at a five pound note today.'

Kathleen was born in 1903, one of thirteen chil-

Left: Bad housing took its toll on all the family but women spent more time in these damp, dark tenements than their husbands and children.

dren of whom seven survived. Their father was out of work, their mother helped part time in a fish and chip shop and took in washing. The sun seldom shone on Kathleen's dark and gloomy corner of Edwardian England. The terraces where they lived were a breeding ground for disease. 'The houses were back-to-backs. There was one bedroom and an attic. Two doors away there was one woman had sixteen children and there was only the bedroom and the attics for 'em to sleep in. There was no scullery, kitchens, nothing like that, only the cellar and there was a little pantry and on the walls there was bugs and fleas.'

Poverty and bad housing took their toll on the whole family's health but hit women hardest. They spent more time in their damp, dark tenements; humping heavy loads of washing and coal up and down stairs, bearing and rearing children and, in between, taking in any work they could find that could be done at home. If there was insufficient food, invariably the women did without. It was common in those days for women to spend as much as fifteen years being pregnant or nursing. Kathleen's mother endured close to twenty years. By thirty most women looked old and tired. As another woman reflected dispassionately, there were times when she felt she had 'only been born to breed children and there was nothing else in life for me'.

The State showed little interest in women's wellbeing except when it thought their bad health might jeopardise future generations of workers and soldiers. In an attempt to reduce infant mortality, voluntary bodies and schools were encouraged to educate the working classes in nutrition and health. School meals for poor children and school medical inspections began in 1906 and 1907 and in many areas clinics were set up to help women during and after pregnancy. Middle-class women were happy to dispense advice, but it was difficult for the average housewife in 1913 to follow the well-meaning tips offered, for instance, by the Women's Imperial Health Association to 'drink good water, eat plain, wholesome food, eat slowly . . . choose a dry house'. Over such matters they seldom had control.

The First World War set a few-alarm bells ringing. Able-bodied women were urgently needed in factories to fuel the industrial war machine. But many of the women who offered themselves for work were pale, thin creatures. The government, shaken into action by reports of listlessness and poor diet among women, ordered canteens to be opened at munitions works. Welfare Supervisors were sent in to see to women's wellbeing, though their attempts to improve time-keeping, diet and moral outlook among their charges made them extremely unpopular. War work in itself did little to improve women's health. It was common to stand for ten hours a day working in overcrowded, unheated factories, often with toxic materials. The state accepted a degree of responsibility for women's health after the 1918 Maternal and Child Welfare Act enabled local authorities to provide free clinics for pregnant women and infants. Many women,

Right: Mother and Child Clinics were often the only free service available to married women. They were initially regarded with suspicion, but became increasingly popular between the wars.

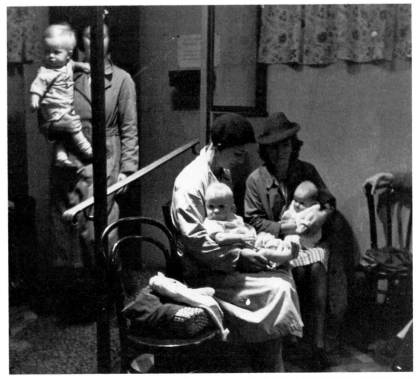

however, resented what they took to be outside interference. They did not think that they needed to be told what to eat when they were pregnant, and they were suspicious of official interest. Hilda Bates, a health visitor between the wars, found this a common reaction in the years before the State played a full part in healthcare. 'They couldn't see why the government should want to register or take any interest in their child. And they wouldn't bring their children to the clinic every month as they were supposed to do. Anyway, the clinic was awful. It was a filthy, dirty public house and, although it wasn't used, it was smelly still. No windows open.' However, it was the only free service available to married women and often the only professional care they ever received.

After the war, home life continued much as before. Despite a drift to new houses in the suburbs, most cities were riddled with overcrowded tenement buildings. In the 1930s Josephine Barnes was a young doctor at University College Hospital, London. 'One did see some pretty horrific poverty, particularly areas like the Caledonian Road where you'd have six families, each living on one of six floors, one water tap half way and a privy in the garden. I remember going to a house one Sunday evening to deliver a lady of her seventh child and the other six were sitting round in the next room eating chips. There were no bedclothes on the bed, because they'd been pawned and were going to be taken out of pawn on Monday when the pay came in.'

Overcrowding was equally bad in Salford where Beatrice Sandys was training to be a midwife. 'Whole families lived in one room and it wouldn't matter the ages of the children or the sexes of the children. They did everything in one room. They ate, they slept, they lived in the one room and they weren't clean either. There was bugs and fleas and all that kind of thing. We were warned by the matron that when we went up the stairs we mustn't touch the walls with our clothes, we must walk in the middle of the stairs.'

Hilda Bates worried particularly about her clothes as she was one of the first to be given the new State Registered Nurse's uniform. 'It cost £7, which was a terrific lot in those days. When we went out on a case we took a hat bag and before we did anything else we took off our uniform carefully and sort of twisted it up so the bugs would not get in. After we finished our case we would stand in the bath and shake our clothes and the bugs would all fall in the bath.'

In such infested surroundings midwives made mothers as comfortable as possible. A pile of newspapers provided the most hygienic bedding to hand. The babies they delivered were as often a source of worry as of joy – another mouth to feed, a danger to the mother's health. Women begged in vain for advice on preventing future births. Midwives had little information and the best doctors could do was to warn the husband he should 'make sure' his wife had no more children. The plight of women worn out

Above: Hilda Bates proudly sporting her new State Registered Nurse's uniform.

by endless pregnancies and thrown into ever greater poverty with each one, prompted the women's sections of the Labour Party and the Co-operative Women's Guilds to demand that information on contraception should be available at local mother and child clinics. In 1924 the Workers' Birth Control Group was set up. Led by feminists such as the writer Dora Russell, and educationalist Mary Stocks, the campaign used a graphic comparison: 'It's four times as dangerous to bear a child as to work in a mine; and mining is man's most dangerous trade.'

The numbers of women dying when giving birth actually rose at this time. In 1924, 3000 women died in childbirth despite having more medical care than ever before. It was becoming more common for doctors to attend births and midwifery had become a more professional business. Although in many homes childbirth was hardly considered a medical matter, doctors and midwives were beginning to see it that way. They argued strongly against home births. A midwife explained, 'It was nothing to see bugs falling out of the ceiling onto the bed when you were waiting for the baby to be born.' With a room full of children, newspapers on the bed, an outside tap, no hot water, nowhere to bath the baby, proper professional treatment was difficult.

There was no pain relief for the working classes. The rich had anaesthetics, the poor a knotted towel to pull on. Not surprisingly most of them believed that they would be better off in hospital in the neat, clean wards they had heard about. However, hospitals brought their own dangers. Jack Suchet, a medical student at St Mary's Hospital, Paddington, in the 1930s, remembers conditions were far from perfect. 'If a woman bled after the vaginal delivery or a vaginal operation, the only method of controlling

Below: Beatrice Sandys in her maternity ward. Hospital births were becoming more common in the 1920s but maternal mortality was still high.

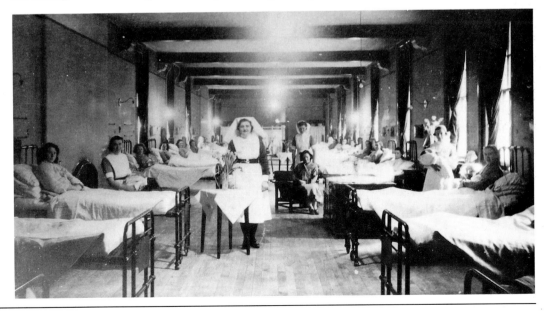

haemorrhage would be by using the curtain of the ward to have sufficient material to pack the vagina. We had no blood transfusions except for our emergency services and then we didn't have the grouping that we have today so that the death rate from haemorrhage was high.'

The greatest risk was puerperal sepsis, childbirth fever. In many hospitals aseptic routines were slack. Ada Finney worked on a gynaecological ward and watched helplessly as infection spread from mother to mother. 'There were absolutely no antibiotics then, absolutely nothing and we used to take any septic cases from the maternity unit and we lost three mothers in a week.' The risk of infection was higher in hospital than at home and as hospitalised births were increasing this may explain the higher maternal mortality rate between the wars. All classes and regions were hit equally – the figures for Middlesex were no different from those in Durham. Campaigners organised a petition with three million signatures calling for fuller maternity and child welfare services, isolation of puerperal sepsis cases and better obstetric training for doctors and midwives.

The need for skilled obstetricians was acute. Victoria Wignall was only one of many scarred by childbirth. Britain's first birth control clinic found that among 10 000 patients, 1 321 had slit cervixes and 1 508 had internal deformations. The gynaecologist, Blair Bell, wrote in *The Lancet* in May 1931 that he estimated 10 per cent of women were permanently disabled by childbirth. The Ministry of Health wrote off the problem as too large to tackle. George Newman, the Minister, said,

Childbirth has always been women's travail and always will be. . . . The broad fact remains, first that childbirth is a heavy strain on the physique of any woman and the bodies of many must, therefore, be impaired. Secondly, that there is in modern civilised nations an insufficient number of organised facilities for effective treatment.

Against this background, it is extraordinary that so little effort went into research and instruction on contraception. The upper and middle classes had been limiting the size of their families since the late nineteenth century. Once their children had a good chance of surviving infancy and they faced the cost of educating, feeding and clothing a large family, Victorian parents presumably had good reason to investigate birth control. Why a parallel trend did not occur among the desperately poor until the inter-war period is not clear. Possibly the high price of sheaths put them beyond reach or couples did not like the idea of them. One Salford housewife, forced into a shotgun wedding in 1927, told us that it never occurred to her to find out about birth control until she had borne four children. Her husband left it to her to take the initiative. 'Finally I got one of those reusable sheaths. I used to wash it, fill it up with water and hold it up in the air to make sure there were no holes in it.' Known as the 'everlasting sheath', this thick, unyielding condom cost between 1s. 6d. and 2s. 6d. in 1920 – a lot of

Above: Mr and Mrs Terry with some of their nineteen children in 1914. Large families were still common in the working classes until the 1930s.

money then. Printed information on contraception was outlawed under the obscenity laws and was therefore very expensive. It seems that *coitus interruptus* was the most common method of limiting families. Yet many older working-class women told us their husbands never liked any form of birth control. It 'undermined a man', threatened his machismo while lots of children proved his virility. What was needed was for public attitudes to change so that husbands could more easily be won over, for more information to be made available and for women to find something simple they could use themselves. To some extent, all this was happening between the wars.

Until the 1920s women had nowhere to go for help. The medical profession did next to nothing about birth control. It was left to an assortment of volunteers, ranging from feminists like Dora Russell and her Workers' Birth Control Group to eugenicists like Marie Stopes, to spread the word and set up clinics to offer practical advice. Dora Russell's group were shocked by the poor health of working-class mothers and believed that contraception was a vital as well as the most immediate way of tackling the problem. Marie Stopes, on the other hand, was attracted by eugenicists' arguments that the strength of the race would diminish if the unfit (by which she meant the lower classes) continued to breed unchecked

Above: An assortment of contraceptive devices used in the 1930s.

while the fit (upper classes) limited their families. Marie Stopes's worries went further. Not only would the British race deteriorate but there was a real danger of the ruling classes being overrun by the masses. Her organisation, the Society for Constructive Birth Control and Racial Progress, opened the first British birth control clinic in 1921 in Holloway. In common with other experts, she did not understand the female cycle, believing that a woman's safe period was the middle of the month – her most fertile time of all. Fortunately for the women visiting her clinic she usually advised them to use what she called a 'racial cap' a small rubber dome which fitted over the cervix. Other clinics soon followed, each run by brave volunteers defying a scandalised establishment and hostile medical profession.

There were a few shining exceptions. William Nixon, the Registrar at St Mary's in Jack Suchet's student days, was anxious to learn as much as he could about contraception. With medical opinion against him, all he could do was to take Jack and some of his other students secretly by night on a Number 27 bus to the North Kensington Clinic where Dr Helena Wright showed them all how to insert Dutch caps, 'thick rubber things made from something like car tyres'. The next week Jack Suchet went to a lecture at the Royal Society of Medicine where, he recalls, an eminent doctor warned 'that all forms of contraception were deleterious and dangerous and that the use of spermaticides – in those days we used a paste called Volpar, Voluntary Parenthood Paste – would result in deformed infants. This doctor also apparently believed that the absorption of semen was necessary for a woman's good health.'

The combined forces of Medicine, Church and State did their best to slow down the development and spread of contraception. In 1923 Dora Russell went to court over the publication of birth control literature. A diagram showing how a woman should insert a cap was considered obscene. It was argued that it might not be the woman's own finger pushing in the cap! A health visitor in Edmonton was dismissed by the Public Health Department for telling mothers at the Mother and Child Welfare Clinic where to go for birth control information.

Mary Stocks came up against unrelenting opposition from Catholics in Salford where she opened a clinic in 1926 with her friend, Charis

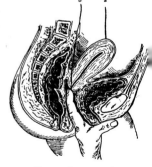

Finger touching mouth of womb.
a—womb ; b—mouth of womb.

Above: This diagram in a family planning leaflet led to a Court case in 1923. The prosecution argued it was obscene.

Frankenburg. Their characters were attacked and they were likened to 'painted women of the worst kind' (to the amusement of Mary Stocks who had always assumed she resembled a rather dowdy social worker). The best premises they could find were above a cooked pie shop. Annie McDermott's mother had the grocery next door. 'Mrs Frankenburg said to my mother she wanted it for a birth control clinic and my mother didn't know what a birth control clinic was, she didn't know what birth control was.' Annie was the youngest of fifteen.

It was not only the Catholics of Salford who were against the clinic. Beatrice Sandys was told firmly by her matron to burn any literature she was given about it. Mothers shrouded by headscarves or wearing hats well pulled down, crept discreetly up the stairs by day or more often by night. One mother admitted that she was begged by a friend to go but was too afraid. She preferred the 'preventive things' she could buy from the local chemist which she took without telling her husband. She had earlier been forced to resort to a back street abortion. Even a trained nurse preferred to turn to her family for advice on an unwanted pregnancy rather than go to a clinic. Her aunt gave her an address and a special number to mention which produced a bottle of pills. 'I took them and, of course, I had rather a nasty period when I flooded. My husband came back and said, "Good God, what on earth have you been doing to yourself?" And he said I should never do it again. But not in all my married life did we have any safe way of stopping children. There was a sort of pessary they sold with cocoa butter, and, of course, there was condoms. But apart from that it was just the withdrawal method.'

It is impossible to put a figure on the number of self-induced miscarriages or abortions routinely resorted to in the absence of anything else. One estimate by the demographer, David Glass, suggested that there were 68 000 criminal abortions in 1935, but that excluded the more common home remedies. A midwife in a mining village, reporting 227 miscarriages among 122 women, suspected few were spontaneous. We found women quite often spoke automatically of abortion when asked about contraception, the two merged inextricably in their minds.

Many women had special pills which they took whenever they feared they were pregnant. In Josephine Barnes's London practice, a variety of concoctions were used. 'There were various types of pills that were sold – pills to regulate you – and some were really poisonous. Some were just strong laxatives, but others would contain lead which, of course, is a disaster. Penny Royal, that's another thing that was used and an extract of parsley called apiole which was a powerful abortifacient. They would buy these from shops – the rather doubtful shops which sold "feminine pills".' Beatrice Sandys saw some horrific consequences of self-induced abortion in Salford. Called to a delivery she would sometimes find women haemorrhaging violently after using a knitting needle to abort a foetus and once found a woman dying from septicaemia after stuffing her vagina with slippery elm. Mail order firms promoted a variety of 'feminine pills to keep yourself regular' or 'cures for female anaemia'. For five shillings women could buy Rene Dubois pilules 'guaranteed speedy and effective even in the most obstinate and unyielding cases. Act like magic and are effective in a few hours.' Salford women understood these codes. Taking precautionary purgatives monthly was common. 'Beecham's used to be advertised as worth a guinea a box, the same price as a back street abortion in Salford,' remembers Beatrice Sandys. 'Now in Beecham's pills, one of the ingredients was lead. So in fact what used to happen was (if they took enough of them) the lead poisoning would in fact kill the foetus with a resulting miscarriage and would make the mother ill too. But she didn't mind being ill as long as she got rid of it.' (Beechams never contained anything stronger than aloes, ginger and soap, but this powerful myth must have done wonders for sales.)

The feminine grapevine whispered that taking tansy, caraway seeds or nutmeg and gin with one's feet in a hot mustard bath would do the trick. Whether they ever brought success is not clear. Some women used highly dangerous mixtures such as gunpowder, turpentine and iron with aloes. Doctors were well aware of the widespread use of abortifacients and in some places routinely examined women's gums for the tell-tale lead stains. A survey of artisan families in London between 1926 and 1929 found married women drenched themselves 'with violent purgatives' monthly as a matter of course.

Induced abortion had been illegal since 1861 unless the life of the mother was in danger. In 1938, Aleck Bourne, a senior consultant at St Mary's Hospital, Paddington, terminated the pregnancy of a fourteen-year-old girl who had been raped by Guardsmen in Whitehall. Aleck Bourne deliberately drew the Attorney General's attention to this operation as he felt the law should sanction abortion in these particular circumstances. In a highly controversial court case he was found not guilty of breaking the law. In summing up, the judge pointed out the difficulty of distinguishing between endangering the *life* of the mother and the *health* of the mother. He thought the law should be interpreted to allow a doctor to abort if he

Above: Women believed Beechams cured greater problems than simple indigestion.

genuinely believed the pregnancy would turn the mother into a physical or mental wreck. After this a doctor (if he agreed with this interpretation of the law) could terminate a pregnancy if he and another doctor considered it would endanger the mental or physical health of the mother. It was an unsatisfactory state of affairs which needed clarification through an Act of Parliament, but this was not to come for another thirty years. Aleck Bourne provides an interesting insight into contemporary opinion. Personally he was against liberalising the law except for rape victims under sixteen, and then only if they were neither mental defectives nor prostitutes, as he did not think those sorts of girls would suffer psychologically from being pregnant.

Abortion and contraception were linked in people's minds with prostitution and venereal disease. They were all lumped together as the sort of things nice people did not know about. Officialdom was more concerned about the falling birthrate than the fact that some women were suffering from multiple pregnancies. Over the country as a whole there was a dramatic fall in births between the wars – so much so that prophets of doom estimated that by the year 2033 England and Wales would have the same sized population as London in 1934. Such forecasts made it even harder for birth control pioneers to rally support and expand their service. However, even if they did not directly reach as many women as they hoped, the fact that they were talking about contraception and showing women that they could control their fertility added to the pool of word-of-mouth knowledge on which so many depended and this helped make the idea more acceptable. The difficulties of raising children during the depression years may also have persuaded some families to use precautions. Certainly, by the start of the Second World War large families were unusual. In 1939, the existing birth control clinics banded together to form the Family Planning Association, with the slogan 'Children by Choice not Chance'. Owing to the vision and hard work of a courageous few, women no longer had to suffer the physical and economic hardship of numerous unwanted pregnancies. The campaign never had official backing and was fought almost exclusively by women.

The tradition of feminine self-help in other areas of health care was also strong. It was, after all, what women were used to. 'Women should take themselves in hand and learn to prevent their ailments, not only by relying on medical cures, but on their own powers of positive health,' proclaimed Mary Bagot Stack, champion of physical fitness and founder of the Women's League of Health and Beauty in 1930. The League was immensely popular. Within a few years there were centres all over the country and 166 000 members. Trained teachers taught women how to keep fit through exercise, diet and hygiene. They held classes in village halls, factories and even in shops. Prunella Stack took over from her mother as President in 1935. 'I think we appealed mostly to working

Above: A keep-fit craze swept the nation in the 1930s.

women. Girls who were working in shops and offices and who really hadn't had the opportunity of doing anything like this. The exercises were all done to music and we used jazz tunes, contemporary music. We had our League uniform which consisted of short black pants and white satin blouse. And that was a good idea because it levelled everybody.' According to Prunella Stack the League never forced a way of thinking on its members, but just used a little gentle persuasion. 'Personal hygiene was mentioned in the classes sometimes. Particularly if we gave displays. It had to be very tactfully done because it wasn't so widespread – knowledge of personal hygiene – then as it is now. But one thing we used to do when we had the classes in deprived areas, before we did breathing exercises, we always made them blow their noses.'

Although the League's organisers sounded remarkably like an earlier generation of patronising do-gooders, they appealed nonetheless to Daisy Carey. She joined in 1933 after watching a class, liked what she saw and has been going ever since. 'I left school at fourteen so I served an apprenticeship in tailoring and this was top class couture work. Most of it, other than seams, of course, was handwork. And you did a lot doubled up on your knee. So this meant that your shoulders were forward and you sank down into yourself. And so really we needed something to stretch us back up again. Otherwise you got all crumpled up and then you could get a chesty cold or something.'

After years of indifference, women's health was becoming a matter for public concern. In addition to the Women's League of Health and Beauty, the National Fitness Campaign and the National League for Health, Maternity and Child Welfare started in the 1930s. A Women's Health Committee was formed in 1933 by women's organisations on a non-political basis. In 1939 they produced a report based on interviews with 1250 working-class women. Only 7 per cent lived in what was considered 'good' housing. Some were living unhappily in new estates, isolated from their old friends. A third lived in appalling conditions. Dampness brought on rheumatism and arthritis. Communal lavatories led indirectly to constipation since women hated using them. Most were exhausted by humping coal, washing, cleaning the house and preparing meals, the domestic grind no different from in their mothers' day. When asked if they were well they said yes, but when asked what ailments they suffered from the list was endless: anaemia, headaches, backaches, constipation, rheumatism, prolapsed womb, bad teeth, varicose veins and so on. Yet married women still had no right to free treatment, so these problems frequently went untreated.

Below: A survey of working-class women in 1939 revealed only 7 per cent lived in good housing.

Research emphasised the importance of proteins and vitamins, particularly the amounts of milk and protein needed by pregnant women, but they were beyond the reach of poorer families. The British Medical

Association brought out a report on nutrition recommending a better and more expensive diet than the Ministry of Health's. Against the advice of doctors and public health officials, the Minister insisted in 1933:

There is at present no available evidence of any general increase in physical impairment, sickness or mortality as a result of the economic depression or unemployment.

Ironically, rationing during the Second World War provided a healthier, more balanced diet than many were used to. Propaganda films preached the importance of sensible eating, fresh air and rest. A glorious world of healthy babies, dry homes and unpolluted green belts around major cities was promised after the war. In 1942 the Beveridge plan recommended a National Health Service with free medicines and treatment for all. At last women would have the same right to free medicine as their men. By a happy coincidence, the day the Health Service was launched in 1948 was Katharina Dalton's first as a fully qualified doctor. Until then women had seldom visited the North London practice where she worked. 'Partly they couldn't afford it and partly it wasn't necessary. You know if a husband is off work, well, they want medical attention because they need the money, they need to get back to work. But the housewife, if she could sleepily carry on with her house duties, didn't go and visit a doctor.

Once the Health Service started, all this changed. Dr Dalton had women queuing for help; women who had suffered for years with thyroid deficiency, gaining weight and growing slower and slower as each year passed, or with gynaecological problems, or with painful varicose veins, or with menopausal difficulties. Within a few months she realised she had only seen the tip of an unexpectedly large iceberg. No one had appreciated the nature or extent of women's ill health.

Mothers were entitled to free ante- and post-natal care. It seemed the State would take care of all women's medical needs. There were other important improvements after the war: antibiotics virtually eliminated childbirth fever and meant tuberculosis need no longer be a killer. New houses were built ending the tyranny of the bug. Central heating and modern gadgets, designed to ease domestic chores, were slowly being introduced. Post-war women were healthier than their mothers. Instead of becoming mere shadows of their former selves, struggling to bring up their latest mistake at forty, they took on a new lease of life. They had the time, energy and opportunity to look beyond domesticity and motherhood. Many went out to work.

Contraception for married women was becoming increasingly acceptable. The Family Planning Association expanded in the 1950s. Still run by volunteers, they were no longer progressive feminists but respectable, rather old-fashioned matrons. In 1958, even the Church of England finally gave its blessing to the use of contraception. The climate was ripe for the

Above: By the 1950s, birth control had become quite respectable but was strictly limited to married women.

"I'd like something vaguely repellent, please."

greatest breakthrough of all: a simple, foolproof contaceptive in the form of a pill. Could this have been developed earlier, if the will had been there? Dr Dalton believes it was certainly possible fifteen or twenty years before. 'At medical school we were taught that a mixture of oestrogen and progestogens is excellent to prevent heavy bleeding or pain with menstruation but, as it is a contraceptive, you never give it to a married woman. That is treatment only for single women and widows. No one realised the demand. There was a feeling that every woman who was married would automatically want to conceive.'

By the 1960s it was clear what a misjudgement this had been. The world population explosion dominated thinking, worries about underpopulation long since forgotten. Women's wish for a simple contraceptive they could use themselves coincided with approved policy. Dr Ellen Grant joined a team working at University College Hospital on clinical trials for an oral contraceptive. They tried out seventy hormone combinations. 'Contrary to what people think we were actually using very low dose pills. We tried low doses of oestrogen, low dose progesterone, low dose of the combinations and, you know, even half got pregnant on the lowest dose of one of the pills we used. So the husbands had to give their agreement. Everybody was very enthusiastic. The husbands were so pleased; one wife came back and said, "My husband brings me flowers now." The change from using condoms and the cap, you see. They were really delighted.'

Dr Grant's hairdresser, Jose Burrough, volunteered to be a guinea pig. She thought the pill was terrific and had never felt better in her life. 'It reduced problems with my periods and I felt just great.' And so it seemed to all of us. Gone were painful periods, sex could be enjoyed without fear of pregnancy and children could be planned. Even spotty skins were transformed in weeks. But there was a price to pay for freedom. Dr Grant began to worry about the pill quite early on. 'The first symptoms we noticed were bad headaches and migraine and depression. Women began to say they stopped being interested in sex. In fact there was a joke in the early days that that was how the pill worked.'

Dr Grant is now convinced that the pill may cause a variety of problems for women, increasing the chance of developing certain cancers and circulatory problems. However, it is a controversial area and medical opinion is divided on precisely what the risks are. Many women have taken the pill for years with apparently no adverse reaction and have been thankful for its simple reliability. Today smokers and women over thirty-five are advised against taking the pill. Jose Burrough had cancer of the uterus, from which she has fully recovered. No one has any idea whether this was caused by the pill trials, the subsequent years when she took the pill or is entirely unrelated.

The pill made birth control a much more complex affair. Amateurs could no longer safely be left to dispense advice. In the 1970s GPs took over, prescribing contraceptives through the Health Service, ending a period when women had looked after their own contraceptive needs. Abortion, too, was professionalised when the law was changed in 1967. The old back street abortionists (until then still performing about 100 000 abortions a year) were finally put out of business. Legal abortion on the Health Service became much easier once all a woman had to do was to convince two doctors that she had strong reasons for wanting one – although women in some areas had difficulties with individual doctors opposed to abortion on moral or religious grounds. Feminists argued that women had the right to make this decision for themselves and that it should not be controlled by possibly unsympathetic outsiders.

However the right to abortion and improved contraception transformed many women's lives. Although the pill, with its threatening side effects, has not turned out to be the perfect contraceptive everyone hoped for, it has brought women – particularly those under thirty – security from unplanned pregnancy, affording extra years betweeen childhood and motherhood. Knowing that women are unlikely to spring a sudden pregnancy on them, employers find it harder to argue that they are a bad risk. Control over fertility has arguably been the most important change for women this century. It has brought a degree of choice and freedom women never had when motherhood absorbed their best years. On the other hand, with outside jobs and higher standards of housekeeping and childcare, women strive to be Superwomen.

Dr John Fry has been in the same practice for forty years in Beckenham, Kent. As he has always kept careful records of his patients' complaints and identified trends, we were interested to know whether the medical profile of women had changed. It seems that as physical ailments lessened, psychological ones became more apparent. Today women are four times more likely than men to come in with emotional problems – depression, anxiety or panic. Dr Fry puts it down to stress, partly explained by new responsibilities they have taken on. 'They have to run the house, bring up a family and many of them now work as well. So much for the weaker sex! They have to be a lot tougher than men to cope with three jobs in one. I don't think women are under any more stress than our grandmothers were, if you can imagine the days when our grandmothers were short of money, living in very poor conditions. I think the stress is different. It's a much more refined stress than it used to be. It used to be gross and grotesque stress in the living conditions.'

Tiredness and depression were not thought of as illnesses in those years and it would not have occurred to an exhausted mother of six to seek treatment, even if she could have afforded the doctor's bill. Besides, the daily grind left little time for women to worry about their nerves. So whether this is a new problem or simply a newly identified one is not clear. What is beyond doubt is that stress plays a large part in women's lives today. Alcoholism used to take a hold of more men than women. Now more women than men are heavy drinkers. In the 1940s 70 per cent of men smoked compared with 20 per cent of women. Today the figure is down to 36 per cent of men but up to 32 per cent of women, with a resulting increase of female lung cancer. Although the number of women smoking has been going down over the last few years after endless warnings about its dangers, it is at a much slower rate than men.

On Merseyside the trends are much the same as in Beckenham. Conversations between women on the Sefton Health Bus reveal that most of them suffer from 'nerves'. As they become more independent, the number who cannot cope increases. Family life is less secure. A woman may be breadwinner, housekeeper, cleaner and single parent rolled into one, with all the pressures that entails. Or she may be isolated in sleepless, unending mothering, with no one to talk to. The easiest way to help herself is through drink or cigarettes. The doctor, on the other hand, might provide a prescription which will do the trick.

Quacks and small pharmacists have been peddling soothing pills for centuries. Opium has calmed generations of troubled nerves, but only in the last fifty years has the drug industry become big business. Antibiotics had shown startling results on infection, and there was huge optimism that some drug could be manufactured which would control mental problems with equal success. The hunt for a 'happiness pill' was on. In the early 1950s chemicals called benzodiazepines were produced which had tranquillising effects. Under brandnames like Valium and Ativan they became the most widely prescribed drug in Britain, with over 21 million prescriptions in 1983.

Many women are now convinced that their doctors were too quick to

Above: Over the century cigarettes were marketed to cure a variety of ills. As time went on, they were seen increasingly as a way of calming nerves.

hand out tranquillisers. One young mother was given Valium on repeat prescriptions after a temporary depression when her two-week-old baby had a kidney infection. At the time her doctor dismissed her child's problem and told the mother she was suffering from postnatal depression. Later, when the baby recovered, the mother was still taking Valium so her own father intervened. 'He put them [the Valium] down the toilet. 'Cos he said I was too young to have 'em 'cos me mother's on them and we've seen me Mum on them.' Her mother had been living for years in a semi-trance, apparently dependent on Valium and Mogadon.

Professor Ian Stanley of Liverpool University made a study of an inner city practice and was horrified to find patients who had been on benzo-diazepines either as sleeping tablets or tranquillisers for more than six months. 'When I looked at the sex ratio there were more women than men and, as a generalisation, it was the younger women who were on the tranquillisers and the older women who were on the sleeping tablets. Often these had been started during a period of life crisis. Typically in an older woman during, or after, a bereavement and they'd just never been stopped. Patients, I think, didn't realise that they were dependent on them and it was only when we actually tried to get patients off them that we became conscious how difficult it was and what a painful experience it was to go through.'

Professor Stanley is confident that doctors are now more circumspect. Yet in 1987 women visiting the Sefton Health Bus were still being prescribed pills without any suggestion that they should try to ease off them. One had been put on repeat prescriptions of Ativan since her husband had lost his job and she had been forced out to work. Another had been on Ativan and sleeping pills for four years, and another on Valium since her parents had split up during her teens – twenty years earlier. Encouraged by the Health Team, they have banded together to give each other support while they cope with the side effects of stopping their drugs. 'A lot of people when they are withdrawing think they've still got their nerves but they're in withdrawal and this is where we're helping them, you see. A lot of people need somebody to talk to. Talk the problem out.'

Self-help groups are spreading. They are a natural legacy of the old community networks which were overshadowed for a while when the State appeared to provide everything. Although the Health Service has brought women tremendous benefits, many find the system unsympathetic. They complain that little notice is taken by GPs of what they may regard as minor problems like period pains, menopausal difficulties and even stress. Some are lucky enough to have an ideal family doctor who finds time to be both medical and spiritual adviser. In Merseyside most are less fortunate. 'I mean, you get there, you have to wait an hour, perhaps, in the surgery. You've got young children. They're crying. Everyone's staring at you. You have to tell the receptionist what the matter is. You could come with a woman's problem, you know, menstruation, whatever it may be and you don't want to tell the receptionist 'cos there's men sitting there.'

Dame Josephine Barnes has noticed, over the forty years she has practised as a doctor and gynaecologist, that women often go to the doctor hoping for a medical solution to a non-medical problem. 'I think that women are a problem to doctors. I think the woman who is the worst problem, in my view, is the woman who's never really ill, but is never really well and she always comes to see you with a sad, drawn face and an "I'm no better, doctor." Now, if you go into it properly, it isn't anything to do with sickness, it's home conditions, marital strife, problems with children, poverty. There are all sorts of causes for women never really feeling well.'

Most of these causes are beyond the scope of the average, overstretched family doctor, hence the need for Well Woman Clinics or some other kind of special health centre. The Sefton Health Bus began when Dr Hilary Hodge, Sefton's Health Promotion Coordinator, thought they needed to find a new way to crack some of these problems. Through the bus they could reach women who might otherwise depend on tranquillisers, smoking or drinking to calm their nerves and who might not bother with cervical smears, breast examination or blood pressure testing. Her lay staff act as a link with the medical services, giving advice, pointing them in the direction of the right professional – if one is needed. Like the League of Health and Beauty, their theory is that prevention is better than cure. They hope women will avoid stress and depression if they are drawn out of their isolation, introduced to others and encouraged to start their own support groups.

Carol Maiden, for instance, in her forties, married with two children, formed a hysterectomy group to help other women get through this operation better than she had. Haunted by her mother's death after a hysterectomy, Carol was terrified when she was told she had to have the same operation. No one had time to find out why Carol was so worried and when she asked the doctors what was going to happen to her they thought she was being difficult. 'Whatever you say to them they take as a challenge to their professionalism as if you're criticising what they're saying to you. So you're frightened even to ask the most fundamental questions of them. You end up saying "I've got a pain, but it's all right really, I can live with it." Instead of saying "I've got a pain and it hurts me."' Doctors and nurses treated her as if she was having a routine operation without emotional repercussions. Their attitude was that Carol was simply 'getting rid of a useless and troublesome organ. It doesn't mean that to women. It's where we've nurtured our children. It's about being sexual. It's about femininity.'

As the State took over the care of women's health, the friendly support women used to give each other was lost. Health buses, caravans, Well Woman Clinics, self-help groups are all trying to revive it. Despite modern stresses and strains, the older women who visit the Sefton bus appreciate the gains of the last fifty years. They are better fed and housed (although a few of them live in highrises). They have had smaller families and access to surgery and medication undreamed of in the past. Menopause did not signal the start of old age but left them extra years of good living. 'Our mothers never lived as long as us. Mine died at sixty-one. We're all in our late seventies. We're living a longer life and a better life.'

This, in turn, brings its own problems. We have an increasingly aging population, predominantly female. Many illnesses associated with women today are those that come with old age. Dame Josephine Barnes warns, 'the biggest problem, of course, is that people like me are going to go on living much too long and then somebody is going to have to look after us and that is possibly the outstanding health problem for women at the moment – the fact that a girl baby born today can expect to live to about eighty. This is the problem which our children and grandchildren are going to have to solve: how to look after granny when she becomes senile.' It is a problem which is becoming increasingly acute as reduced state funding returns responsibility for the elderly to the community. And the community, in this context, means women. It would be an ironic and bitter twist if the better health which has brought longer life to one generation deprived another of freedom. Women who look forward to getting out of the house and starting something new once their children grow up may now have to stay there to look after mother.

CHAPTER FIVE

The Good Mother
The Changing Face of Motherhood

'COULD have done without the last six,' Leah Chegwidden used to mutter when contemplating her ten children. Dolly, the ninth, was born in 1911 in a four-room house in the East End of London. Dolly remembers her mother ruled her boisterous brood with infinite patience, never favouring one above the other, always sticking to her favourite saying that 'a child's first need is love'. For thirty years – from the birth of her first child, until the youngest was ten – Leah was immersed in motherhood. She had no books to guide her, just a fund of common sense and good humour. To Dolly she was the 'perfect mother' and many agreed. All ten children grew to be adults. All ten 'turned out well'.

It is as a mother that a woman is often most harshly judged. No matter what else she does, if her children are inadequate in any way, there will be plenty who will shake their heads wisely and say, 'she never was much

Below: Leah Chegwidden with her husband and ten children. To Dolly (ringed) she always seemed a perfect mother.

of a mother'. People have always been quick to praise good mothers and quicker still to condemn bad ones, but what seems good mothering to one generation may seem neglectful to another. This century has seen an enormous growth in advice to mothers. A welter of agents in the shape of health visitors, doctors, school teachers and social workers keep a watchful eye on mothers, and you could fill a library with manuals on mothering techniques, with one set of instructions often contradicting the next. Fashions in mothering change as often as fads about food. A Good Mother in this century has at different times been encouraged to leave her children in the care of an expert nanny; to look after them herself, sticking to a rigid time-table and rationing her cuddles; to leave her children at a nursery to free herself for war work; to devote herself entirely to her children, feeding her baby whenever he cried and turning the house into an adventure playground for his elder sisters. With such sharp U-turns, it is hardly surprising that women are frequently riddled with guilt about the way they have brought up their children.

At the beginning of the century, when Leah Chegwidden was busy producing her ten children, mothering was thought to be an uncomplicated business. Working-class mothers knew their job: to feed, clothe, house their children and teach them to behave. The middle and upper classes paid some attention to childrearing fashions, but the tasks of motherhood were largely delegated to a nanny or a nursemaid or both. Mothers convinced themselves that nanny would do a better job as she would be less emotionally involved – although, quite often, it was the mother who remained the more detached of the two. 'Nanny was my life. She was my authority,' explained Mary Lutyens. 'Mother was a goddess. It was unthinkable that a goddess should bath me.'

Mary was brought up in the years immediately before the First World War by her much loved nanny, Louisa Sleath. The children's world revolved around the nursery, tucked away on the top floor far from their parents. They had all their meals in the nursery, their lessons in the nursery and their mother visited them in the nursery after tea to read to them. As a child, Mary was much closer to Nanny Sleath than to her mother who seems to have defined maternal duty as purely educational. Mary 'couldn't have borne the shame' if her mother had seen her without clothes and when, at fifteen, she was sick in front of her, she was 'terribly ashamed' and amazed that her mother could hold her head without appearing to be disgusted. Nanny had always been the one who comforted and nursed her when she was ill – a perfectly happy arrangement as far as Mary was concerned. The best nannies compensated for a mother's shortcomings, provided an extra shoulder to cry on and gave the mother freedom to develop interests beyond her family circle. Although Mary's memory of her mother is far from the fairytale aproned and rosy-cheeked provider of meals, she worshipped her all the same. Mrs Lutyens inspired

Above: Nanny with charges 1911. At its best the nanny system allowed mothers to develop interests outside the family circle and gave children an extra shoulder to cry on.

her children with her own love of literature and as they grew older they became closer. On the other hand, Helena Wright, the eminent gynaecologist and birth control campaigner, remained bitterly critical of her mother who had, like other Good Mothers of her generation, been more bound up in her social life and charitable works than in her children. 'To me you were merely a shadow,' she wrote to her mother, 'a shadow with three characteristics; you were always "busy" and you were always either ill or worried. . . . I don't remember that you once spent time actually playing with us in the nursery. Nurse Minter was our chief companion. . . . Why didn't you get to know your children a little?'

In working-class families, there was no such division of labour: children were left entirely to mother. In the early years of this century, there was no talk of stimulating play or entertaining or amusing children. On the contrary, one or two elderly ladies remember that when they were toddlers they used to be strapped into a chair for hours on end to keep them 'out of harm's way while mother got on'. Children were left to their own devices and by the age of six or seven were expected to look after themselves and, when not at school, run errands for the family. Ideally, they kept out of the way, bothering grown-ups as little as possible.

Some writers suggest that mothers in the past loved their children less than today, that either they were afraid of becoming too attached to a child who might be 'taken from them' or that, in a large family, there was less room for individual affection. Our own interviews suggest this is far from the truth. Women still speak with tears in their eyes of a child lost sixty years ago. At the beginning of the century, it was quite common for children to die from infectious diseases and babies were particularly vulnerable. One in six, registered alive at birth, never reached its first birthday and the number who died at birth without ever being registered is unknown.

Rose Ashton's baby sister was one of many whose births went unrecorded and whose death was unmarked by any headstone. In 1904 Rose was called to her mother's bedroom where she saw her newborn sister lying dead on a pillow, 'looking like a little doll, a beautiful thing'. Rose was told by her mother to collect a soap box from the grocer, put the baby inside and take it to the gravedigger for burial. Wanting to do more for her tiny sister, Rose tore the lining out of her father's coat to upholster the soap box and only when she had it looking pretty did she set off to the graveyard with her baby sister tucked into her makeshift coffin. The gravedigger was not at all surprised to see Rose, clutching her small box, and pointed her towards a heap of similar boxes and packets near the church. Upset and puzzled, Rose asked where he was going to bury all the tiny babies. ' "Well, lass," ' Rose remembers the gravedigger explaining, ' "Y'see, people can't afford to buy graves these days so when a public grave is full and ready for filling we put one on each end till we get rid of them. They can't afford a private grave so we put them in at the foot or the head," ' he said and I came back broken-hearted for this little doll.'

Officials at that time were not too worried about babies who were stillborn or who died in their first month like Rose's little sister. Most assumed when babies died in their first few weeks that they had a congenital weakness and their dying was simply part of the process of natural selection. They were more concerned about those who died in the following months.

The Second Boer War (1889–1902) focused attention sharply on the ability of mothers to rear fit children. The fate of the Empire depended on tomorrow's soldiers and an unacceptable number were not surviving infancy. Many of those that did were not up to much: there were far too many puny volunteers, with weak hearts and lungs, offering to fight for King and Country. An inter-departmental committee, set up to examine the apparent physical deterioration of the race, reported in 1904. The report brought the first official recognition that poverty had social causes and suggested slum clearances and other environmental reforms. It also included a long section on infant mortality. From that time official interest in mothering began in earnest, but the emphasis was on improving child welfare through educating mothers and building a healthy, imperial race, not on the indirect causes of poor health such as poverty and bad housing.

Concern about the wastage of infant life intensified in the years preceding the First World War. Medical officers of health were convinced that if

Above: Schools for Mothers were seen as a way of countering old wives' tales and teaching mothers about hygiene and nutrition.

Left: Officials blamed infant deaths on mothers' incompetence rather than on indirect causes such as poverty and bad housing.

mothers were better educated in the art of mothering, fewer babies would die. They were convinced there were too many incompetent mothers who, through ignorance and carelessness, jeopardised the lives of their children. Diarrhoea, thought to be caught from germs on dirty feeding bottles or dummies, was the main killer of small babies. The cheapest and simplest solution seemed to be to educate women in hygiene, encourage them to breast-feed their young and keep their houses cleaner, particularly by getting rid of flies (a huge menace in the days when the horse was the main means of transport). In fact, sub-standard sanitation caused many of the problems – towns like Hull, which had a large percentage of insanitary privies, also had high infant mortality – but improved sanitation was a long-term and far more costly project than teaching women how to be better mothers. Motherhood was to be looked on not just as a personal duty but as a national one. Women were expected to take pride in being mothers of the race and they had to learn how to do the job properly.

Health visitors seemed to be the perfect agents for reform. Originally known as 'lady health missioners', these well-intentioned volunteers visited the poor distributing advice, disinfectants and religious tracts, but in the early twentieth century, they were becoming increasingly useful to local authorities. They taught up-to-date methods of babycare to mothers in their own homes and countered the 'bad advice' offered by grannies

Above: Schools for Mothers were gradually taken over by the State and renamed Infant Welfare Centres.

and neighbours. They also encouraged mothers to go to the new Schools for Mothers. The first of these opened in 1907 in St Pancras, London, and was rapidly followed by others. The Schools ran cookery demonstrations, sewing lessons and provided numerous helpful hints on feeding schedules as well as warnings about dirty dummies or bottles and buying the wrong kind of clothes. The advice was always practical but sometimes left poorer mothers in a dilemma. Should they buy cheap flanelette for clothing so their babies could have a change of clothes more often or heed the health visitor's warning that it was highly flammable? Should they break the habit of generations and not take their babies to bed with them? A health visitor remembers this was one of their strictest rules. 'On no account must the baby be placed in bed with its mother because the mother is in danger of going to sleep, rolling over and suffocating the baby. So it was my job to see that the child was placed in a drawer – or, usually, a wicker clothes basket – but you knew jolly well when you left the house that it had to go in with mother for warmth because there was no fire.'

To begin with the Schools for Mothers were run by volunteers but, like health visitors, they were gradually taken over by the State and renamed Infant Welfare Centres. Rather more mothers used the centres to have their babies weighed and checked over than to take advantage of the classes they offered. They resented the high-handed manner of the nurses and doctors who often failed to appreciate the difficulties mothers faced through poor housing and lack of money. Marjorie Jones remembers going to the local Infant Welfare Centre in Hornsey with her mother and baby brother. 'The prams were left outside in the yard of this rundown, yellow brick building, with its wire-protected windows. Stone-throwing by small boys was a favourite pastime.... My mother didn't like the idea of going. I know that she was very tense about it. In those days we weren't used to coming in contact with nurses and doctors like we are now.' Marjorie's mother had lost a baby from meningitis and was nervous about her other three children. In the past she had relied on tips from a friend or relation, but seeking professional advice was increasingly considered the right thing to do.

The State's involvement increased with the Maternal and Child Welfare Act of 1918, enabling local authorities to provide a wide range of services, including health visitors, infant welfare centres and day nurseries. They were not actually *required* to provide any of these and, while health visitors and infant welfare centres became an accepted part of municipal life, day nurseries did not. A small number of crèches had been set up during the war to enable mothers to work, but they were seen as a necessary evil in time of national emergency. Paid work was thought by officials to get in the way of good mothering. Even Mary McArthur, the most prominent woman trades unionist at that time, insisted mothers should be given every 'encouragement' to stay at home.

After the war mothers were given more attention than ever before, with ante-natal advice and post-natal visits from the health visitor. By 1925 the number of babies dying in their first year was half what it had been in 1900; and the network of health visitors, doctors and other experts was

Right: Baby Week in Dublin, 1917. During the war infant welfare became a fashionable cause. A jewel fund encouraged the rich to sell a jewel to save a child's life.

well entrenched, though not necessarily well loved. In Deptford Nellie Finley resented the health visitor's suggestion that her child should be given a nice bowl of chicken. 'Chicken in them days, well, you nearly had to be the Queen to have chicken.... I used to go by my own instincts or I used to go to my mother or my mother-in-law. She was very good, very clever with children and I used to copy her, do what she told me. In one ear, out the other with health visitors, definitely.' Experts shuddered when they heard mothers say they would 'just act natural' with their babies or they were following 'Mum's advice; after all, she's raised six and buried four.' In their view, mother did not know best and grannies who laid down nursery lore got in the way of the correct, scientific approach.

Dorothy Campbell, a health visitor in Birmingham, used the offer of subsidised 'twopenny lunches' as bait to persuade nursing or expectant mothers to come to the clinic. 'A lot of them came and then a lot of them thought the Public Health Department were interfering in their lives.... The people we really wanted – the very ignorant – often wouldn't come. We wanted to teach them hygiene because a lot of people fed their babies from the milkman's milk which was delivered in a jug from a can. There was no pasteurisation of milk. Women had to be taught to sterilise their bottles. There were no pellets to put in jugs, you had to boil the bottles and keep them in cold water. You see, when you have to go out in the stormy weather to the tap or to the lavatory, it's awfully tempting not to wash your hands. A lot of mothers kept the baby's bottle warm on the hob if the baby didn't finish the feed [for the next feed four hours later]. The mother in those days didn't realise the importance of keeping the bottles cool. Some breast-fed but a lot bottle fed. The breast-fed baby, as a rule, didn't get diarrhoea and vomiting. The breast-fed baby was better off.'

A Good Mother breast-fed her baby and stuck to carefully prescribed feeding routines. How often she should feed her baby was a matter of changing fashion. Before the First World War, Eric Pritchard, a specialist in infant care, recommended three-hourly feeds but nothing at night. Sir Frederick Truby King, who became chief guru on infant care in Britain between the wars, preferred a four-hourly schedule. Truby King's reputation was made in New Zealand where his scientific approach dramatically reduced the number of babies dying from infantile diarrhoea. In his eyes, mothercraft was more important than motherlove which hampered routines. Besides, kissing and hugging carried the risk of spreading germs. Truby King babies were fed every four hours on the clock no matter how much they cried. They were expected to sleep through the night and not to be fed if they woke up. Unlike modern babies they were left alone between feeds. Nothing should be allowed to excite or spoil babies. They were not given much love or attention. Forming the right habits and building character seem to have been the guiding principles.

All of which could hardly have been more different from the way Leah Chegwidden had brought up Dolly and her nine other children. But when Dolly had children of her own, she turned to the experts for advice. Her baby daughter cried a great deal, 'a spoilt baby', she was told, 'which I'm sure she wasn't. I couldn't believe I would have a bad-tempered child and they said, "just leave her one day, let her cry it out". And she cried and cried and I sat behind the door listening. I didn't want to spoil her and I cried as well. It was absolutely awful.' Many other mothers found Truby King's methods hard to follow. They remember listening to heartbreaking sounds of their baby crying while the milk gushed through their tightly fitting maternity bras. But they knew they must do nothing until the next four-hour feed was due, otherwise they might harm their baby's digestive system. 'You didn't lift a baby up when it's crying – ever,' remembers a mother who suffered a year of misery bringing up her eldest child to the Truby King formula. 'You just didn't handle the baby, if possible.'

Leah Chegwidden, who believed in 'nursing and cuddling a child' whenever it seemed unhappy, could hardly believe her ears. Dolly was torn between her mother's words of wisdom and the professionals' advice at the clinic. The professionals won, mainly because Dolly was concerned about her baby's health and, quite reasonably, thought the professionals knew all about germs. 'Not having an education myself, I assumed people in authority must know better.' The local clinic was particularly strict about hygiene and the spread of infection and discouraged mothers from kissing their babies. 'Of course, other people wanted to kiss her – the relations. "Oh, let me," you know. And I couldn't have that. So I bought a badge, because I didn't want to hurt their feelings by saying "don't breathe on her". "Please Do Not Kiss Me" it said.'

Depriving children of kisses and cuddles may have reduced the risk of infection and put backbone into a future generation of soldiers and rulers of the Empire. Certainly Truby King's disciplines fitted in rather well with the traditional middle and upper-class view of mothering, where the baby adapted to the mother's or nanny's routine and children were kept on a nursery floor, apart from the family. In the 1920s the behaviourist, J. B. Watson, seemed to suggest that mothers were actually a potential hazard to their children as their protective instincts got in the way of a child's self-development. He recommended that mothers should play down love – 'there are rocks ahead for the over-kissed child' – and treat children as young adults, leaving them to learn on their own and develop self-sufficiency early on. Watson discouraged all cuddling and suggested parents should shake hands with their children in the morning.

In this climate a determined professional woman could pursue her own interests – even a career, if the marriage bar did not interfere – without feeling guilty about her children, and there were still plenty of women willing to work as nursemaids and nannies. However, there was a growing

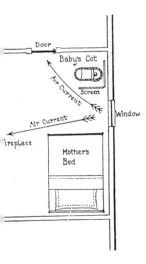

Above: The obsession with germs in the 1920s and 30s led mothercraft manuals to recommend a safe distance between mother and child to protect the baby from 'impurities breathed out by parents or nurse'.

feeling among the middle classes that a mother should be at home, on hand in case her intelligence was needed in the management of her young. In 1934, the writer Winifred Holtby felt obliged to defend working mothers in her book, *Women, and a Changing Civilisation*:

Mothers who can share their children's interests, mothers who have some knowledge of the wider world outside the family circle, are far better equipped than purely domestic housewives, to help their sons and daughters as they pass from school to the shops and offices and factories and universities in which they complete their education.

Writing of her own mother who, as an alderman, had always had interests outside the home, she said:

I can visit or leave her without compunction, knowing that she has her life to live as much as I have mine; yet when we meet there is none of that awkwardness, that 'making conversation' which I see between so many parents and children. In the future the child will be as much interested in the mother's career as the mother in the child's.

But Winifred Holtby was ahead of her time. In the 1930s, a Good Mother did not go out to work. Yet often it was only through working that mothers could provide for their children. Kathleen Dayus was widowed when her fourth child was only two days old. She had no right to a pension, all she could get was assistance towards the cost of coal and food which did not cover the costs of keeping her and the children. 'I sold everything,' Kathleen remembers, 'pawned everything, even me wedding ring and I got a six-penny brass one from Woolworths and then went on for a few weeks. Then I went back to the Parish and told them I wanted some more and they said they couldn't give me any more. So I went chopping firewood while the children were in bed. I chopped firewood on the night-time; and next morning, about 7 o'clock before they were awake, I went downstairs and I used to get the bundles of wood and go and sell 'em to the customers.' Kathleen never told the authorities about the few extra coppers she earned this way but was found out all the same, threatened with prosecution and given no money for the next fortnight. Completely destitute and thinking she might be fined or imprisoned, Kathleen went to Dr Barnardo's in Mosley and asked for help. They persuaded her to leave the children temporarily at the Home until she had found a new place to live. When Kathleen saw the children a few days later, 'they came in and [the older girls] curtseyed to the Matron and then we clung together and cried. Then she said that if I upset them I wouldn't be able to come again.' It appeared that in asking for help, Kathleen had signed away her rights to her children. They were not allowed to go home with her and were moved to another Barnardo's home without her consent. Kathleen then made matters worse by trying to kidnap her own baby and was threatened with prosecution again. Despite doing her best for her children Kathleen was branded a Bad

Mother. The only way she could provide for her children was by finding work, but if she worked, she had no one to look after them. Kathleen had to wait eight years before she was allowed to have her children home.

A Good Mother was expected to have a home for her children, a father for her children and, above all, a ring on her wedding finger. An unmarried mother who became pregnant at eighteen remembers that, in the eyes of her family, she had literally suffered a fate worse than death. Her mother tried to perform an amateur abortion on her own daughter. 'I was terrified. It hurt like hell. It was unsuccessful but what hurt most was that my mother's sister had died as a result of an abortion and I couldn't bear to think that my mother was willing to allow this to happen to me.' This young woman was forced into a home for unmarried mothers and when her baby arrived was told to have him adopted. Before they were parted, she secretly took his photograph which, forty years on, she looks at frequently. Another unmarried mother admits she still sheds secret tears on her daughter's birthday. She was born in the war and they were together for only seven days. 'She must think that I never loved her. The truth is, society robbed me of a precious daughter whom I desperately wanted in the bad old days when to be unmarried and pregnant was to be an outcast, a bad woman, a pariah.'

Muriel Duff had an illegitimate baby in 1941. She was working on the buses and 'had a romance as you called it in those days' with a married bus driver. Her parents disowned her so she went to a Mother and Baby Home. Before they accepted her, she was examined for venereal disease. 'You were made to know you'd done something that was wrong in everybody's eyes. You were there for a punishment; even the jobs that you were given were menial little things that needn't have been done every day. If you went to sit of an evening in the little sitting room you were made to sit on a hard chair. You were not allowed out, only in the grounds of the Home itself. It had got great big high boardings all round. Nobody knew what it was, only us that was inside.'

When Muriel went into hospital, she was shunned by the other mothers. None of them spoke to her the whole time she shared their ward. The hardest part of all was deciding what to do with her daughter. 'I very nearly changed my mind three times while the adoption was going through the courts, and then I sat down and thought it out and I thought it was better for her. These people had got her and they loved her, they treated her as their own. But I did love her. I gave her as much love as I could while I'd got her.' Among the many women who wrote or talked to us about having a child as an unmarried mother, almost none had any help or sympathy from their own parents. As Muriel remembers, 'my parents didn't even want to know anything about her.... They just ignored her, as if she wasn't there.'

Some women, however, noticed that during the Second World War

there was more tolerance towards unmarried mothers. 'Women without men were a common sight. I was just one of many coping with war work and a young baby at the same time,' explained Asphodel Long. As a single parent with a baby son, Asphodel was delighted to find a subsidised nursery to take her son and a job for herself at a nearby factory. 'Women's work was valuable. You were required to work and the war effort depended on women. Help was given you at every point to go out and work.' In fact, during a short spell when Asphodel did not work, she was made to feel she was letting the side down. The nursery made it easy to be a working mother. 'The child got meals there and got looked after there. And you were told it was good for the child, that the child would be socialised and would sort of become more intelligent. Or if it were not exactly more intelligent it would learn more and it would have the society of other children. And there would be experts there who would look after it and know what to do for it. And so you had a lot of confidence about that.'

The rigid regime of Truby King suited these times and worked like a dream for Asphodel Long. Her bible was *Mothercraft*, written by Truby King's adopted daughter. 'It told you that the child would learn, if you started early enough, to regulate its times with yours and so you had to feed at certain times: Six, ten, two, six, ten. And the extraordinary thing

Above: Nurseries were not merely acceptable during the war, they were seen as positively beneficial for children.

was that the child did actually wake at about five minutes to each of these hours wanting to be fed and did, in fact, sleep the rest of the time.'

While earlier wars had drawn attention to the physical health of children, during and after the Second World War the focus gradually shifted to their emotional wellbeing. Although many children seemed happy enough to be evacuated to the country, some even seeing it as their greatest adventure, others suffered badly from being separated from their parents. Dolly Scannell's daughter was sent to an aunt in Suffolk. She was only eleven months old and Dolly, determined not to be parted from her for long, soon joined her. When they were reunited, she found her daughter considerably altered. 'They said she'd never smiled while I wasn't there. She just got thinner and thinner and more and more miserable and she's not miserable. She's a happy person.'

With so much concern over the physical needs of children, their emotional needs had been overlooked or misunderstood and the special bond between a mother and child was often underestimated. When Freda Davis took her youngest child into hospital for a few days, the doctor made it quite clear that he thought the child would be better off if she did not visit him. Freda knew her son would be anxious and unhappy, 'but the doctor said, "You mustn't go and see him. You mothers spoil your children and he will get on quite well with the nurses there. It'll only be three and a half days and you'll have him back." Very much against our will we

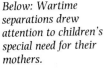

Below: Wartime separations drew attention to children's special need for their mothers.

allowed it to happen. When we went to fetch him he was completely blank. He didn't look at us or speak to us or keep his head rigid. He just dropped his head like that and that's how he remained for several weeks. He had nightmares every night. He cried absolutely non-stop. When he didn't cry he lay in an absolute coma. We really thought that he was going to die of lack of will to live. Gradually, after a great deal of loving and caring, he came back to himself.'

This was exactly the kind of trauma that psychiatrists were beginning to associate with children separated from their families and which prompted the World Health Organisation to invite Dr John Bowlby, a paediatrician and psychiatrist, to study the needs of children in institutions. The Second World War had left millions of children without homes or families. In Britain Lady Allen, Founder and President of the World Organisation for Early Childhood Education, was appalled by the cruelty she witnessed to children in residential care. She saw 'children forcibly fed by holding noses' or punished by being put to bed in a dark room. One seven-year-old was left to stand all day in a cold room, partly clothed, as a punishment for wetting his pants. Lady Allen published her findings in a pamplet, *Whose Children* in 1945 and the public anger it caused, together with the new evidence of psychiatrists about problems in institutions, led to a new Act of Parliament to lay down a kinder system for children in care, emphasising the need for them to have some kind of mother-figure.

John Bowlby's report, 'Maternal Deprivation and Mental Health', became a classic. It challenged the 'spoil-the-child-at-your-peril' theories of Truby King and Watson whose books gathered dust or were consigned to the dustbin. Bowlby maintained that infants and toddlers needed the continuous care of their mothers and found a statistical correlation between a disrupted childhood and a delinquent personality. In a more readable paperback, *Child Care and the Growth of Love*, Bowlby's ideas were incorporated into a new Mother's Bible. Although Bowlby had been writing about children in institutions, his theories were expanded and applied to mothers at home. A Good Mother did not leave a child under three years of age with anyone else at all, except perhaps with Granny while she had a few days' annual holiday. In fact, a conscientious mother was now afraid to leave her child at all in case it developed signs of 'maternal deprivation'. Looking back, Bowlby says he was misinterpreted. 'I said a continuous relationship of mother and child, in which both find happiness and satisfaction, promotes mental health. And if you get disruptions of that relationship, you get all sorts of trouble – mental, psychological trouble. Now the word "continuous", in my context, was "not all these frightful disruptions" [a long spell in hospital, different foster parents, time in an institution], but some people interpreted it to mean 24 hours a day which, of course, was not what I intended.'

But this was how he was interpreted at the time. The idea that a Good

Mother stayed at home fitted in with the general philosophy at the end of the war. After the evacuation of children and forced separation of married couples, families needed rebuilding and women were wanted as home-makers. The very week the war finished, Asphodel Long went as usual to pick up her son, Joe, from the nursery. 'The matron was there – and I shall never forget her – she was standing there and I see her now with her glasses on her nose, looking straight at me. She said "Well, the nursery is closing today at 6.30. Take all your things away." We had a little locker there where we put the child's things. "Remove all your things, don't come back, the nursery shuts at 6.30 today." And it was a dreadful moment, absolutely dreadful. The world sort of came to pieces for me.'

Asphodel found being a single mother in peacetime was extremely difficult. As she could not find any satisfactory arrangement for Joe during the day, she had to stop work; but then she could not make ends meet, so had to start working again. Both of them became ill. 'It was like running from pillar to post and on top of everything else, there was the guilt – the massive guilt because I felt that bundling Joe up to go from one makeshift arrangement to another was no way to bring up a child.' The same people who had made her feel bad during the brief spell when she had not worked in the war now made her feel bad for working and leaving a little boy with other people. 'I had a stock answer after a while. It was about the period when the royal family were gadding all over the world and Prince Charles was being left at home. I used to say, "Well, if it's all right for our own dear Queen to leave her little boy while she goes about her business, then it'll do for me!"'

At exactly the time Asphodel was struggling to find work and a nursery for Joe in the south, the Lancashire mills were begging women to return to work. For the first time in her life, Annie Holt found being a working mother quite easy. 'The nursery van used to come at 6 o'clock and pick us up and they'd go round and pick all the other children up. It were lovely at the nursery for the children. They had two ladies and they used to make games up and take 'em out, put playtime on for 'em, give 'em their meals. So they were really better looked after than what they was at home. So you could work because you knew that your children were happy.' Annie had always managed to fit work around her eight children. Her husband had never fully recovered from being gassed in the First World War and they needed her wages. In the past she had been obliged to leave her children with a minder for twelve hours every day. After the war, her two youngest children were given a place in a nursery attached to the mill and the older ones were looked after during the school holidays by the two ladies who ran the nursery.

It was unusual for a mother in the late 1940s and 1950s to be supported and encouraged to return to work. Asphodel Long's experiences were more common. Up and down the country nurseries were closing. In Pudsey,

Yorkshire, mothers staged a sit-in to protest at the closure of the local nursery. They locked themselves in the nursery over the weekend and sat tight until police stormed the building and forced them out. Thirty mothers refused to go to work at the local textile factory to register their protest. Pudsey Council was adamant that it could not afford to keep the nursery open. It closed. Conflicting national needs left women in a dilemma. They were wanted at work but a Good Mother was supposed to stay at home happily baking while her children played at her feet.

If the success of motherhood is judged by the health of the nation's babies – and, after all, it was concern over this that first drew the State to set standards of mothering – then post-war mothers did a good job. Dorothy Campbell had a fifteen-year break from health visiting while she brought up her own children. Returning in 1956, she found her practice had changed dramatically, largely due to better housing and improved medicine. Babies were no longer dying from diarrhoea and bronchial pneumonia; one in fifty died in their first year compared with one in six at the start of the century. But Dorothy also felt modern mothers were more responsible about their children's health than mothers in the 1930s. 'I saw women from the problem families that I'd first seen when they were five years old; I saw them at twenty bringing their own babies spotlessly clean to the clinic, making sure the children had the right amount of teeth and they had all their injections and all their intelligence tests and hearing tests and so on. Of course, they'd been brought up to come to the ante-natal clinic, you see, so they had a better start than their grandmothers.'

Above: 1947: fourteen-year-old girls being taught infant care at school.

The welfare state had freed mothers from much of the worry about the physical welfare of their children but mothers now felt that their competence to cope with the psychological and social development of their children was being questioned. Emotional care was not something easily taught in a scientific way, but mothers picked up the essential requirement: that their children needed a great deal of their mother's time and attention.

Many found child-rearing a lonely occupation. Post-war housing schemes were quite different from the old communities of small streets, squares and terraces where everyone knew her neighbour's business. The post-war mother often lived in a new estate, far from her own mother and her old friends, and looked increasingly for guidance from experts.

The psychological theories of Sigmund Freud and Jean Piaget which had been around for thirty years seemed to suit the post-war mood. Freud emphasised the importance of early development and not repressing a child; Piaget believed in constant stimulation and education. The liberal views of the child psychologist, Dr Benjamin Spock, provided new guidance for mothers. Spock children were radically different from the pre-war well-disciplined models. What a child enjoyed, Spock said, was good for him. Cleaning up after a child who enjoyed experimenting with tipping his cereal over the high chair or pulling the stuffing out of his toys or playing

Dropping is a new skill

Above: Guided by Dr Spock mothers learned to try to enjoy what their children enjoyed.

at 5.30 in the morning was a lot more work for mother than Truby King's disciplinarian approach. No allowance was made for mothers who could not cope with the demands of small children because they were too involved with housework or spent their days in sullen depression. Yet children are sensitive to their mothers' ups and downs. In some instances it might have been better for the child if the mother had shared her mothering with a minder, a nursery, or the father.

A professional woman who gave up work when she had two children in the 1950s discussed the possibility of resuming her career with another mother. 'It's our duty to stay at home,' her friend replied. 'If people like us cannot stay at home with our children, then who can!' The implication being that as they could afford not to work, they should set an example to the rest. Having 'sacrificed' themselves for motherhood, these former professional women were often loudest in their criticisms of working mothers. The more they had given up, the more they needed to idealise motherhood. They were probably the first generation of highly educated women to look after their children exclusively themselves. In the 1950s domestic help was expensive and hard to come by. Graduate mothers in the past had usually afforded someone to help mind the children and had no hesitation in doing so. 'Forget about your intellect,' Berry Mayall, who had her first baby just after getting a degree at Cambridge, remembers hearing on the radio. The speaker, the respected psychoanalyst Donald Winnicott, explained, 'The only thing that matters for you as a mother is your instinct.' Berry was told it was vital that she stayed with her child all the time, providing constant stimulation and attention. She 'scanned through Bowlby to see if it was all right to go out for half an hour and certainly, below the age of three, you were not really meant to leave the child at all.' As a mother, Berry decided, she had no independence whatsoever.

Fathers were shadowy figures who were seen briefly in the morning and at weekends and often not at all in the evening. Their idea of childcare was a quick game of snakes and ladders or a story at bedtime. Berry's husband left home at 8.30 and did not return until about 7.00 in the evening. It was a long day to fill with activities for her daughter, a little cooking, waterplay, plasticine, a trip to the park or the shops or the library. Berry was frustrated and bored a great deal of the time. 'I had some of those feelings they call being depersonalised. I didn't know who I was any more and I didn't find myself enjoying anything very much. It was more a sort of endurance test getting through that time. I knew that the minute she went to proper school, it would be OK to go out to work and that is exactly what I did.'

At what point could a Good Mother assume that her children no longer needed her continuous presence? In the 1950s a mother spent, on average, only four years pregnant and nursing. Once their children were at school, some found they had time on their hands and looked for a job, particularly a part-time one to fit in with school hours. Yet the notion that a working mother was a neglectful mother prevailed. Rising juvenile delinquency was blamed on mothers leaving their 'latch key' children to roam wild after school. A London magistrate, Basil Henriques, complained that:

The family is not considered to be so important as it used to be and it is because of this that we have in our midst so many suffering, unhappy and delinquent children.... Legislation regulating the working hours of mothers of school age children is one of the most urgent reforms required for the creation of good homes.

It seemed particularly ironic that just as families had shrunk to a size where women would not, like Leah Chegwidden, have to spend all their best years immersed in mothering, childcare was turned into a full-time vocation. Ironic, too, that more women than ever before were educated and trained to do something else. The American anthropologist Margaret Mead thought this was no coincidence and criticised the new theories of childcare in the *American Journal of Orthopsychiatry* in 1954, saying they were a 'new but subtle form of anti-feminism in which men – under the guise of exalting the importance of maternity – are tying women more tightly to their children'.

Above: Rising juvenile delinquency was blamed on mothers leaving their 'latch key' children to roam wild after school.

One woman who had children in the 1960s decided not to be merely a good mother, she wanted to be 'an incredible mother. I was a kind of earth mother and could not deny the children anything. I gave them food when they wanted and if they wanted to come into our bed, I let them and just bought a larger bed. I breast-fed the first for nine months, the second for a year and the third for eighteen months. The living room was completely given over to the children. There were no carpets for them to spoil and there was a large climbing frame and swing in the middle. The room was organised around and for the children. I never said "no".' She was submerged in motherhood until rescued by the Women's Movement. She joined a local group where they discussed mothering and challenged the 'accepted views'. Women were beginning to argue that 'what children required in order to grow up into healthy adults was a stable, stimulating and loving environment but that that didn't need to be provided by the mother only. It could be provided by the mother, the father and other friendly adults. Feminists argued that childrearing should be the equal responsibility of both parents. Multiple attachments, as the psychologists call it, are the norm. It's a very obvious and simple idea but at the time it was a really revolutionary idea.' Fathers were no longer to be allowed to be shadowy figures. As their wives took on more outside the home, feminists insisted men did more inside it.

As the divorce rate rose, an increasing number of men, too, found themselves bringing up the children alone, strengthening the argument that women were not the only ones capable of looking after children.

Above: A sitting room turned into an adventure playground. In the 1960s mothers were encouraged to give their children free rein.

When Eric Clark's wife left him in 1971, he became father and mother to five children. His idea of a Good Mother was someone who did the 'washing, ironing, cooking, shopping, housework ... I realised that it was important to try and play with the children sometimes, but obviously I just didn't have the time. At the end of the day I was so physically exhausted I used to fall asleep.' Unlike most of the mothers who talked to us, Eric did not mind admitting that although he was devoted to his children, he 'seemed to need to get away from them – screaming and questions and all the other problems that they was throwing up at me'.

If mothers seem unique in the amount of guilt they feel, it is hardly surprising. In the post-war years they have been blamed for their children's delinquency, anorexia nervosa, homosexuality, frigidity, schizophrenia, dropping out of school and a host of other problems. As they were the dominant figures in their children's upbringing, they bore the brunt of criticism. Even some of the happier products of these times have complained of being stifled by their mothers who, having 'sacrificed' themselves for their children, smothered them with overprotective love or resented the chains their children imposed. Clearly the idea that a child would grow up contented just so long as his mother was there was as daft as the theory that a mother should keep a child at a distance.

John Bowlby admits that 'looking after children is whopping hard work. It's a very important job and unfortunately much under-valued.' He is all in favour, he says, of mothers having as much assistance as possible, but the British way of life does not allow for this. 'In the traditional extended family, in India, for example, the majority of girls have their own mother around, or perhaps an aunt or an elder sister or someone, and they have a lot of assistance for looking after their baby and that's a good thing. But to stick a young mother with two small children up in a tower block is disastrous. It's bad for her, it's bad for the children.'

One of the most dramatic changes in recent years, despite the counter-pull of childrearing fashion, has been in the increase of working mothers. Today 27 per cent of mothers with children under five go out to work compared with only 6 per cent in the 1950s. Hardship during the inflationary years forced many women to seek a second income. Convenience food, household gadgetry and small families made it possible. Domestic isolation made getting out of the house agreeable. Despite this, many children are getting more mothering than they were in the past. The sociological review *Monograph* (January 1987) shows that in the last ten years the amount of time working mothers spent on their children doubled. The majority of working mothers with young children work part-time; in some cases because they prefer to, in others because of the lack of childcare facilities.

The State's attitude to motherhood is ambivalent (as any social worker, given the responsibility of deciding when to interfere between mother and child, must know). Compared with some other European countries the government does little to help working mothers. In France, for instance, childcare is subsidised by the government, with crèches for children up to the age of three, kindergartens for three- to four-year-olds and special arrangements at elementary schools for older children. Parents are able to leave their children any time from seven in the morning until seven in the evening, including at elementary schools, which are open for longer than the normal school hours for parents' convenience. In Britain, mothers are expected to make private arrangements and receive no tax concessions for the expenses they incur.

Janet Fordham, a teacher in Manchester, has two children. She found a place in a nursery attached to a training college for nursery nurses for her elder child. But when her second child was born the nursery had no room for her. Manchester City Council runs twenty-five nurseries but they are mainly for deprived or other 'social services cases'. Janet's child is not the sort they normally take. (In the 1960s, married women teachers were desperately needed because of staff shortages and their children were given priority for day nursery places.) Vacancies at registered childminders seldom come up. Besides, she has heard stories about minders not stimulating children and leaving them for hours on end. Janet cannot afford

Above: Despite more mothers working than ever before, there are fewer nurseries today than in the last war.

a nanny or a private nursery, either of which would cost about £60 a week.

In London, the position is as difficult. A television production assistant decided that a childminder was the only available childcare she could afford. When she asked to see the list of childminders kept by her local council, she was told she was not allowed access to the list, but officials would find a childminder for her. She was given one name only. When she visited, she found the minder had her own toddler who showed extreme jealousy at the sight of another baby, so much so that he struck out at him several times. Feeling this was not the ideal daily home for her baby, she asked the council for another name. 'That is your childminder,' she was told, 'What is wrong with her?' When she explained, she was told that if she was such a worrier, she was not the sort of mother who should go back to work! The implication in 1986 was still that a working mother was the kind not to mind what happened to her baby while she was away.

The State may subtly discourage mothers from working, except when the economy needs them, but there are other influences pushing women in the opposite direction – financial need, personal fulfilment and, particularly in the middle classes, peer group pressure. A successful personnel officer, who had twins last year, automatically resumed her career. It never occurred to her to do anything else. 'I love my work. The children aren't suffering because I'm out at work, but *I'm* suffering. They don't miss me. They have a delightful nanny who plays with them all the time and is in fact much more patient than I would be with them. But every day, since I came back to work, the feeling that I should be at home with the children has grown stronger and I've given in my notice.' The hardest part has been the hostility of her female colleagues who feel she is throwing in the towel and 'just going to be a housewife'. When picked up on the 'just' she said, 'It's awful. I already have problems even saying it. I'm going to be one of those women who invent jobs for themselves like being a freelance writer or something just so I won't have to say "mother" or "housewife" at parties.'

After several decades of exalting full-time motherhood, the pendulum has swung the other way. Today a Good Mother contributes to the family purse, has that 'knowledge of the wider world' recommended by Winifred Holtby *and* spends every spare moment stimulating and amusing her children. Full-time housewives and mothers are, therefore, left feeling rather inadequate. They should not.

Fashions in mothering come and go, leaving far too many women feeling guilty. Dolly Scannell and her mother, Leah, were both Good Mothers. Yet Dolly left her baby to cry when Leah would have picked her up. Dolly's daughter was evacuated as a baby while Leah's children were never separated from her. Dolly had two children, her mother had ten. Now Dolly watches her daughter with her own children. She is still worried

Above: Liz Macann gave up a successful career to spend more time with her children. Colleagues thought she was throwing in the towel.

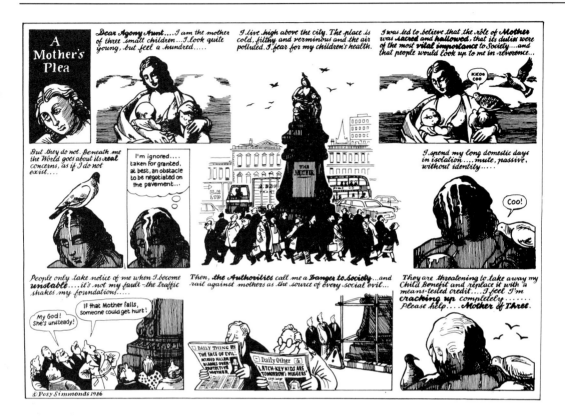

that she was not a very good mother and yet her daughter seems to be perfectly well adjusted. 'My daughter will cuddle her children however old they are and she'll say, "Oh, give us a kiss," and they're all lovely. She came in Saturday and sat on the settee and stroked my face and said, "You know, you're an absolutely lovely mother. Put your head on my shoulder, you look tired." I felt so embarrassed, I said, "Don't be silly," and she laughed. But I think mothers today can sort it out. It was my fault because I'm not a woman who can think for herself. But there were hundreds like me. I mean I wasn't the only one to feel anxious.'

Most mothers are uncertain whether they have done the right thing, whether they work or stay at home, whether they cuddle their babies or leave them to cry, whether they feed them whenever they look hungry or impose strict mealtimes. History has shown there is no blueprint for a perfect mother.

CHAPTER SIX

Thinking of England
Sex and Marriage

OR DOLL'S house women, the approved love was maternal. Sexual love was a forbidden secret. The Victorian female body, hidden by voluminous clothes to save men from temptation, was almost as much of a mystery to women themselves as to the men it was hidden from. Whatever the very rich and the very poor did, the accepted ideal for the vast majority of women was a chaste respectability. The Angel in the House had to be pure and innocent, knowing nothing of sex and certainly not enjoying it. The advice to Victorian brides to 'lie still and think of England' implied duty not pleasure: duty to produce more sons, duty to let a husband have his way. Man had his desires and woman had to service them. *His* sexual urges made him a gallant or a bit of a lad. They proved his manliness. *Hers*, on the other hand, made her a floosie, a trollop,

Below: Victorian women were expected to be pure and innocent.

a tart. A Good Woman was supposed to find her satisfaction in being a good wife and mother. It was only a Fallen Woman, a courtesan or prostitute, who could admit to sexual feelings. The worst transgressor of all was the woman who committed adultery, for whom no punishment was too great. She could lose her home, her children and all financial support while her husband could get away with adultery as much as he pleased and not even risk a divorce suit unless he was cruel to her or deserted her as well.

At the end of the nineteenth century, feminists began to challenge the double standard under which wives were expected to lead virtuous married lives while women were 'constantly annoyed and imperilled by the solicitation of profligate men in the streets' and child prostitution and white slave traffic flourished. A campaign, led by Josephine Butler towards the end of the last century, against the 1860s Contagious Diseases Acts brought prostitution into the public eye – from which it had been well hidden. The Acts allowed policemen to arrest prostitutes in ports and army towns and bring them in to have compulsory checks for venereal disease. The excuse was that this was the most hygienic way of protecting men from 'unclean women'. (No mention was made of 'unclean men' infecting the women in the first place.) Many of the women picked on by the police were not prostitutes at all, but the police were empowered to bring anyone they suspected of prostitution to the police station for examination. This involved having their legs clamped apart while surgical instruments probed their insides. If they struggled, they were put in straitjackets; if they were virgins, they bled profusely. After continuous pressure from Josephine Butler and the Ladies' Association against the Contagious Diseases Acts, this brutal practice was abolished in 1886.

As Naomi Mitchison remembers in her autobiography, feminists this century continued to attack male hypocrisy about sex. 'For instance, my mother told me that if anyone proposed marriage (no other proposal would conceivably have been a possibility!) I must ask whether he had ever had anything to do with another woman and if he had I must refuse him. This was straight feminism of the period, an attack on the double standard of men and women, which was still, of course, socially accepted.' It was also a sensible precaution in those years just before the First World War when Christabel Pankhurst was warning that between 75 and 80 per cent of men who had sex outside marriage had gonorrhoea. 'Women – and there are so many of them – who have never been well since they married are victims of gonorrhoea,' she wrote in her booklet, *The Great Scourge*.

Women have suffered too much from the Conspiracy of Silence to allow that conspiracy to last one minute longer. It has been an established and admitted rule in the medical profession to keep a wife in ignorance of the fact that she has become the victim of venereal disease.

Christabel's slogan 'votes for women and chastity for men' had some appeal for the feminists of her day. It seemed only reasonable to demand something from men.

Behind their closed doors Edwardian families concealed many of the problems we discuss today as if they were new. Violence to women was common, as was sexual abuse of children. Margaret Bondfield, who in 1929 became the first woman cabinet minister, interviewed the head of a home for unmarried mothers in Bradford in 1908 and was told of a number of cases of sisters bearing children to brothers and daughters to fathers. Although it had always been a social taboo and a sin in the eyes of the Church, incest only became illegal for the first time in 1908. Social reformers recognised the risks brought by overcrowded houses where parents slept with their children and children of both sexes had to share a bed.

In Nellie Boulton's house, the sexes were kept rigidly apart. Nellie, one of thirteen children, was born in 1909 in Stoke-on-Trent. She and her sisters shared a room but if any of them went near their brothers' bedroom for as little as to borrow a book, their mother pounced. 'I'd never seen a man in the nude,' Nellie remembers. 'I'd got seven brothers and I didn't know they'd even got ankles.' Stella Morgan, the same generation as Nellie, came from Southport, 'a very narrow-minded middle-class place', and could not remember ever seeing her father 'without a tie on, let alone anything else missing. I'd never seen a man in bed and at home smalls would never be seen on the line, and underwear would certainly never be mended in front of father.'

These memories may evoke a charming picture of lost innocence but beneath the surface girls were afraid of things that were hinted at but never spoken of. They were told that being alone with a man was dangerous, but not why. A student teacher hoped she would learn something at training college. 'I should have liked them to have mentioned sex but they seldom did. At twenty I had never heard a dirty story, did not know of their existence. Each girl thought the others knew more than she did and was afraid to talk for fear of showing her ignorance. Once when the science lecturer was absent the education lecturer took her place and to the amazement of the girls she unwove the story of the human embryo to a silent, thirsty class. I was grateful for that lecture, but I was still puzzled. What did my mother mean when she said, "Now I have warned you against men. You've been warned so you can safely go anywhere." That was all my mother ever told me.'

There was no common vocabulary of sex – pubic hair, clitoris, orgasm were words which were never spoken, much less understood. The most a girl could hope for was to pick up a few rudimentary facts of life from her sisters, friends or workmates. There were no words to describe making love. It was presented in a bald, unromantic light. Husbands would 'want their way' or, if you were lucky, you might find a 'good' husband who did not 'press his attentions' too often. Kathleen Dayus's accidental discovery of the facts of life when she was a young girl of seven in 1910 did little to inspire an ideal of romantic love. The youngest of thirteen, Kathleen crept past her sleeping siblings to get a glass of water one night. Passing her parents' bedroom 'I heard Mum say, "You can put the bloody thing away. I've had enough." Her says, "I've had a baker's dozen and you ain't having no more." That's how she used to talk and I didn't know what she meant by a baker's dozen so I asked me sister and she told me that Mum had had thirteen children and I was the scraping of the pot and Mum didn't want any more.' Knowledge of birth control was also limited. A variety of dubious pills or a dangerous, illegal abortion were the only safeguards available to women. Otherwise they relied on their husbands to use condoms, to withdraw, or to leave them alone.

Many of Kathleen's generation grew up totally ignorant of the facts of life. A nurse remembers going to her first confinement expecting the baby to come out of the navel and both men and women remember bewildering and embarrassing moments on their wedding nights. Nearly all of the older women who talked to us were virgins when they married. They had to be. Until they married they lived at home. Courting couples came under the watchful eye of their parents or, in middle- and upper-class circles, had varying degrees of attention from a chaperone. Some sympathetic chaperones did not bother to take their duties very seriously but there was little opportunity for intimacy. Besides, a girl knew she would be in trouble with her parents, shunned by society and considered damaged goods by all other men if she were found out. It was not worth the risk of being thrown out of home for, unless she was convinced her young man would marry her, there was nowhere else to go. For most girls, dependence on their parents was total so they did as they were told. Nellie Boulton's mother seems to have been fairly typical. 'I'd got that kind of matriarchal mother that didn't tell you anything at all. She always warned you against what *could* happen but she never told you what *did* happen. But you wouldn't have dared to have come home, you know, so you just didn't get involved in sex. It wasn't that girls were any different than they are today. It wasn't because they didn't want to do these awful things (that we used to think of as awful). It was just because they daren't.'

In the early years of the century, working-class marriage often seems to have been a practical affair, based on compatibility of temperament rather than sexual attraction. Women married rather older than today – on average in their mid-twenties. 'I got married at twenty-nine', one explained. 'Girls didn't get married so young in those days because they were expected to help out at home and contribute their wages to bringing up the rest of the family. Girls didn't get engaged, at least not in working-class families.' But they often had long courtships, saving up until the man could support a wife and family. A man needed a wife as manager of his

Right: Working-class weddings were unfussy occasions. Women married rather older than today, often after a long courtship, waiting until the man could support a wife and family.

house, provider of his meals, mother for his children. Marriage gave girls a ticket out of their parents' house and a nest of their own. It was not so different in the upper and middle classes, except that marriage was presented in a more romantic light. The trappings of romance diverted a young bride, making up for the fact she might be marrying a virtual stranger. The custom of chaperones made friendship almost as awkward as physical intimacy. Yet, once married, it was for life. In 1911, less than one in five hundred marriages ended in divorce.

The 1914 War changed the moral climate far less than is popularly imagined. Certainly there were more whirlwind romances and hurried marriages. The major worry for self-appointed guardians of the nation's morality was the large numbers of unprotected women – girls living away from home for the first time, and wives with husbands at the front. But there were plenty of busybodies to keep an eye on them. Welfare supervisors, sent into the factories to look after woman at work, were also told to make sure their moral standards did not slip. Policemen were asked to list all the women on their beat receiving separation allowances, the idea being to stop the allowance of anyone 'unworthy' – although after public protest this was never enforced. There may have been a few girls like the heroine of Warren Chetham-Strode's play about war-time love affairs, *Sometimes Even Now*, who thought it 'wonderful to be able to give so much without

caring about the cost ... Noel and I sat talking by the fire ... he was lonely, he was going back ... he didn't plead for my body, I gave it to him of my own free will.' But the majority stuck to the old morality. The idea that it was almost patriotic to make a man happy before he returned to the front was not generally held.

Above: The sexes were kept carefully segregated. Even during the First World War WRNS serving alongside men found few opportunities for social contact.

Irene Angell worked in her father's firm in London before the war. She remembers that as soon as war broke out 'things eased up'. Her tyrannical father abandoned war-stricken England for Australia, and Irene left her secretarial job to work as a VAD. Hospital life was far more worldly than the office had ever been. For a while Irene had a boyfriend but there was no question of any sexual hanky panky. 'We had parties but there was no hugging and cuddling at all. We all conformed. People wouldn't do it in front of other people.' Courting couples exchanged kisses in a darkened doorway or snatched their opportunity for a quick cuddle in those rare moments when they were alone. ,

Daisy Noakes's husband-to-be, George, 'never had any thoughts of us sleeping together or getting together before we married. Never even entered his mind. He never took very many advances to me at all.' Daisy and her young man 'walked out' for six years while she was in domestic service in Brighton. Long courtships were quite common until the Second World War and, if Daisy is right in thinking most followed the same pattern as her own, were models of self-restraint. 'When we went out together we mostly went on hikes or visits. The only time he made any fuss of me was when we met. He used to give me a kiss and we walked arm in arm. In those days that was the fashion. Perhaps if we went to the pictures he'd put an arm around me and the only other time we got in contact was

Above: Working as a VAD opened a new world to Irene Angell.

Above: Daisy and George Noakes. Over a six-year courtship George never made advances.

when he was saying goodnight to me when I was going back into service. He might give me a nice big cuddle and one or two heavy kisses, you know, on your cheek and your lips and that sort of thing and then "goodbye, goodnight, see you tomorrow" and that was all.' When Daisy took him home, she was charged sixpence for the tea. (Her mother believed in teaching her children the value of money.) They asked Daisy's father's permission to get engaged and always behaved themselves during their long engagement because 'my father would have bristled and we would have had a darn good thrashing and beaten out of house and home if anything had happened. After we were married my husband said "I knew I couldn't muck about with you because you were brought up too strict." I wasn't the first girl he had, but he never did make any advances at all and after six years I think that was pretty good.'

When Dorothy Marshall went up to Cambridge in 1918, chaperones were still the order of the day, but the following term the university was overwhelmed by men coming back from the war to take up postponed places. The authorities abandoned all pretence of keeping up the chaperone system. The new rules allowed couples to go out unsupervised but always in foursomes. Dorothy was a complete innocent. 'Sex in the physical sense of the word really meant nothing. It was a romantic concept of falling in love and true love and marriage. But what that involved I had not got a clue. I belonged to this little dance club. It really was set up by the men because they wanted dancing partners and we were always invited. We never paid. We used to go at eight o'clock at night and had to be back in college by eleven. We had one general chaperone. It was all very beautifully and decorously run and the whole time I was there I languished for one young man. But I would have been absolutely horrified if any man had kissed me at a dance or in any way kissed me. I should have thought that he hadn't honourable intentions, that he was holding me cheap. And I spent a lot of my time not taking the opportunities that I might have had because I was so anxious. You see, in those days if you allowed a man to know that you were too interested in him, you were holding yourself cheap. And so you had these romantic fantasies. But – this is a dreadful confession to make – do you know I must have been almost verging into my thirties before I ever really got kissed. Kissed by anybody who made me realise what it might all be about. And I think there were a great many of us.'

In the 1920s Irene Angell and Dorothy Marshall were living in what Ruth Adam, in her book *A Woman's Place*, describes as a mutilated society. Their generation had lost husbands and fiancés in the battlefields of Europe. Of the men who returned, many were physically and mentally maimed by their experience. Neither Irene nor Dorothy ever married. As Irene remembers, their chances of finding an eligible partner were not good. 'All our tennis club from up to 1914 who were cadets were killed in Mons and

Ypres and all this. I go down to the church and I see the notice board and I knew every one of those boys. I used to play tennis with them and go to school with them. But there were no more. You see, there wasn't anybody left over except men who came back from the forces and then they had somebody. My sister was lucky, she got her friend's brother. He was twelve years older than she was. You really had to work hard to get a husband, I think, in those days. It wasn't the kind of work I was looking for.' No longer needed for nursing, Irene found an office job and later fell in love with her boss. He had been the innocent party in a divorce that had taken place some years earlier and was keen to marry Irene, but she refused. 'It just wasn't done. We never heard about divorce, even in the papers.' A divorce caused scandal and anyone associated with one was tarnished so Irene remained single, living at home until her mother's death in 1926. Irene decided she was unlikely at thirty to find a husband so she took a Social Science Diploma at London University and started a new career in Poplar.

Being a social worker took Irene into a world she had never known. She worked with prostitutes and runaway girls, trying to find them jobs to get them off the streets and running an overnight shelter. Prostitutes were treated more kindly than in the days when they were dragged off the streets and examined for VD. There was less talk of punishment and more of rehabilitation. Unlike the 'respectable' working classes, most of Irene's girls came from miserable, overcrowded homes, where they slept four or

Below: Women tending war graves in 1919. Two million women would never have husbands.

five to a bed. Many had been abused by brothers, uncles, even their own fathers. It could hardly have been more different from Irene's own background and she kept quiet about the exact nature of her work. During the ten years she worked in Poplar, Irene never talked to her sisters about what she did. It was another of those subjects that were never mentioned. 'Good women' did not want to hear about the 'other sort'.

Some of Irene's girls had gone on the game to get away from their families. Almost anything was better than sharing a room with a drunken, violent father and several brothers and sisters. There were not many ways for a young girl to get away from home. Domestic service was one, but getting pregnant and 'having to get married' was often thought an easier alternative.

Winifred Routledge deliberately became pregnant to escape from her Cinderella-like existence. Illegitimate and treated as the family skivvy, Winifred was brought up by a grudging grandmother along with her uncles and aunts. She had a job cleaning and helping in a sweet shop but was not allowed to leave home as she was expected to do all the cleaning there too. Her grandmother bullied her and her own mother, living a few streets away with a separate family, ignored her. One of her uncles sexually abused her when she was young. 'I felt very frightened and I felt everybody knew and I wouldn't mix much with my friends. I felt everybody knew that I was a wicked, terrible person. Yet I wasn't the one that done it. It was the most traumatic experience and stayed with me right till I was about forty-two. I never told my grandmother because of what Philip would have done. When I said to my grandmother about wanting to get married and she said "Oo, nobody'd ever want to marry you", I thought it was because I was illegitimate; but thinking back it was probably because she knew about Philip and had condoned it because he was her favourite.'

Above: Winifred Routledge deliberately became pregnant to escape home.

Determined to keep her at home, Winifred's grandmother would not let her marry her boyfriend, Reg. They had been courting for two and a half years, 'having a little cuddle but nothing else', and both wanted to get married. When it became clear that her grandmother would never be won round, Winifred decided to force her hand by having a baby. The opportunity presented itself on Sunday nights when her grandparents went out to the pictures. Winifred eventually became pregnant but her grandmother still would not give her consent. So Winifred persuaded her real mother, 'Aunt Marjorie', to do the only good turn she ever did her and agree that her under-age daughter could marry. Winifred and Reg went to the registry office by tram, had lunch afterwards with Reg's aunt in a pub and then went to see Fred and Adele Astaire dancing at the Alhambra.

A ballroom-dancing craze swept the country in the 1920s. The pre-war generation, brought up on Viennese waltzes and the military two-step, condemned jazz as a degrading 'nigger dance' and were totally baffled by

Above: Learning the charleston was a must, even for Society matrons.

the charleston, but they were enjoyed in the new palais-de-danse halls. Those who went alone could hire partners of either sex for sixpence a dance. Bright Young Things who sipped cocktails and smoked cigarettes in public did not give a fig for their parents' fuddy-duddy inhibitions. They considered themselves the first generation of liberated women and were much more attracted by the arguments of feminists that women should be allowed to express their sexuality. Dora Russell, for instance, advocated free love: 'It was free ... instead of forced love, we were advocating where a woman could choose to love instead of being purchased for it.' There were not many women going this far but in the more open post-war society, there was growing agreement that women could and should enjoy sex. Avant-garde circles discussed Havelock Ellis's *The Psychology of Sex* which was finally completed (there were seven volumes) in 1927. Havelock Ellis called for 'erotic rights' for women, though he still believed women were naturally passive. Sigmund Freud's theories were gaining fashionable currency and he also recommended abandoning self-restraint. Some feminists thought this line of argument potentially dangerous – another excuse to turn women into vehicles to suit men's sexual urges. However, the tide was against them. In the 1920s their preference for celibacy sounded like spinsterish prudery.

Instead young women turned eagerly to Marie Stopes's book, *Married Love*. Best known today for her pioneering work in birth control, Marie Stopes had only become interested in contraception through studying feminine sexuality. She was a well-travelled doctor of botany but, like others of her generation, she was an innocent. When, after five years of unconsummated marriage, she had no idea why she had not produced babies, Marie Stopes acquainted herself with the facts by reading nearly every book on sex in English, French and German in the British Museum. Fortunately for her contemporaries, she published the results of her research in the book, *Married Love*, in 1918. Although this book was initially turned down by a publisher on the grounds that 'there are few enough men for girls to marry and I think this would frighten off the few', *Married Love* was an overnight best-seller. Thousands of couples bought it and were grateful for the first serious sex-instruction book they had ever seen. Its main message was that:

Man, through prudery, through the custom of ignoring the woman's side of marriage and considering his own whim as marriage law, has largely lost the art of stirring a chaste partner to physical love.

Once Marie Stopes had broken through the prejudice surrounding this kind of book, others followed. Dr Helena Wright published *The Sex Factor in Marriage* in 1930. In both books women had a new duty to enjoy sex but as fairly passive partners, waiting to be 'awakened' by their husband. The emphasis was on male technique. But as the Reverend Gray's introduction to Dr Wright's book made clear, women had a duty to co-operate.

If you do not consent to be awakened your husband will be deeply disappointed. ... He will not call it purity, he will call it prudery; and he will be right.... He will know that you have not fully *given* yourself in marriage: and married joys are for those who *give* with royal generosity.

'Thinking of England' was out of date. However, the search for successful physical love in marriage was largely confined to the privileged classes. Their families were smaller, couples spent more time alone together and women had energy to channel in new directions. But this was not true in large working-class families. When Dr Wright asked women visiting her North London Birth Control Clinic whether they enjoyed sex, they looked at her blankly. What was there to enjoy? They had not the faintest idea what she was talking about.

Improved technique was only part of the equation. Women were unlikely to enjoy sex while they associated it with unwanted pregnancies. The work of Helena Wright, Marie Stopes and the other birth control pioneers of the 1920s and 30s played a crucial part in liberating women. But their attempts to spread information about contraception were frequently hampered by their opponents, who feared that once sexual intercourse could be separated from procreation, men might behave less responsibly and women might be tempted to stray from their doll's house world, endangering the institution of marriage itself.

As women found their political voice, they made it clear what they thought of allowing men to divorce women for adultery without giving women the same right in return. Divorce reform became a major issue between the wars. When the Matrimonial Causes Act in 1923 finally allowed women to use their husband's adultery as a sole ground for divorce, the notion slowly grew that marriage was not necessarily for life. But infidelity was still the vital element in ending a marriage. Divorce, therefore, implied naughtiness so respectable people, like Irene Angell, fought shy of it. Couples who had simply made a mistake had to commit adultery, pretend to commit adultery or stay married. However, by the 1930s Hollywood film stars were beginning to lend glamour to divorce. In their eyes divorce was not a squalid hole-in-the-corner affair but an inevitable step in the search for the perfect marriage. The avant-garde embraced American permissiveness but the British public did not. When the King tried to marry a divorcee, he found the weight of the establishment against him. Britain would not accept a divorced Queen.

However, coaxed by the well-known playwright and MP, Alan Herbert, the establishment was prepared to accept wider grounds for divorce. Herbert ran an eloquent campaign against the old laws which included a witty novel, *Holy Deadlock*, about a couple who longed to divorce but were foiled by the system time and time again, and which exposed the hypocrisy of arranged adultery in hotels. In 1937 Parliament passed an Act, affectionately known as the Herbert Act, enabling divorce for cruelty, after three years for wilful desertion and after five years for insanity.

Attitudes to marriage were slowly changing and so, too, were attitudes to women's sexuality. As it became more acceptable for women to acknowledge sexual urges, a lesbian sub-culture emerged which, until the 1920s, had never found a form. Unlike male homosexuality, female homosexuality was not unlawful. Queen Victoria is rumoured to have refused to agree to ban it as she could not believe such a thing existed. An attempt to make lesbianism illegal failed in 1921. Those opposed to outlawing it argued that silence was stronger than law. If people did not know about lesbianism they would not think of such acts while legislation would only draw attention to them and give people ideas. Silence was quite effective. Dorothy Marshall, resisting advances from a friend of her brother, was puzzled when he asked if she was a lesbian. 'What's that?' she asked, and only discovered what the word meant when she had turned fifty. The banning and prosecution of Radclyffe Hall's lesbian novel *Well of Loneliness* in 1928, probably did more than anything else to bring lesbianism into the open and to give lesbians a sense of group identity. But in a society discovering the joys of heterosexual love, they were largely dismissed by such writers as Havelock Ellis as 'perverted' and 'abnormal'.

By the late 1930s a young woman had a better chance of getting married than for several generations. Children from the war years were grown men and another half million had drifted back from the Empire. They found Britain hugely altered. Middle-class life seemed particularly different from pre-war days. Chaperones were a distant memory, girls had their own

Right: By the 1930s there were far more opportunities for couples to be alone.

wage-packets. Some even drove cars. There were far more opportunities for couples to be alone. They might take a spin to a country pub or roadhouse, or while away an hour or so in the car on the way back from a dance or the pictures. The cinema brought glamour, romance and excitement into every provincial town, providing not only an evening's entertainment but the chance for many an awkward youth to chance his luck when the lights dimmed.

Patricia Elton, the daughter of a surgeon living in the West End, had no shortage of boyfriends. By day she had a good job running a wholesale dress company and modelling her wares. At night she went home to her parents who were always ready with a meal or spare bed for any of her friends. She had use of the family car and drove her 'crowd' to charity dances at the Hammersmith Palais. She had plenty of freedom to have a good time but no more. 'One didn't want to sort of rock the boat. You see, we were living at home and you had to obey the rules.' She was expected to stay pure until she married. Parents like Patricia's worried about their daughters 'going the whole hog'. There was still great fear of pregnancy. The contraceptive advice available was exclusively for married women who wanted to limit their families. It was not given to young girls wanting to experiment. Patricia's mother warned her that there were zones of the body that should be kept to herself. 'You see, if you got into trouble, very often the boy had to marry the girl and they hadn't got jobs. There was a lot of unemployment even in the middle classes. It would have been rather kept under dust sheets and if anyone had got pregnant they'd have been sent off to stay with granny in the country and the baby would have been adopted or something. It would have been very, very traumatic.'

In 1939 war shattered Patricia's carefree existence. She had to abandon her coveted job as a mannequin and join up. Choosing the Air Force because the uniform was the nicest colour, she found herself at a training camp with thirty other women who had never left home and who had not the slightest idea how to cope with the thousands of airmen at the main camp. Patricia, used to a greater degree of freedom than most, was not thrown by all the attention. There were tales of girls being harassed and teased by bands of servicemen but most managed to steer clear of trouble. Patricia made sure she always had an escort, even when crossing camp to the 'ablutions'. There was safety in numbers so girls usually went out in foursomes. The innocent had to learn the facts of life fast. 'One of the girls thought you couldn't get pregnant the first time you did it and I said, "I think you can, you know, I wouldn't bank on that if I were you." But I don't remember any of the girls in my group getting pregnant. I think we just kept the men at bay and they were often frightened of getting a girl pregnant. You know, they did take a feeling of responsibility and some of my young men that took me out didn't want to get married. They couldn't afford to get married. So you just sort of gritted your teeth and kept your legs crossed and waited.'

Above: Patricia Elton (right) joined the Air Force. It had the nicest uniform.

Patricia knew one or two progressive women who were not prepared to wait and took the initiative themselves. They apparently went to Dr Helena Wright's clinic and spun a line about getting married next month and asked to be fitted with a Dutch cap. But they were a tiny minority. Far more girls left contraception up to the man or threw caution to the winds or simply did without sex.

As in the First World War, illegitimacy went up. Much was blamed on 'the Yank factor'. When one and three-quarter million Americans and Canadians passed through Britain during the war, the local population was dazzled. Our own men were away fighting on other fronts, leaving their wives, sweethearts and daughters open to American cigarettes, chocolate and charm. Kathleen Atwell was fifteen when the Yanks arrived in Bristol in 1942. 'We were brought up on the pictures, you see. Hollywood was a mecca. I wanted to be like Marlene Dietrich, you know, but I was more like Judy Garland, very sort of bubbly personality. When the GIs came marching into Bristol, it was like Hollywood was coming to us. It was just great. Any one of them could have been a film star, you know. They had the accent and they had the smart uniforms and they were so full of life. We fell for them in droves. It was like being in a movie.'

Oversexed, overpaid and over here, grumbled British soldiers, miffed at the Americans' obvious success with women. Kathleen's gorgeous GI friends in their tailored uniforms looked like officers and were paid about five times as much as their British equivalents. Kathleen was introduced to nylons and American cigarettes like Lucky Strikes and chewing gum in sticks. She soon paired off with Louis, a second generation Italian American, known to his buddies as Dago, Her best friend, Mary, dated his pal, Henry. They both came from the South and the girls loved to hear them shout, 'Come on, chicken, grab a wing.' The well-stocked American PX (their Naafi) ensured a steady supply of wartime scarcities like scented soap, chocolate and oranges which Louis brought her mother whenever he came for a meal. For Kathleen the Yanks' spell in Bristol was a time when the sun perpetually shone, with walks on the Downs and fun at the local fair. Best of all she had an engagement to boast of. Nothing did more for a girl's reputation than a handsome GI fiancé. Seventy thousand babies were said to have been fathered by Americans during the war and in 1945 20 000 women applied to be wives of American soldiers. Mary married her Yank. Kathleen did not. Once Louis had gone to France, the Hollywood magic disappeared and Kathleen's life returned to normal. Crossing the Atlantic and not seeing her family for years seemed rather frightening, a dream that was over. All the same, the American episode still stands out as the highlight in Kathleen's war. 'It was part of your self-respect to find that there was somebody that would go to the altar with you and put that thin gold band on your finger. It was important. You don't hear the term

Below: American soldiers dazzled British girls. 'It was like Hollywood coming to us.'

"old maid" so much now, but you were less than a woman if you couldn't get yourself a man then, I think, than now.'

The worry about ending up an old maid was not simply fear of not marrying. Many spinsters of the First World War talk in a roundabout way of not wanting to 'miss out'. Although they never married, they were anxious we should know they were not old maids. Virginity, once so highly prized, was an embarrassment as they got older. Having accepted they would never marry, they wanted at least to have experience of sex. War offered some of them a last chance. Twice the average number of illegitimate babies were born to spinsters between the age of thirty and forty-five during the war. Amidst all the chaos, a few barriers were lowered and some inhibitions disappeared. Irene Angell was forty-three when war once again disrupted her life. By day she worked in an office, at night in Clapham she took shelter from the bombs wherever she could. Speaking of her contemporaries and, rather shyly, of herself she explained 'Life was different. They were so glad to be alive, they let themselves go. And they didn't know whether there mightn't be another.... Yes. Morals went. Everybody slept in shelters and they came to you for comfort and that sort of thing. I mean we lost touch with the ordinary principles of life, I think, in the Second World War. 'Cos I was older then, a lot older and I was quite on my own. My people all fled to different places, I was left with a flat of my own. We all sort of cuddled in together, if you know what I mean.'

Below: Kathleen Atwell married in a grey suit. In austerity Britain, bridal gowns were hard to find.

Irene feels that she is indefinably richer than those of her generation 'who have never loved. I don't think you ever learn to love, unless you have lived with a man. Oh, no, you can always tell, I think, a person who has and a person who hasn't.' Her only regret is that she never had a son. Had she been born fifty years later, she could have had her dream child. She could have put her name down for a council flat and claimed a single parent allowance. Instead she devoted her best years to running a shelter for outcasts: prostitutes, unmarried mothers, runaway girls.

Despite the feeling of liberation during the war – the sense of being let out, the secret romances, jitterbugging with GIs – when it ended most people were glad to get back to normal. In 1947 wedding bells sounded more often than ever before as 401 210 couples settled down to married life. Patricia Elton married a Master Mariner in the Merchant Navy who had spent most of the war in a prison camp and who tragically died a few years later from TB. Kathleen Atwell, her GI romance well behind her, married a local boy. They had a typical austerity wedding. Kathleen could not buy a white dress anywhere so she made do with 'a little dove-grey silky kind of suit I was rather fond of, and some nice little dove-grey shoes'. In the event, her wedding day was not quite all she had hoped for. 'People weren't as knowledgeable then, they hadn't tried things out that applied to men and women. Not all of them, of course, but it was far more widespread that a man hadn't slept around either. It was romantic in that we went to the Lake District for our honeymoon and we were in love and all that but we had to learn and we had to learn together. As I say, there was a great, great deal that could have helped. Today people are so much more knowledgeable and that's why I'm all in favour of it.'

Between 1948 and 1953 the American zoologist, Alfred Kinsey, conducted a survey of sexual behaviour in North America. The resulting 'K Bomb' report exploded on an astonished British public. 'Sex is here to stay' concluded the *Daily Mail* on 20 August 1953. The Kinsey Report suggested that 50 per cent of Nice College Girls were not virgins when they married, that homosexuality was more common than anyone had believed (incidences of overt lesbian contact to the point of orgasm were 13 per cent) and that sexual acts publicly regarded as perversions (such as fellatio and masturbation) were widely practised in private. The more sex was talked about, the more couples were impatient to experiment. Long engagements gave way to early marriages. Daisy Noakes's six years of innocent courting in the 1920s would not be repeated by her children in the 1950s.

Marriage, it seemed, was as popular as ever. People were marrying younger and younger but they were also divorcing more often. After the 1914–18 war the number of divorce petitions increased by fifteen hundred a year; after the 1939–45 war they increased by twenty thousand. Legal aid enabled people who previously could not have contemplated the cost of a solicitor to go ahead with proceedings. In 1954 it was estimated that one in fifteen marriages would end in divorce (compared with one in sixty in 1937 and one in five hundred in 1911). In 1955 the Morton Commission reported on the state of divorce law. The commissioners were alarmed at what they saw as mounting evidence that the institution of marriage was taken less seriously than formerly. They blamed youthful mistakes in the choice of partner but also the changing position of women:

Women are no longer content to endure the treatment which in past times their inferior position obliged them to suffer. They expect of marriage that it shall be an equal partnership; and rightly so. But the working out of this ideal exposes marriages to new strains.

They went on to note that there had been rapid changes in attitudes to sex brought about partly by the upheavals of two world wars. People were more likely to pursue their own personal satisfaction, regardless of the consequences to others. Modern psychology was widely interpreted as stressing the dangers of repression; and, the report suggested, the wider knowledge of sexual matters, while of great value, might 'have produced in the popular mind an undue emphasis on the over-riding importance of a satisfactory sex relationship' at the expense of 'the other stable and enduring factors of a lasting marriage'. The threat to marriage was seen only as a trend to be checked – the report emphasised that most people still believed in working hard to make their marriages a success.

The popular image of the 1950s is of a prim period preceding a permissive one. A few trendsetters jived in basements in Oxford Street, but homely girls with bobby socks, neat shirtwaister dresses and pony tails far outnumbered them. 'No one ever had sexual intercourse (which are two words that were never used anyway) before they were married,' remembers June Rendle about her own circle of friends. 'You were quite well aware that some girls did have babies and they weren't married but they were beyond the pale, I mean, like from another world. All girls went to the altar virgins and had "it" for the very first time on their wedding night and that was what you kept in your mind throughout. You made sure that you were never in a position that anything could possibly happen. So you didn't go on holiday with your boyfriend.' June lived at home in Staffordshire, where her father owned a garage. Her boyfriend was a paying guest in someone else's house. There was never any good reason for them to be alone at either house. They went out to the pictures or to the pub and parked the car somewhere on the way home. Girls in her circumstances had limited opportunities for 'going all the way' except in a car. 'If your boyfriend said, "Let's get in the back," forget it. That was tantamount to you'd definitely had it, because you couldn't fight back so easily in the back. After the pictures I would be driven home, that is to outside the gate and the engine would be switched off. I always had to be in by eleven. Always! So by this time it's getting up to 10.50 and usually you'd have a cigarette and I can tell you exactly how long it takes to smoke a cigarette because I'd think "I've only got ten minutes". And then you would kiss and then you'd got to be in by eleven, so there wasn't a lot of opportunity.' If June did not arrive at eleven, her father would be looking out for her and if he spotted her he would knock on the car window and summon her indoors.

June had been brought up believing men were naturally aggressive as far as sex was concerned and it was up to girls to say 'no'. 'That was the battle, because they wouldn't marry you if you said "yes". They married the girl that said "no".' With this drummed into them, girls played a careful game. After all, they risked not only losing their virginity but their chance of marriage too. On the other hand, June expected her husband to

Above: 1950s' primness personified by model Zoe Newton, in a campaign to get people to drink more milk.

Above: Rock 'n Roll. From the late 1950s teenagers asserted their growing independence from their parents' generation.

be experienced. 'He hadn't got to be a virgin, that would be awful. You couldn't have two of you not knowing anything. But where he got his experience, I don't know. With these other girls, the ones who said "yes", but then he would come to me with all this wonderful experience that he had and he would teach me what he knew.' The double standard was never discussed. Girls assumed that boys needed sex so it seemed reasonable for them to find it somewhere, but nice girls did not – or if they did, they kept quiet about it.

It was a sign of the growing attention paid to sex that it was thought important that schools should provide some sort of grounding. Sex education varied enormously from school to school. At Cheltenham we were sent out into the world with a clear warning not to lead men on but were told little else. We had a talk from the school doctor, an elderly spinster, who gave us two pearls of wisdom. One was that you could not catch VD (something clearly to be avoided, but none of us knew precisely what it was) from public lavatories and the other was how to stop men 'going too far'. She said that in the tolerant climate of 1963 we would probably find tempting opportunities to be alone with men. There was to be no 'thinking of England' for us. We, being girls, she explained, must not get carried away during love-making like the weaker sex. It was up to us to keep our minds on other things, ready to say 'no' at an appropriate moment. She drew up a suggested thinking list for us: shopping for the next day, drawers that needed tidying, letters to be written and so on.

At the Winkley Square Convent, Preston, the facts of life were still explained through the reproduction of a frog. Theresa Williamson picked up what she could from the other girls at school. When her own daughters went to the same school recently they were shown explicit videos and taught about contraception. In Theresa's day, despite the best efforts of the nuns, boyfriends dominated school life. From the moment Theresa met her husband-to-be at the ripe age of fourteen, her school grades slumped. Though her parents' generation thought she and her girlfriends were fast and forward, they always waited for the boys to make the first move, egging them on only a little. 'If you fancied someone you let your female friends know, and they would tell their boyfriend to tell his friend that you fancied him. And the message would come back along that line. He would tell your friend's boyfriend that he fancied you and he would tell the girlfriend and the girlfriend would say, "My boyfriend's friend says he fancies you, do you fancy going out with him?" And that is how it worked.' Without a boyfriend you were nobody. Girls went to the cinema with boyfriends, dancing with boyfriends, out to coffee bars with boyfriends. Unless you were one of a couple, you felt you were missing out.

There was no shortage of boys in the 1960s. For the first time this century there were more marriageable men than women. Mothers no longer warned their daughters to 'work hard at getting married'. The main aim of most young girls was to have a good time. With the benefits of a welfare state – better food, better housing, better health care – they were maturing earlier. Youth was in fashion. Teenagers were cultivated as a new consumer group, with their own style of dressing, their own music, their own magazines. By the end of the decade even the voting age had been brought down to eighteen. Teenagers had a clear identity between childhood and adulthood which their parents had not known and far more generous wage-packets to boost their sense of independence. Parental authority weakened. The numbers in colleges and universities doubled during the 1960s and these young luminaries owed their way of life to the State, not their parents. They could afford to ignore strictures to be back by eleven. The threat of being turned out of home had become a rather empty one. The last thing parents wanted was their darling daughter disappearing into digs where they could no longer keep a watchful eye on her. Yet that is exactly what she did if living at home grew awkward. She could probably afford to move into a place of her own or, at least, share with others. Knowing this, bemused parents learned to tolerate the habits of the young.

Unlike other generations who had modelled themselves on their mothers, this one was proud to be different. The pampered post-war bulge was growing up. Whether the impact was greater because there were so many of us I do not know. (There were one million more between the ages of fifteen and twenty-four than ten years earlier.) At the time it seemed we were always making the running. We had more disposable income than our parents, and salesmen and advertisers flocked to serve us. Our music, our fashion, even our views appeared to be taken seriously. Sex was regarded as natural and liberating. There were, of course, outraged voices protesting that the young were getting out of hand. In 1963 Sandra Cowlam was seventeen, still living at home and deliberately shocking her middle-class parents whenever possible. She dyed most of her clothes purple, took to wearing men's shirts, plastered her eyes with black make-up and refused her mother's pleas to have her hair cut and permed. She used the house like a hotel, coming and going whenever she pleased. 'There seemed to be a party just about every weekend and I worked in a coffee bar so I was in a very good position to find out where they were. Most of the friends I had were middle-class and their parents went away often and that was the perfect opportunity to have a party and we just used to take over the house.'

Behind the bold facade, Sandra was quite unsophisticated. Permissiveness was more talked about than indulged in. Although the pill had arrived it was not freely available on the National Health. Besides contraception of any kind was awkward for a single girl. Family Planning Clinics were staffed by formidable matrons who cross-examined their patients in such detail about their private lives that they appeared to be questioning their morals (and probably were). Girls had to pretend to be married, or about to be, and give details of their husband or fiancé. So many took risks. Sandra was amazed to find herself pregnant. 'I was totally shocked. I couldn't believe it. It really didn't have anything to do with having sex. . . . I thought it was something that happened to older people. I thought I was too young somehow. Contraception wasn't something I'd discussed with anybody. The only things I'd discussed really were the kind of jokes about Durex. Even after I'd had my baby I didn't know much about what was happening to my body and how I could prevent being pregnant again.' Convention triumphed. Sandra's parents insisted that she married her lover and all the uncles, aunts and cousins came to the wedding, pretending not to notice she was eight months pregnant. The marriage did not last.

During the 1960s the illegitimacy rate rose from 5.8 to 8.2 per cent of all live births. Many girls in Sandra's shoes refused to marry their child's father. Virginity mattered less in the marriage stakes than formerly and they had their own high expectations from marriage. Girls talked about sexual compatibility and the risk of marrying a man without sleeping with him first. Not having to grab a man or be left a surplus woman, they could afford to be choosy and they were.

In 1966, aged fourteen, Brenda Mayo was filmed for a BBC documentary. She appeared to the producer to be a typical product of her generation. Her father worked as an assistant foreman in a local factory in Swindon. Brenda went to the Dove Secondary Modern. She came across as a confident extrovert, with clear ideas about what the future held in store. First she wanted to make pop records with her friend Joy and to have a good time, then, at around twenty-one she would settle down and get married. In the documentary she sounded worldly and street-wise – a representative modern girl. She had known the facts of life since she was twelve and poured scorn on girls who 'got into trouble'. A year later Brenda, herself, was pregnant. Keith walked into her life and she fell in love. 'We never actually slept together. You know, it was just really at parties and this type of thing. It's the old myth, I never thought it would happen to me and it did.'

Although Keith was prepared to stand by her, Brenda did not want to get married. They both decided the baby should be given to Keith's sister (who had suffered many miscarriages but produced no children), and planned to leave the baby in a basket outside her front door. Despite their sex education lessons at school, they both thought babies came from the navel and that childbirth was a relatively uncomplicated affair which they could manage between them – Keith playing obstetrician. Brenda concealed her pregnancy by wearing a tight corset and, since she was quite chubby anyway, no one noticed her swelling figure. Six weeks before the baby was due her mother thought she might be 'suffering from glands' and sent her to their family doctor. 'I said to the doctor "I think I'm pregnant." And he took this dreadful corset off (which hadn't been washed because I was too frightened to wash it because my mother would recognise it) and found I'd turned the baby.' Once her parents discovered the truth, Brenda was bundled off to a home for unmarried mothers. She was given a wedding ring to wear and the nurses insisted on calling her 'Mrs'. After her son was born, everyone tried to persuade her to let him be adopted. Despite her parents' objections, Keith visited her daily and agreed they had to keep the baby. 'I wasn't allowed to breast-feed which was very sad because I did make plenty of milk. I was given tablets to dry myself up because they didn't want the bond between the mother and the baby to grow.' A generation earlier she might have passed the baby off as her mother's, but times had changed and adoption societies had huge waiting lists of childless couples desperate to adopt. A generation earlier she might

Far left: Brenda Mayo only married her son's father after his birth, when 'sure of her feelings'. Shotgun weddings were decreasing by 1970.

Left: The Rolling Stones. Pop songs and singers were blatantly sexy.

have felt obliged to marry Keith. But girls were becoming less submissive and Brenda both kept her baby and refused to marry Keith until she had time to 'check her feelings'. Eighteen months later they had a church wedding. The bride wore blue.

'Fashions changed, changed again, changed faster and still faster,' wrote Bernard Levin of the 1960s in *The Pendulum Years*. 'What had lasted a generation now lasted a year, what had lasted a year lasted a month, a week, a day. There was a restlessness in the time that communicated itself everywhere and to everyone.' Attitudes to sex changed as fast as everything else. The trial of the publishers of D. H. Lawrence's *Lady Chatterley's Lover* in 1960 set the scene. It turned out to be a test not merely of what could be published under the new Obscene Publications Act but of how far public taste had changed. The sensational trial and acceptance of Lawrence's book marked the start of the Permissive Society. Plays on television became more daring. In the cinema, the ultimate good girl, Doris Day, was replaced by the sixties' darling, Julie Christie. While sex in films became more explicit and erotic, the back seats of the cinema no longer attracted rows of amorous couples. Presumably they were curled up in front of their own television sets. Pop singers and songs were openly sexy. 'Why don't we do it in the road,' sang the Beatles. 'I can't get no satisfaction,' moaned the Rolling Stones. In 1967 abortion laws were relaxed and homosexual acts were permitted in private between consenting adults. Drugs, previously the undoing of a small minority, became widespread. The pill, as one sixties' swinger remembers, was something more written about than taken

Right: Carnaby Street fashions reflect what was becoming known as the Permissive Society.

but 'it encouraged us to think that we too could have sex like the boys did and get away with it. It encouraged us to think that there was something out there that would enable us to have an abandoned sex life.' The same message rang out from pulp novels girls could buy even in their local W. H. Smith's. Lying back and thinking of England was as outmoded as stays and bustles. At the start of the decade girls who slept with their boyfriends kept quiet about it. By the 1970s (a more universally permissive decade), they were quite open about it.

Virginity, no longer a prized commodity, weighed heavily on a young girl. Sheila Jeffreys, at Manchester University in the late 1960s, found that freshers were expected to lose their virginity within six months. Sheila did not and felt she was regarded as a rare 'sort of exhibit. Even though I looked the part and I had the long blonde hair and all of that, I couldn't transform myself into the sexual object that I was expected to be at the time.'

Saying 'no' was harder than it had ever been. Pregnancy, the great deterrent, had also been the best excuse. With liberal abortion laws and the pill available to unmarried girls at family planning clinics from 1967 (and free on the National Health from 1974), it was now barely a worry. Even the plea that nice girls did not do it had vanished. A trendy girl changed her men as frequently as her brother bought a new tie. Those who did not go along with the easy sex of the times were labelled 'frigid' or a 'tease'. The pressure to conform was enormous. Sheila Jeffreys remembers that 'one boy described me as a bottle of disinfectant, which is something I must have found very shocking at the time because I've always remembered it'. Another insisted she saw the university psychiatrist because she did not want to sleep with him. Eventually she decided, quite clinically, to

Above: Sheila Jeffreys resented being seen as a sex object.

Left: Family Planning Leaflet. When unmarried girls became entitled to contraceptive advice, the Family Planning Association changed its stuffy image to move with the times.

lose her virginity. She sized up the men she knew, picked a medical student on the basis that he ought to know what he was doing and determinedly stayed the night with him. After that she fitted in. 'I was involved with a large number of men, mostly in a very casual way, because I had agreed with the sexual revolution philosophy around me that you should be able to engage in sexual activity without falling in love or being tremendously emotionally involved.'

For a while equality in sex, like equality at work, obliged women to prove they could do precisely what men do. If this involved quelling a natural instinct to act differently, it was stifled in the name of progress. As one put it, 'I saw men rather like buses. You kind of got on one and you went along a bit and then you got off that one and you got on another one.' When the Women's Movement questioned whether this permissiveness often implied submissiveness, it found plenty who agreed. 'In the safe space of small groups, women started to share their secrets,' wrote Anna Coote and Beatrix Campbell in *Sweet Freedom*, 'and what emerged, among much else, was an epidemic of sexual failure.' When women were supposed to be having a terrific time, many were privately miserable. 'Women were bored with their husbands in bed; or their husbands were bored with them; or they only had orgasms when they masturbated; or they felt awkward and humiliated; or they hated their own bodies; or they feared they were frigid.'

What had appeared as a new way of women pleasing themselves had turned out to be yet another way of women pleasing men. All their newfound sexual freedom had merely increased the pool of available crumpet. Talking it out rescued Sylvie Pierce from being swept along on a succession of men's arms, never feeling she quite came up to scratch.

"I'm afraid I got a boy in trouble."

'That area of women's lives is so important and it has been kind of kept in the closet as something you didn't share and so there were these amazing groups going on all over England, of women actually talking together about these things. I suppose women had talked about them before but they had never been named. They had never been given words. It was like finding a new language and naming things. A rather obvious example is things like sexual harassment. There had been no names for that. And how women have orgasms and all that kind of thing. Was it vaginal orgasm or was it through the clitoris? It was incredibly exciting. It was incredibly liberating and, of course, for a lot of women it had quite an impact on the relationships they were having with men.'

In 1969 Anne Koedt published a paper called the 'Myth of the Vaginal Orgasm' arguing that the route to sexual rapture lay through the clitoris not the vagina and that, therefore, penetration was not necessary for a woman's satisfaction. Many disagreed with this analysis. Germaine Greer, for instance, argued in *The Female Eunuch* that 'the substitution of the clitoral spasm for genuine gratification may turn out to be a disaster for sexuality'. Bemused spectators were puzzled by the intensity of the debate about the relative merits of one orgasm over another. The argument centred on whether women really needed men at all for sexual gratification. This was a crucial development for those feminists who believed they should not waste their closest emotions on men. Although lesbians still felt they were treated as oddities and in certain jobs, particularly those involving children, had to conceal their proclivities, many were coming out of the closet. Havelock Ellis's dismissal of lesbians as 'abnormal' or 'perverted' no longer carried much weight. Some women discovered their lesbian leanings through the women's movement. Sheila Jeffreys had never contemplated having any kind of sexual relationship with women, but she felt that living with a man was inconsistent with her growing commitment to revolutionary feminism so asked her lover to move out. 'I assumed that I was making a decision to dedicate myself to the revolution for women and that I would be celibate for ever. Only it didn't work out like that because once I had made that break, I found very quickly that I was able to recognise something that I'd felt for women for a long time, that actually it was attraction towards them, but because there hadn't been a name for it and it hadn't been sort of described in a heterosexual way, I hadn't recognised that. Eighteen months later I fell in love with a woman and have been a lesbian involved in relationships with women since then.'

Sheila prepared a paper on the way men maintained power over women for the annual Women's Liberation Conference in 1977. 'The main line of analysis was around male sexuality: a social control of women, seeing the way in which men, through sexual violence, controlled women's lives through harassment in the street, sexual abuse in childhood, sexual abuse and rape in adulthood, pornography. The whole way that women were constructed into sexual objects and their freedom and opportunities were limited.' Feminists argued that as women had grown more independent, men had used more sexual violence to keep their position of power and pointed to the enormous growth of material which degraded women, from Page Three Girls to hard pornography. In 1980, after the death of the thirteenth victim of the Yorkshire Ripper, a new campaign was formed, Women Against Violence Against Women.

One of the most successful earlier campaigns carried out by feminists was against domestic violence. They revealed that wife-battering was not an occasional problem but widespread and worrying. They raised money for shelters for battered wives and lobbied MPs about it. In 1976 the Domestic Violence Act enabled a woman to obtain an immediate injunction to exclude a violent husband from the house and gave the police powers of arrest without a warrant in specific circumstances. With more liberal divorce laws, women are now no longer legally bound in sexual relationships they do not want, though there may be a dozen other reasons why they put up with being knocked about.

The fears of the Morton Commission in the 1950s proved well-founded. The concept of marriage as a life-long commitment is no longer widely held. Then the number of marriages ending in divorce was one in fifteen, today it is one in three. (Though in many ways family life was just as unstable one hundred years ago: a sixteen-year marriage, for instance, had the same chance of being broken by a death then as by a divorce today.) Illegitimate births are more numerous than they have ever been this century. Seventeen per cent of babies today are born out of wedlock, though well over half of them are registered by both parents, possibly suggesting that although an increasing number of people may not want the ties of marriage they prefer to produce children within a stable union.

None of the young women who talked to us were in a hurry to get married. After some initial disappointments, most were remarkably relaxed about sex – their present contentment justifying the change of partners and experience along the way. Sacha Cowlam, Sandra's 25-year-old daughter, explained the difference between herself and her mother. 'She was part of that generation in the sixties who believed sex was a vital part of their experience and you weren't a free person until you had experienced lots of sexual partners. They slept with someone first and then hoped that a long-term relationship would come of it.' Sacha makes friendships first and only then allows a sexual relationship to develop. But she finds the double standard is still strong though moulded to the 1980s. 'The men you meet aren't naive enough to expect virgins but they certainly don't want to hear about the "ghosts" of your past life. Yet I can't imagine a man sticking around much after two or three months if you hadn't slept together.' The increase in venereal disease, especially Herpes II, and, above all, the AIDS epidemic have made people more cautious – but only a little. 'The whole

"THEY'RE AWFULLY FIDDLY TO PUT ON. ISN'T THAT HALF THE FUN?"

thing has been blown right out of proportion,' was the common reaction among those who talked to us. The most tangible result is the sight of young women throwing Durex into their supermarket trolleys along with washing powder, instant coffee and sliced bread. As an 18-year-old girl put it, 'Girls do sleep with their boyfriends today. To get a reputation they really have to go flat out and sleep around. It's really a question of numbers.' A woman is no longer 'bad' if she shows she has a sexual appetite or has several lovers in her lifetime – in fact she might be considered something of an oddity if she did not. She has come a long way from the days when she was treated like an unresponsive, passionless doll. Some (mostly men) will argue that something has been lost – a magical quality that set women apart. An aspiring Conservative politician told me that he would never let any wife of his read Court cases in case they coarsened her. It is a sentiment echoed by Stella Morgan, a former marriage guidance counsellor, now in her seventies. 'Women have lost a lot – there are a lot of brittle women around. I think they've lost a certain charm – whether it was of any value or not, I don't know. Now they have short hair and wear trousers. There used to be something gentle about being a woman. Those women who are gentle now are totally useless.'

On the other hand, that shrewd pioneering gynaecologist, Helena Wright, before she died compared modern girls with women in the 1930s, who had blinked uncomprehendingly when asked what they got out of making love, and said 'the contrast is extraordinary. The girl's face shines brilliantly and she says, "Oh, Doctor, it's glorious."'

Above: No longer the picture of innocence, with the spread of sexually transmitted diseases, girls are targeted by condom manufacturers as much as boys.

CHAPTER SEVEN

Mirror, Mirror
Following Fashion

'PRIDE can be painful,' explained a retired mill worker, 'we go through all sorts of agony to look nice. I mean, when you pluck your eyebrows, which I did when I was younger, it really hurt. But when you see the finished results, it's worth it.' What makes millions of women do daft things in the name of fashion? Certainly sex has something to do with it but that takes women in different directions. Modesty pulls one way; sensuality pulls another. Women just as often have a clear idea of what they do *not* want to look like as of what they *do* want to look like. Fear of 'looking a tart' has, for instance, at different times this century, kept ankles from view, cleavages hidden, colours sombre and figures rigidly controlled by inhibiting underwear. On the other hand, the desire to be seductive has bared legs, revealed backs and even breasts have been visible through see-through blouses and cut-away tops. In every age clothes reflect the ideal man and woman. The high public morals of the Victorians were displayed in the men's dark suits, fit for offices and dark satanic mills, and the women's modest and matronly crinolines and bustles. The twentieth-century emancipation of women – out of the doll's house and into the bracing world of the street, office, and factory – has been mirrored in the greatest revolution in dress since people first started wearing clothes. For the first time, in the West at least, women have taken to wearing skirts above the ankle and even above the knee. As women have grown physically more active and sexually more liberated, their way of dressing has reflected their growing freedom, but only up to a point. For example, a fashionable woman at the beginning of the century had a plump, curvaceous figure. In the 1920s she pretended to have no breasts or waist and, taking on a tubular appearance, looked much like a young boy. In the 1930s, it was fashionable to look feminine again. In wartime lines were austere and rather masculine. In the 1950s a fashionable woman was almost as curvaceous as her Edwardian grandmother had been, but in the 1960s she was flat-chested and long-legged. Each decade had its own style, dictated by a variety of factors apart from sexual display.

In Edwardian days, it was essential to wear the 'right' clothes. In the middle classes, suitability was more important than elegance. The right clothes for the country were not the right clothes for the town. A high-necked dress was 'suitable' for a young girl; a low-cut one was not. Obvious

Above: This 1912 advertisement could be simply reversed to achieve the ideal slender shape for 1988.

make-up was associated with prostitutes. Pale, natural skins were admired. In the summer, ladies carried parasols to keep the sun off their faces. The upper classes had fashionable and pretty clothes, changing from day-wear into a tea-gown, usually a negligee made in a loose, voluminous style so the lady could rest from her corsets before changing back into them as part of her formal evening wear. The styles they adopted were dictated by famous fashion houses, mostly in Paris, and were frequently full of elaborate detail such as pleating, tucking, lace inserts and embroidery.

The lower orders had neither the time nor the money to worry much about clothes except that they should be hard-wearing. Hannah Greenwood, brought up in Lancashire, remembers that her mother, 'very beautiful, Spanish-looking, had a completely natural look with no make-up or decorations in her hair. She couldn't afford anything. She wore dark clothes to her ankles and a rough hessian apron over everything.' Despite heavy physical work as a washer-woman, Hannah's mother wore stays which Hannah used to tie for her before she dressed. These corsets were made of cotton, or satin for the rich, and were reinforced by whalebones with steel busks and laces which could be drawn as tightly as the wearer wished. Rich or poor, if she wanted to look a 'stunner', a woman nipped in her waist as much as possible to accentuate her bosom. Edwardian beauties were generously endowed, with a monolithic bosom suspended over their stays to the front and a generous bottom to the rear – rather more of an 's' shape than an hour glass. Whether stars from the stage or society beauties, the admired women of the time, such as Camille Clifford or Lily Elsie, or even Queen Alexandra herself, all dressed in much the same fashion.

Traditionally ladies had little physical activity – nothing more strenuous than archery or a game of croquet, but bicycling and tennis were becoming popular. Women began to wear knickerbockers or bloomers for cycling but somehow managed to play tennis in their everyday clothes, including their corsets.

The First World War brought visible change. Materials were plainer as people talked about economising. For working girls skirts went up, stays went out. The pre-war layered look of tunic over underskirt was adapted by replacing the underskirt with breeches or doing without it altogether. Trailing skirts were impossible in many jobs. Chauffeuring or bus conducting required agility which was difficult in a long dress, and women landworkers wore breeches because:

Dainty skirts and delicate blouses,
Aren't much use for pigs and cowses.

Women remember that they enjoyed the somewhat military appearance of the new fashion and the sense that, for the first time, class distinction was not immediately discernible from the clothes they wore. Many of them had enough money in their wage packets to be able to follow fashion for the first time. Brassieres and pull-on girdles took the place of corsets, to allow women easier movement. However, many women who had grown up with corsets never abandoned them. My own grandmother, who died in her nineties in 1977, wore them all through her life and felt so strange without them that she even put them on over her nightclothes if she had to leave her bedroom during the night.

It was not only their appearance that changed with the war. Women

Above: Camille Clifford. Edwardian beauties were more of an 's' shape than an hour glass.

Opposite: Women's clothes restricted outdoor activities to one or two genteel pastimes.
Right: The pre-war layered look of tunic over underskirt was adapted for warwork by replacing the underskirt with breeches.

began to feel different. They had new confidence and new horizons, and reacted violently against the lingering Edwardian values which surrounded them. They did not want to be sweet, gentle, brainless creatures who were good for nothing but looking decorative. They wanted to be free. The most common gesture was to cut off their hair. A bobbed or shingled hairdo saved hours of elaborate curling and coiffing. Daphne Elwin, newly married to an extremely rich husband, was one of the first to adopt the new fashion. 'I used to go to a hairdresser called "Douglas", where they would press my hair into waves by hand. I wanted to look like Gladys Cooper who had her hair done there. "Could you do my hair like Gladys Cooper?" I asked. I was very disappointed when they told me it was too fine.' Women often got their inspiration from well-known beauties from the screen. As well as Gladys Cooper, Clara Bow, the 'It' girl, was the biggest box office draw in the cinema and a renowned expert on the charleston. Society beauties also attracted attention and devotion. Lady Diana Cooper had her carriage stormed by enthusiastic women fans on her wedding day in 1919.

Hemlines went up, but cautiously, as for the first time in recorded history, women revealed their legs. For the first few years after the war they were still below the calf. The most daring fashion in 1920 was the backless dress. Young girls outmanoeuvred their disapproving mothers by leaving the house modestly covered only to pin their dresses back in the cloakroom before appearing at the dance. In 1924 Paris dictated that skirts should be above the calf, that waists should be on hips, while hips and bosoms vanished altogether. By 1926 hems were up to the knee and a woman's outfit weighed, on average, one tenth its Victorian equivalent.

Above: Clara Bow, the 'It' girl, was the biggest box office draw in the cinema. Film stars in the 1920s were popular trendsetters. Below: Punch, 1918.

First Officer (in spasm of jealousy). "WHO'S THE KNOCK-KNEED CHAP WITH YOUR SISTER, OLD MAN?"
Second Officer. "MY OTHER SISTER."

In her autobiographical account of those years, *We Danced all Night*, Barbara Cartland says:

I think the reason my generation bobbed and shingled their hair, flattened their bosoms and lowered their waists, was not that we wanted to be masculine, but that we didn't want to be emotional. War widows, many of them still wearing crepe and widows' weeds in the Victorian tradition, had full bosoms, full skirts and fluffed-out hair. To shingle was to cut loose from the maternal pattern; it was an anti-sentiment symbol, not an anti-feminine one.

They were not a cynical lot, she insists, they were just putting on a front to forget the war-time telegrams bringing news of a father killed in action, or a fiancé missing. They did not want anything which reminded them of the intolerable tension they had lived through during the war.

So they danced. They one-stepped, waltzed, tangoed and did the new charleston. They danced to the music of black American jazz groups. They danced at tea-time and they danced through the night. They danced almost everywhere. Audrey Withers, who later became editor of *Vogue*, remembers dancing at Covent Garden. 'They put a floor across the top of the stalls and we danced there and we also went to Olympia. That was so big that they had two dance bands and they were rather far apart and one danced right past both of them. They weren't always synchronised so you had to alter your steps as you went along so as to work in with the band in whose orbit you were at that particular time.'

It was a dizzy time for the Bright Young Things, rushing from dance to dance and dressing to dazzle. Their flimsy chiffon dresses suited the mood perfectly. Daphne Elwin had her clothes made at Chanel's. 'Everyone, not just rich people, had their clothes made for them. They all had little dressmakers who would make things that had the most perfect fit. So people really did look marvellous.' (A view reflecting her position in society – dressmakers were actually becoming more scarce in the 1920s.) Ironically Gabrielle 'Coco' Chanel's first successful designs were known as the 'poor look'. She has been called 'the inventor of twentieth-century woman', the creator of the simple, boyish look of the 1920s. In the post-war years, her preference for simple lines and plain cloth nudged fashion in a direction it wanted to go. The fabrics she chose, such as cotton, jersey and flannel, were a far cry from Edwardian opulence, but they were affordable and lent themselves to being copied for the mass market, bringing haute couture a little closer to the High Street. For her own clients she added elegant details, a silk lining here, an exquisite button there, or a perfectly made matching blouse. She turned the cardigan, first made for warmth on the battlefield, into a fashionable jacket.

Working in one of the famous fashion houses was many a young girl's dream. 'It was endlessly entertaining. Every day was full of glamour,' remembers Sheila Wetton who worked as a model at Molyneux. 'Women used to come in with their maids who'd say, "You don't want that, you haven't worn the other one yet," that sort of thing. And when it came to big occasions, like a coronation or a jubilee or a wedding or whatever, the maids would come bearing the jewels and possibly someone would come from Garrard's with the tiaras. It was better than any play.' Sheila had glamour not only by day but also by night, as Molyneux used to let her borrow anything she wanted to wear in her time off.

New Paris collections were eagerly awaited by the home dressmaker. The simpler lines meant that you no longer had to be very rich in order to be fashionable. Those who could not afford dressmakers' prices often ran up their own little numbers, buying pattern books such as Vogue's or Butterick's or Mabs Fashions. Women's magazines advertised their own 'special offer patterns'. 'I used to make all my own clothes,' remembers a Lancashire mill worker. 'I made a dress, I thought it had just come into fashion, with a low back and I were going to be such a toff with this low back. Well, when me Dad saw it, he said, "If you don't get some stuff in that back, every time you have it on, I'll put soot on your back." So that was the finish of that, I had to put a piece in it.'

There was also a boom in ready-made clothes. Although dressmakers had been dealing in them since the nineteenth century, off-the-peg dresses were not common in Britain until the 1920s. Improved machinery and simple styles enabled wholesalers to cut and copy fashionable outfits. Even the Paris couturiers recognised the importance of *prêt-à-porter* and by 1929 Chanel, Patou and Lelong had all opened small retail outlets for ready-made clothes.

Above: Sheila Wetton modelling a dress from Princess Marina's wedding trousseau.

In Rochdale, Hannah Greenwood also tried to keep up with the latest trends. 'They had this second-hand dress agency called Vine House and the lady used to keep size sixteens for me because I paid every week – it was a shilling a week – and she saved me the most marvellous clothes. So, although we were poor, I had some nice clothes. I never told anybody where I got them from. She bought off the theatricals, you know.'

Neither Hannah nor any of her friends could afford magazines. Hannah got all her ideas from the cinema and, like women through the ages, used fashion to realise fantasies of a better or, at any rate, different body. 'Unfortunately, I was well endowed on top and the fashion was for flat chests. My sister used to ask me where I'd put my bosoms. "I've shoved 'em under me arms and I've put a stocking round and pulled it," I said. I remember being a flapper, well, in as much as I could afford to be. I'd wear a dress with fringes on, cut high at the front and then low at the back, and maybe even a charleston cap – if the agency had one. Lots of girls smoked at this time and they had long cigarette holders and fancy boxes to carry their cigarettes in. But, because we were always short of money we didn't really participate fully with all the changes in fashion.'

None of the women we interviewed seemed to have cared very much what their boyfriends thought of their clothes. Usually they copied women

they, themselves, thought beautiful – the popular heroines of the stage and screen. They dressed to please themselves or impress their girlfriends. Remembering how much her boyfriend, later her husband, hated the dresses which were high at the front and low at the back, a woman explained, 'everybody had 'em, so he had to go along with it. They looked very nice, well I thought so, but he says, "I never liked you in that dress." Years after he told me that.'

Hannah Greenwood always tried to keep her hair fashionable which, with do-it-yourself perms, was a cheaper business than running a wardrobe. However, one day she won a pound at work. The mill ran a 'Diddle-'Em Club', a sort of lottery, and Hannah's ticket was picked out. She decided to blow the lot on a trip to a professional hairdresser. 'I always wanted to look like Betty Grable and I went to Lewis's in Manchester to have my hair made blonde. It was peroxide but, my God, it was red when they'd finished and it was burning all over. Somebody said, "Open that window and put her out." This is at Manchester, and I've got me head out o' t'window. I had a sore head weeks after, all because I wanted to look like Betty Grable.'

Another mill worker remembers that trips to the hairdresser were far too expensive. 'I used to marcel wave my hair at home.' Nor did she

Opposite: Underwear, 1930. Between the wars both waists and bosoms went out of fashion.
Right: Hannah Greenwood, longing to look like Betty Grable (far right), had a disastrous experience with early peroxide.

attempt to follow fashion, she 'even went out courting in my black clogs and thick stockings'.

Stockings were still woollen, lisle or artificial silk, unless you could afford real silk. Nylons came in just before the Second World War but were not generally available until after it. Synthetic fibres were being developed and had been trying to break into the fashion world for some time. As early as 1910 a non-iron material called Riplette had been on the market, but until Paris started using synthetic fibres in the late 1930s, they did not catch on.

Between the wars, make-up came out of the closet, though still frowned on by the older generation. A little powder was permissible. There were basically only three shades: dead white, yellow and almost brown. Although vamps on the screen rimmed their eyes with kohl, eye make-up was not generally worn. By the 1930s, Hannah Greenwood remembers that bright red lipstick was all the rage, with a little rouge on the cheeks and ear lobes. For sixpence, Woolworth's sold a lipstick called Tangee which looked orange but claimed to tone into a natural colour when applied.

Unlike their Edwardian mothers, modern girls were not afraid of the sun. Coco Chanel set a trend in cultivating a tan after she bought herself a house in the South of France and allowed her skin to darken. A healthy outdoor look was becoming a sign of affluence, suggesting sunbathing in the Riviera rather than potato picking in Essex. As sunbathing became more fashionable, beachware grew briefer, revealing legs, arms and backs, though hiding everything else. No longer constricted by clothing and fear

Left: Sunbathing became fashionable between the wars. Beachwear grew briefer, revealing legs, arms and backs but no more.

of the sun, women enjoyed sports as never before. As well as the established sports such as tennis and golf, crazes came and went. Pogo-sticks had women hopping about like kangaroos, roller-skating and ice-skating had them racing round the new rinks. The Women's League of Health and Beauty had them lying on the floor bicycling their legs in the air.

It is not clear what pulled fashion back to a less boyish look in the 1930s, whether a new generation reacted to the excessively stylised look of their mothers, or whether the Edwardian influence was not quite as dead as it appeared, or whether the fashion houses were casting around for new ideas to outbid each other's collections. For whatever reason, egged on by a plethora of new women's magazines, the 1930s woman was more feminine. She grew her hair, nipped in her waist and dropped her hemline. She was encouraged to make herself attractive to her husband and she did not go out to work. It looked suspiciously as if women were returning to an updated mock-tudor doll's house.

According to the couturier Hardy Amies, the Second World War interrupted a fashion trend. 'Just before the war, one was conscious that one's role was in bringing shape back to clothes and bringing bosoms back. The Hollywood ladies helped. We showed corsets to open our show in 1938. We felt that was coming, and of course it did come in 1947 with the New Look, after that rather flat plateau of fashion which was the war.'

The war certainly put the dampers on the fashion scene. Material was rationed and the Board of Trade brought out regulations for 'utility clothes' and rationed everyone to twenty clothes coupons, twice a year. A suit alone used up eighteen coupons. Clothes took on a functional, military

Right: In the 1930s fashion became more feminine again.

"I WISH YOU WEREN'T SO MODERN, MOTHER. IT'S TERRIBLY
OUT OF DATE."

look, with padded shoulders and straightish skirts, using as little cloth as possible. Sheila Wetton, still working for Edward Molyneux, remembers the restrictions placed on designers. 'He worked under enormous difficulties because he was supposedly designing things for America and just as he got it all going and we were doing the fittings and he'd be looking at the garment, then in came the "Gestapo", a girl called Maudie whose responsibility was the Board of Trade documents. Every day they'd send in amendments like "Now you can't have a three-inch hem, it can only be two inches." or "You mustn't have a pocket." Or "You can't have five buttons on there, you can only have three."'

Hats escaped rationing so girls concentrated on their heads, cultivating elaborate hairdos and inventive hats. Before the turban became fashionable, the government was anxious about the danger of long page-boy hairstyles on the factory floor. So they approached the women's magazines. Audrey Withers was then editor of *Vogue*. 'I remember them telling us they were horrified that girls were going into factories with hairstyles that were totally unsuitable and being too fashion-conscious to wear the caps that they were given and they got their hair caught in machines and some were literally scalped. So they said, "Can you persuade them that the chic thing would be to have your hair cut short?"' Audrey sat on a committee formed from the editors of a dozen magazines which was used by the government as part of the propaganda machine. 'They used to call us to the various ministries when they had something they wanted to put over – if they wanted women to do or not to do certain things such as join up,

Below: Not surprisingly, women were reluctant to adopt these government-approved hairstyles for warwork.

Women are winning the War — of Freedom

England has always been a "free country" but grandmother's mother would have been surprised at the spacious activities of girls in 1941. It was not "polite" when she was young to do a man's job—and it was not possible. Women were still largely restricted by natural disabilities. Tampax—sanitary protection worn internally—has changed all that. In doing so it has liberated women of today for the strenuous struggle for freedom; the task that allows no time for "off-days".

TAMPAX
Regd. Trade Mark
worn internally
PRICES 7d. 1/2 & 1/9
NEW FAMILY PACK 40 FOR 6/-
Sold by BOOTS, TIMOTHY WHITES & TAYLORS, and other chemists, departmental stores, drapers, WOOLWORTH'S, MARKS & SPENCER LTD and THE N.A.A.F.I.
For further information regarding Tampax please write to The Name, Tampax Ltd., Belvue Rd., Northolt, Middlesex.

or go into factories or to evacuate children or whatever it was they wanted. Of course, *Vogue* was a very minor thing, our circulation, but the mass circulation people had got enormous power and the ministries used to say, "they will listen to what you tell them when they won't read our pamphlets" which was absolutely true.'

The magazines ran useful advertising campaigns, such as one to persuade women to use Tampax instead of 'the old clumsy and uncomfortable methods'. Thanks to Tampax, women were 'winning the war of freedom'. The hope seemed to be that the more modern methods of sanitary protection would stop women taking time off work.

Wearing trousers, or slacks as they were called, became common, spreading from the workplace to become casual wear at home. Girls still liked to dress up to go out, however. Many remember the shortage of stockings and painting their legs instead. 'We'd use camomile lotion with gravy browning. Then we'd get a good friend to draw the pencil line down the back of our legs. I always remember when it was a hot day you'd have both legs covered in flies. They flocked to the gravy browning.'

The cardigan had captured the popular imagination in the First World War; in the Second, it was Field Marshal Montgomery's duffle coat which caught on and, probably to his dismay, became part of the uniform of protest – a reaction to the formality of fashion in the post-war years.

In 1947 Christian Dior's New Look turned the fashion world upside-down. To professionals, like Hardy Amies, it may have been possible to see it coming, but most people were caught by surprise. Joanne Brogden was

Right: The New Look. Many protested it was taking women back forty years.

at art school when Dior launched a new feminine shape with a tiny corseted waist, rounded bosom and hips and enormously full, petticoated skirts only twelve inches above the ground. 'It was the most exciting, wonderful, invigorating thing in one's life and I think in many people's lives, not just an imaginative and excitable teenager. I was determined to try and do something. I had seen fantastic illustrations of these extra-ordinary clothes with tremendous amounts of material in the skirts and wonderful sloping shoulders and tiny, tiny, minute little waists. Of course, everybody brought up in the war had a mannish, boyish sort of figure and it wasn't easy for people older than myself. However, what I did was to make the biggest skirt in the whole world, apart from a genuine Dior, out of blackout material.' Many women remember *Gone with the Wind*, one of the most popular films ever, left them longing to look like Vivien Leigh playing Scarlett O'Hara. The New Look was not only a welcome change from austerity, but also brought them nearer to looking like their idol.

As clothes and material were still rationed, the Board of Trade was not pleased by the new fashion. At *Vogue* Audrey Withers welcomed the contrast to austerity. 'What amused me, though, was realising how changes of fashion change your whole posture and your whole attitude and your movements. Suddenly I found myself having to pick my skirt up in two hands to go up the steps of a bus and I realised that I hadn't seen that gesture since I'd seen my mother before the First World War.' Outraged feminists wrote letters to the press, protesting that, once again, fashion was limiting women's freedom of movement and taking them back to the beginning of the century.

In the north, the Lancashire mill girls tried hard to keep up. Gwen Hughes thought the New Look was lovely. 'I had a navy blue coat, nipped in at the waist and ankle length with a very full skirt. With it I wore strap-round-the-ankle lizard-skin, wedge-heeled shoes and huge fur-backed gloves. Of course, I always wore a hat, that goes without saying. I can remember wearing flat hats. They were all the rage then.' Two sisters remember wearing the New Look. 'Our frocks would show a yard below our coat. We never could afford to buy a New Look coat.'

The lady-like figure launched by Dior dominated the 1950s. Women wanted to look glamorous and mature. At the start of the decade young people had no style of their own. They went straight from children's clothes into dressing as if they were thirty-five. Hairdressers remember that their clients came in for a weekly shampoo and set. 'You could just look at the client and know what day it was and what time it was. It was so rigid, like the hair was rigid too. The whole attitude was completely different.' Janet Reger, who reintroduced silky, sensual underwear after decades of stiff and dull functional corsetry, remembers that underclothes were also rigid at that time. 'Bras with huge bands of elastic everywhere and roll-ons. Everybody wore them whether they were fat or thin. It was the thing to wear. I'm not quite sure why. I think perhaps it gave a firmer outline.' At boarding school, girls were forced into tight roll-ons and the merest suggestion of movement or 'wobble' was greeted with dismay. Bottoms and breasts had to stay firmly in place. Anything else suggested 'tartiness'. Even art students like Joanne Brogden were expected to dress elegantly and have a pair of white gloves handy, in case they were whisked off to view a fashion show in London.

Cherry Marshall, a top model in the late 1940s and 1950s, felt she was always on parade. She was expected to be well-spoken, well-groomed, elegant and superior the whole time and, above all, never to sweat. She was the woman all others wanted to be like. In fact, she was looking after two small children and an unemployed husband in a 'pretty grotty Hampstead flat'. When *Woman's Own* wanted to photograph her at home, she panicked. The flat was sparsely furnished and damp with mushrooms. Fortunately, she had friendly neighbours living upstairs who suggested she was photographed in their flat. So surrounded by icons and statues of the Virgin Mary she was photographed polishing her neighbours' floor. 'Somebody rang me up and said, "I can tell you've never polished a floor in your life because you haven't got the polish in the lid."'

In many people's eyes, Fiona Campbell Walter was the most beautiful girl of the 1950s. She typified the well-bred model of the period. Her father was an admiral and she did a modelling course at Lucy Clayton's. 'We were supposed to be ladies. The only people in those days who bought couture clothes were the upper classes or people with money. It was the time of the coronation so everything was very regal. There were a few of us who had longer necks than the others and could look a bit snooty and haughty and, you know, we were only eighteen and full of the exuberance of youth. It was very constricting and constraining to be dominated by somebody else's attitude. We were really playing the role of wealthy, elderly women in ermines, in sort of Ascot clothes, in dignified ball gowns and so on which left no room for the young people we really were.'

But young people were beginning to rebel. Fiona single-handedly changed an absurd and outdated custom in one of the top London hotels. Dressed in an elegant Balenciaga black cocktail dress and a rose in her hair she went to collect a friend from the hotel. She was stopped from entering because she had a 'hat' on, a reference, apparently to the rose she wore at the top of her chignon. 'I said, "But this is actually just a cache-chignon and, anyway, I don't want to stay for dinner, I've just come to fetch somebody."' Unmoved, the Head Porter blocked her way, so eventually she asked for a message to be sent in to her friend and they left. The next day Fiona gave the story to the *Daily Express* who immediately called the hotel and were told that it was an old rule, dating from the eighteenth century, that women were not allowed in wearing hats. In those days, ladies arrived at hotels by private carriage and, therefore, did

Above: Fiona Campbell Walter typified the well-bred fifties' model but found playing the part very constricting.

Opposite: 1950s' underwear. Bosoms and waists were in fashion. Underwear was rigid to eliminate any sign of 'wobble'.

not wear hats. Any woman who did, was assumed to have walked in from the streets. The rule was dropped.

Despite her stunning looks, Fiona was quite large which was becoming unfashionable. 'I couldn't get into anything and most of the dresses were open at the back. Fortunately, the style of photography in those days was that you were totally immobile. You were pinned to your dress or pinned to the wall.' Leading couturiers such as Givenchy preferred waif-like figures to shapely ones and their clothes reflected this. Fiona thought he should be made to realise that he was catering for a very limited market and possibly bringing gloom to millions of well-endowed ladies who would never have such slender figures. So she bought a copy of *Playboy*, opened it at the centrefold and said, ' "Now you've got to take account that some ladies have boobs and this is what a lot of normal women look like. They have huge breasts." He looked as if he had been struck in the face with a wet fish and staggered back and said, "I don't believe you. Are there really women like that?" ' Thirty years later, fashion houses are still designing clothes for waifs.

A social revolution on the High Street brought women more choice of clothes than ever before. By the late 1950s Marks and Spencer operated a large network, with a store in most large towns and six million customers a week. They offered inexpensive but good quality dresses, practical but attractive underclothes and easy-to-iron blouses and shirts. At times they even had to withdraw popular lines which threatened to become a national uniform. However, they were not exciting clothes.

In art schools, fashion students were fed up with conformity. 'It would be very difficult for most people to understand now that it was not acceptable, even for a fashion student, to wear mascara or eye shadow,' Joanne Brogden recalls. 'Lipstick was fine, but very little else. It was considered "common" and "tarty".' Bursting with ideas which they had not been allowed to express as students, once they left college, they started opening their own small boutiques and creating their own styles. 'The beginning of the mini skirts era was extremely important because, before the name of Mary Quant was very well known, students from the fashion school at the Royal College were all round South Kensington in their mini skirts. The only thing that was not so good about it was that you could see stocking tops 'cos tights hadn't really come in as a cheap commodity.'

Many of the small boutiques failed, but others became successful and had an enormous impact on the fashion world. Foremost among these was Mary Quant's Bazaar. Initially, Mary intended to buy her own small collection but could not find anything she liked so she set to, designing her own simple shifts and pinafores. Her King's Road boutique became a focus for a new, young look. Girls stopped copying the timid fashions of their mothers, abandoned permanent waves for Vidal Sassoon's straight, dramatic short hair-cuts, whitened their faces and blackened their eyes.

Right: 1965 fashions. For the first time haute couture followed street fashion.

In London the fashion centre shifted from the West End to boutiques along the King's Road or near High Street Kensington. Mary Quant's clothes grew increasingly distinctive. She experimented with stripes and checks and spots and squares, turned evening materials, like satin and velvet, into daytime ones, used new fabrics like PVC and made 'fun' furs. Teenagers had money to spend and they wanted clothes that suited them.

Lucienne Phillips, who owns an exclusive dress shop in Knightsbridge, remembers that, for the first time in history, Paris fashion houses did not dictate fashion but followed it and adapted it. 'In 1964 I went to the second Courrèges show and we were all in for an absolute surprise. We'd never seen anything like it. The decor was very spare and we saw a collection which was really like outer space and girls wearing little bootees in sort of soft leather, flatter than flat. One had never seen that at the couture and for the first time ever Courrèges used music. We were just entranced and, of course, those skirts above the knee and all those tights in pearl grey, lettuce green, pearl pink. Any woman would have been delicious in them. What an experience! It was glorious to be there.'

Couturiers had recognised that in the 1960s fashion no longer belonged to an élite of rich or titled ladies. The affluent middle and working classes and the young were setting trends. Old class barriers were breaking down. 'Hairdressers were taken from being what were really – to be honest with you – servants to the public and were suddenly treated as people,' remembers Leonard, owner of the most fashionable London salon of the 1960s. 'We were invited to parties. If we went to the Duke of Bedford's to do his hair, you know, their hair, we were invited afterwards for dinner. We went to the American Embassy and were invited there afterwards. When Kennedy was in town with Lee Radziwill and Jackie, they said, "Do you want to stay?" I suppose it was the Kennedys that caused it because Americans accept people more and it just followed from there.'

Models were no longer expected to look well bred, nor were they any longer photographed pinned to the wall in set poses, but moving about, with their hair blowing freely. Lesley Hornby, an ungainly, working-class schoolgirl with an urchin look, was brought into Leonard's salon. 'Justin de Villeneuve said, "I've got this girl, she wants to be a model," and there was this kid, very skinny, a complete contrast to the other models, great tall leggy girls. We looked at her, and the hair was long and lanky, and I said, "Well, the best thing to do is just cut her hair off like a boy." And we did and took photographs; and Deirdre McSharry, who was then fashion editor of the *Daily Express*, was in the salon and saw the photographs and said she was the face of the year. She was launched and she took off like lightning.' She had as androgynous a look as the cropped flapper of the 1920s. Nicknamed Twiggy because of her skinny figure, she never looked back and a disgruntled generation of women were left feeling distinctly overweight.

Left: Twiggy: an overnight success story. In the fifties daughters wanted to look like their mothers. In the sixties mothers wanted to look like their daughters.

The explosion of new talent in the fashion world crossed class barriers: working-class photographers mingled with old Etonian photographers; dress designers, magazine owners, hairdressers, models, restaurateurs were the 'in' crowd and came from all walks of life. 'It was a time when people became liberated. It was smart to be seen with your hairdresser,' remembers Michael Rasser of Michaeljohn, the hairdresser's. 'The fashion business, "swinging London" – a term that *Time Magazine* coined – really happened and you couldn't believe the impact it had. I mean it made life so exciting. Until that point daughters wanted to look like their mums. After the sixties, mums wanted to look like their daughters. Skirts went up, everything, it was just sheer madness.'

In 1965 Jean Shrimpton, Britain's top model, scandalised the world by appearing at the Melbourne races carrying no gloves and in a dress several inches above her knees. But no matter how much it was criticised, the mini became regulation wear, at least for a few years, as the annual cry became, 'How much off this season?' and hems were turned up yet again.

Hardy Amies, dressing the Queen the following year, failed to persuade her to adopt the shorter fashion. 'We tried. We said, "Oh, ma'am, we must have it a bit shorter." But she would sit down and see what happened when she sat down and that was that; the crux of the matter. She was perfectly right. "I'll have it the length of the last ones," she would say or something, always immensely polite.'

Sheila Wetton, then fashion editor of *Vogue*, also preferred the more elegant fashions of the 1950s to the trendy look of the 1960s. 'Some of them were very out of proportion. I mean, OK, the skirts were short but then the hairdos were too big. I mean nobody got it properly together. I look back at some of my sittings and I think, God, how could anybody have ever published them.'

However much people thought the mini skirt had brought freedom and a chance for individuality, it often felt like a uniform. 'Hairdressers were the place where you went to catch up on all the fashion news,' remembers one woman. 'They'd get all the magazines and you could browse through them and get an idea of what was in and what was out.' 'Fashion was dictated by the girl next door,' remembers another. 'What she had, you had, and if she had a shorter skirt, you had a shorter skirt, and if she had a bell-bottom, crimplene, psychedelic trouser suit, you got one too. I was always checking up and saying, "well, I think I can do better than that". We had enormously heavy accessories. They were lime green or they were purple or they were orange. They were really revolting colours. We bought them in Leicester market and then we'd paint them for ourselves.'

Enterprising individuals, short on cash but not on ideas, started raiding second-hand clothes shops and creating a new, eclectic style of their own as Min Hogg spotted. 'When I was on *The Observer* we noticed that young people had started to get out the dressing-up-box and put on extraordinary things. Also, I think it was the beginning of all those funny clothes coming in from Afghanistan and the hippy trail, so that it became more and more fancy dress, the look. So we decided to record the fact because before fashion pages had always been what's in the shop, never a report of what's going on.'

David Sassoon, now a designer of clothes for the royal family, was 'very much part of the Swinging Sixties. I had an Afro hairdo – it's all gone now but at that particular time I had an enormous, wonderful head of hair. I remember having stencils on my face, flower chains round my neck, velvet trousers and ruffled shirts and, of course, the shoes! As I am not very tall, I got a tremendous kick out of wearing very, very high-heeled boots. It was the biggest boost to my morale.' David remembers that there was enormous overlap between the sexes. 'There was less discrimination between men's clothes and women's clothes. Unisex became very strong. You went to the same hairdresser, you wore the same shirts, the same trousers. There was a tremendous combination of fashion.'

Anything would do. Hippy and flower-power styles were adopted by young people to detach themselves from what they saw as the materialism and aggression of the late 1960s. Paris was designing denim and studded leather copies of working clothes. In complete contrast, Laura Ashley was making demure, old-fashioned, cotton print peasant dresses and in 1968 Saint Laurent startled everyone at his spring collection by introducing a transparent blouse with braless breasts clearly revealed beneath it. It was the final kiss of death to the rigid outline and the pointed, uplift bra. Girdles and roll-ons had been going out of fashion for some years as tights replaced stockings. At the same time feminists had begun to abandon their bras as they saw them as symbolic harnesses. In the 1970s, even girls who did not want to stop wearing bras bought soft ones to give them a 'braless look'.

During the 1970s many women reacted against dressing-up. They argued that they could not be truly liberated if they followed the dictates of the fashion world or dressed to please men. Unisex blue jeans provided a way of opting out of fashion altogether.

The most extreme reaction against conventional fashion was seen in punk dressing which was aggressively ugly and anti-establishment. Street fashion had already produced teddy boys and skinheads, but girls had been less influenced by these styles than they were by punk. Vivienne Westwood, who designed the first 'punk couture', says, 'we were encapsulating a cult. To me, street style is something with a content. Establishment clothes are just about the architecture of garments or re-working of what's gone before. Street has always got something to do with the support of people who are outside establishment approval.'

Another trend in the 1970s was to cultivate a healthier image. Make-up became more natural and an outdoor look replaced pale faces and dark eyes. Women became generally more health-conscious. A diet no longer implied starvation but a healthier approach to eating. Exercise was seen as the fastest route to glowing skin and a beautiful body. By the end of the 1970s aerobic classes and health clubs were popping up all over the country. Leonard altered his salon to cope with the new demand. His clients used to come in every week to have their hair cut and styled. 'Nowadays women come in, have their hair cut, washed, conditioned. They have facials. They can use a gym to exercise. They go through the whole treatment. They'll spend a day here but then we won't see them for maybe another six or seven weeks.'

Today women choose fashion to suit their lifestyle, whether it is punk or classical, Marks and Spencer or boutique, casual or severe. Every woman we interviewed said firmly that she dressed for herself, though most admitted they preferred to swim with the tide and keep abreast of the latest trends, choosing the ones that best suited them. Few were prepared to be positively uncomfortable to look fashionable. Most liked clothes that were easy and functional and hairstyles that did not take time.

'Women want to look more feminine,' explains the London hairdresser John Frieda. 'They've finally begun to realise that they're different from men. All that stupid competitiveness is over. Women now want to grow their hair longer. In the late fifties, women had a much softer look. They were more feminine and sophisticated. Then in the sixties, it was the

Below: Women today have a greater range and variety of fashion to choose from than ever before. Distinctions in dress style between the sexes are often blurred.

"young" look that was all the rage. Now we're in the eighties there's no specific look around. Women now have other priorities to worry about as well as the way they look. They're career women and mothers. Time is the most precious commodity these days.'

There is a consensus in the fashion world that British women dress badly compared with their American or European counterparts. Designers blame the upper classes who, they say, would rather spend money on their houses, children's school fees and their time in their gardens. Some say the British prefer everything to be understated, not wanting to look as if they have tried too hard. Perhaps the British have got their priorities right. Hardy Amies thinks that people too preoccupied with their clothes are 'cracking bores'. After all, as Janet Reger puts it, people really dress to fit in. 'If you know that everybody is going to turn up in trousers and a great big t-shirt, you tend to dress accordingly so you look part of what is going on.'

Women dream as much as ever about looking like somebody else. In that sense, little has changed but at least their favourites – the Princess of Wales, Madonna and Joan Collins – offer a range and variety of styles that would have been impossible for earlier generations of conforming women.

CHAPTER EIGHT

Breaking Free
The Road to Equality

W HEN we asked Britain's oldest surviving suffragette, Elizabeth Dean, whether she thought the vote had yet brought equality to women, there was not the slightest doubt in her mind. It had. 'Now a woman can get married or not as she likes, she doesn't mind. Nobody throws things at her, or sneers. It has allowed women to be themselves, to choose their own future, or their own present; to choose things for themselves and not to be tied up by tradition. They're free agents to act as they want and as they feel they really need to act, without people sneering or people talking. It's a marvellous feeling to feel free to do just what you want to do after being down so long.'

Over her lifetime, Elizabeth Dean has seen women gradually break free from their restrictive doll's house world. When she was born in 1885, women were expected to be obedient, selfless and retiring. They depended largely on the goodwill of their husbands or fathers and, no matter how miserable, they had little chance of escaping their authority. Their position of dependence was underpinned by laws, tying them to their husbands and their homes. Few spoke out in public about their position, for politics was men's business and a woman who was seen to interfere brought disgrace to her husband. Most accepted their lot uncomplainingly. Looking around her today, Elizabeth sees a different breed of women, free to develop in whatever direction they wish. In her view, they have come a long way.

On the other hand, there are those who argue that this is a rose-tinted view, that equality has come only for a lucky few and that until there are radical changes in the way we work and organise our families, the world will continue to be controlled by men to their own advantage and women will always be put in second place.

Throughout this century there have been women campaigning on behalf of their sex: spreading information on birth control, defining the need for family allowances, lobbying for the end of the marriage bar or for equal pay, protesting against violence and pornography and – the most unifying struggle of all – fighting for the right to vote. They have not always agreed about priorities or tactics but, as every milestone was passed, determined feminists pointed out that there was still much to be done and charted the next course, ensuring their cause never died through complacency.

The first peak of public activity came in the early years of this century when suffragettes split from the main suffragist movement and ran a militant campaign to give women a voice in the affairs of state through the parliamentary vote. The suffragists had sprung from the nineteenth-century movement for social reform. They were supported and given intellectual weight by John Stuart Mill, the radical reformer and philosopher and, as a Member of Parliament, Mill attempted to amend the 1867 Reform Bill to give women the vote. Although only eighty MPs supported him, the women involved in the first suffrage societies were cheered by the result and assumed victory was only a year or so away. None of them in their most pessimistic moments dreamed it would take another fifty-one years to persuade the House of Commons to change its mind. Millicent Fawcett was a young bride when she first heard Mill call for votes for women in the House of Commons, a doughty seventy-one-year-old widow when she heard MPs give the vote to women over thirty, and eighty-one when it was finally extended to all women.

Above: Millicent Fawcett was a young bride when Parliament first voted against giving women the vote, and an 81-year-old widow when the battle was finally won.

The early suffragists were a well-connected group of women who used their influence to try to persuade powerful men to take up their cause. Millicent came from a liberal-minded family, committed to the Women's Movement. Her sister, Elizabeth Garrett Anderson, became one of the first British women on the Medical Register. In 1897 Millicent brought the various suffrage societies together under the umbrella of the National Union of Women's Suffrage Societies. From this moment, the suffragists

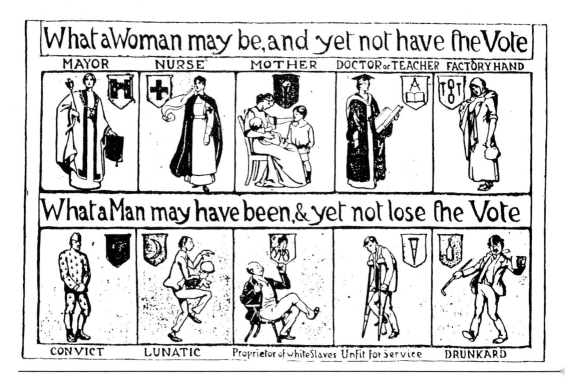

Above: Suffragette marches were both dignified and imaginative.

became a national movement, with Millicent Fawcett at the helm.

By this time, other campaigns and years of patient lobbying had already achieved some notable successes: women householders could vote in local elections, girls schools were springing up all over the country, universities were beginning to accept women undergraduates, married women were allowed to keep their inheritance and some professional barriers were tumbling as, for instance, a few women became doctors and accountants. However, progress was slow and women were as far away as ever from getting the vote.

The vote was seen as the most significant hurdle of all. Until women could vote, they were dependent on the whim of an entirely male parliament for action in any of their varied causes such as divorce reform, equal pay, prostitution, sweated labour, birth control and many other matters which concerned women. The suffrage campaign brought together a wide, and often ill assorted, collection of women who all hoped the vote would further their particular ends. There were Conservative women, Liberal women, Labour women, Catholic women, Anglican women, society hostesses, mill girls, the eugenic movement, the Co-operative Women's Guilds and many others.

It was at this stage that the suffragettes entered the fray. In 1903 Emmeline Pankhurst, a longstanding member of the suffragist group in Manchester, decided to break away and form a separate society. Mrs Pankhurst thought the suffrage campaign needed an injection of new blood and a change of tactics. She had grown impatient with the old-fashioned, respectable ways of the suffragists so, with her daughters Christabel and Sylvia, and some working-class sympathisers, she started the Women's Social and Political Union. This suffragette movement brought excitement, enthusiasm and, above all, publicity to the cause. Their tactics had as much in common with modern urban guerrillas' as with the temperate activities of their suffragist sisters and deeply shocked Edwardian society. Enraged by the prime minister, Sir Henry Campbell-Bannerman, who, while accepting the principle of suffrage, counselled them to exercise 'the virtue of patience' but 'go on pestering', they took him at his word and pestered. They burned letter boxes and buildings, hurled bricks through shop windows, heckled parliament and generally made a nuisance of themselves. At the same time the suffragists continued their quiet campaign of winning over MPs and public figures. The story of both suffragettes and suffragists is one of frustration and dashed hopes as the vote seemed often very near, only to be blocked time and again by opponents in parliament.

The more they were rejected, the angrier they became. As one elderly suffragette explained to us, 'by attacking property we were getting at men who believed that if you hurt a girl child you should get off but if you destroyed property you deserved a sentence'. The campaign became far more bitter as thousands of suffragettes were imprisoned for their crimes. Many went on hunger strike and suffered the agonies and indignities of forcible feeding.

Only a handful of women alive today remember being behind bars for their part in the suffrage campaign. Victoria Lidiard is one of the last of a tough breed. At ninety-six, she manages her roomy Brighton flat entirely on her own, her respectable neighbours little suspecting that in her youth this sprightly and pleasant retired optician did time in Holloway. Yet in 1912 Victoria was gaoled for two months for taking part in one of Emmeline Pankhurst's days of action. At a pre-arranged time, suffragettes smashed windows all over central London. Victoria's beat was Whitehall; her target the War Office. She looked as demure as possible, deliberately walking in step with a policeman to allay suspicion. When she suddenly threw a stone through one of the War Office windows, the policeman could not believe his eyes. 'He just looked at me. Meantime another policeman rushed up towards me and then an inspector on horseback came. So I was escorted to Bow Street, a policeman each side of me, clutching my arm, and one behind. Well, I had eight stones, but I'd only used one (unlike Mrs Pankhurst who was renowned for her inaccuracy, Victoria was a good shot) so on the way to the police station I dropped them one by one and to my amazement when I was taken down at Bow Street, this police-man that had followed put the seven stones on the table and said, "She dropped these on the way."' The case against her was complete.

Above: Victoria Lidiard, gaoled for throwing a stone at the War Office in 1912.

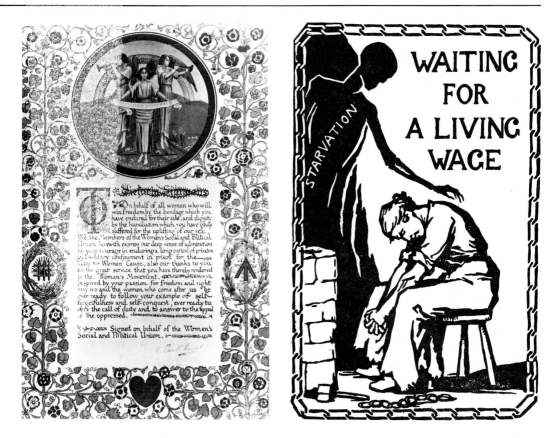

Above left: Victoria Lidiard's certificate of thanks, signed by Emmeline Pankhurst.

Above right: There was a strong working-class suffragette movement in the North West, fighting for better conditions and wages for women at work.

Victoria spent the next sixty days in Holloway but remembers little of her time there. It was a numbing experience. All she can say is that it was as if she had 'a nasty steel band' around her head. On her release she was awarded the suffragette brooch for bravery – the culmination of two years of personal protest.

The drive came from Victoria's mother who organised all her daughters into joining the suffragettes in 1910. Victoria cannot recall her mother ever having a good day's health. She had a child every thirteen months for around ten years but, though physically frail, she had an iron will and was a determined believer in women's rights. She and her daughters joined the suffragettes to fight not only for the vote but also for proper education for girls and for the end of the white slave trade. Living in Bristol, they heard stories about girls being kidnapped and whisked down to the docks to be shipped away to slavery overseas. They were convinced that this was yet another issue which would be ignored until women had the vote.

Elizabeth Dean joined the suffragettes in 1912 because she wanted to change the world. There was a strong working-class movement in the north-west where she lived, fighting for better conditions and wages for women in factories and mills. Elizabeth Dean was nearly 102 when we talked to her. Although she has poor eyesight and hearing and relies on a pacemaker and walking aid, she has a crystal clear memory. When she describes her Lancashire childhood, it is easy to understand why she had turned fighter.

'My mother died at thirty-eight. She left six of us. I was only six years old. She died with childbirth. There was a little boy younger than me. There was no information at all on birth control. If it happened, which it did very, very often in my younger days, that when a woman went into a hospital for confinement, and the doctors said if there was a recurrence of pregnancy the woman would die, that woman was sent out without any information as to how to avoid that. The law forbade them to give information on birth control.' As Elizabeth grew up she saw that poverty fell hardest on women. 'They was expected, wages being very, very low in those days, to make a pound go a marvellous long way. Oftener than not they found it didn't. Families too large, more than they could afford to keep, tempers rising and quite a lot of cruelty on the part of their husbands through frustration and irritation with conditions. Now if this got unbearable and the wife had the courage to summons her husband for cruelty, when she got that summons there was a time to wait before she had to appear in court. A lot of the injuries was fading, there was no women magistrates allowed, no women solicitors allowed. That woman stood in a court alone in a man's world and got man's sense of justice.' If she was lucky, she got her separation and a miserly, unenforceable allowance of 5/– a week for herself and her children. Some of the local women went blind after years of sewing in badly lit workshops to earn ten shillings a week to support their families. Elizabeth Dean was not 'born a rebel', she became one.

Most militants need a catalyst. For the suffragette leader, Emmeline Pankhurst, it came in middle age. 'When I began this militant campaign I was a Poor Law Guardian, and it was my duty to go through a workhouse infirmary, and I shall never forget seeing a little girl of thirteen lying on a bed playing with a doll. I was told she was on the eve of becoming a mother, and she was infected with a loathsome disease, and on the point of bringing, no doubt, a diseased child into the world. Was that not enough to make me a militant suffragette?'

However strong the provocation, Elizabeth Dean did not really approve of suffragettes using violence, especially when they put women out of work by bombing the Bolton cotton mills. She played her part by going to rallies in Alexandra Park where they were pelted with cabbages, oranges, eggs and other missiles, often hurled by unsympathetic women who 'liked hugging their chains'. Elizabeth's most militant moment came when she attacked a polling station, shouting 'votes for women' at the top of her voice, toppling the table with its neatly stacked electoral rolls to the surprise of the elderly tellers on duty.

Right: Emily Wilding Davidson's funeral. Supporters from all over the country formed an impressive cortège.

In the suffragettes' most heroic act, Emily Wilding Davidson threw herself under the king's horse at the Derby in 1913, shouting 'votes for women'. She died a few days later. She had been to prison eight times, on hunger strike seven times and been forcibly fed forty-nine times. People who initially had little sympathy with the suffragettes were growing to respect the sincerity of women prepared to sacrifice so much for their cause. Supporters came to her funeral from all over the country and suffragettes dressed in white formed an impressive cortège through London. But true to British form, some passers-by showed more sympathy with the dead animal and greeted the procession with shouts of 'the king's 'orse'.

Many opinion-makers were also openly hostile. Beatrice Webb, the great Socialist reformer, although a champion of women's education, was at first opposed to giving herself and her sex the vote. Leading politicians such as Winston Churchill and Herbert Asquith, prime minister from 1908 to 1916, were against women's suffrage. The press depicted suffragettes as ugly and mannish, strident and obsessive, despite the obvious femininity and good looks of the Pankhurst women and many other supporters. Critics dismissed them glibly as frustrated spinsters. Some even suggested the problem could be sorted out by shipping surplus women to the colonies to be married off.

In 1914 war broke out and put an end to suffragette activities more promptly than any solution dreamed up by their opponents. The movement lost impetus as its leaders went their separate ways. Christabel and her mother became superpatriots, vigorously supporting the war effort, while Sylvia Pankhurst sided with the pacifists. Millicent Fawcett and most of

SUFFRAGETTES
WHO HAVE NEVER
BEEN KISSED

*Left and below:
Suffragettes were
viciously lampooned in
the press.*

the suffragists, on the other hand, continued to lobby politicians while making themselves useful to the war effort, funding ambulances for women to drive in France and organising women's voluntary work.

The war shook many traditional views about women but perhaps none so much as the notion that they were not responsible enough to be given the vote. The enormous burden they carried through the war, doing men's work, running their homes alone, feeding the nation, won over most of their opponents. The whole question of the vote was re-examined towards the end of the war. Although property qualifications had been lowered, they had not been abolished and only 58 per cent of the adult male population was entitled to vote. There was a general feeling that sailors and soldiers who had valiantly served their country should all be given the vote. Millicent Fawcett and the suffragists drove home their advantage. Surely women, too, had played their part in the war effort? Was this not the right time to reward them? Even such old enemies as the former prime minister, Herbert Asquith, admitted that 'some of my friends may think that ... my eyes, which for many years on this matter have been clouded by fallacies and sealed by illusions, at last have been opened to the truth'.

On 6 February 1918 British women were finally given the vote. But only six million out of a total of thirteen million were actually enfranchised. Women over thirty who were householders, or the wives of men house-holders, or had been to university, were allowed to vote and by the end of the year women could also stand for parliament. However, millions of women were still denied the vote. No one was sure what effect women voting would have: would they always vote Labour or Liberal? Would they only vote for other women? The fear of a 'petticoat government' proved farfetched but at the time, with women far outnumbering men in the population, a gradual approach was preferred.

Within two years of the war ending, women seemed to have gained enormous ground. They could vote, stand for parliament, be lawyers, jurors and magistrates. The suffragette wing of the Women's Movement

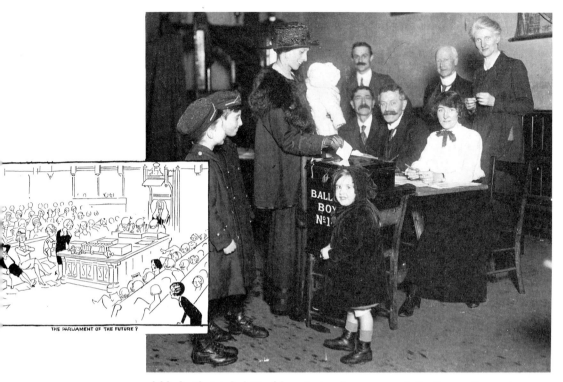

THE PARLIAMENT OF THE FUTURE ?

folded. Christabel Pankhurst stood unsuccessfully for parliament, representing the Women's Party in Smethwick. The Women's Party never took off. Christabel ended her days in the United States, preaching about Christ's Second Coming. Sylvia Pankhurst threw herself into pacifism, internationalism and Labour politics. Victoria Lidiard married and joined her husband in training to be an optician. For over forty years they ran separate businesses, doing a day in each other's practice once a week for patients who preferred an optician of the opposite sex. Victoria lost touch with her suffragette friends but never lost her feminist zeal. In her nineties she is a vocal campaigner for the ordination of women. 'You know,' she explains, 'the ordination of women is meeting with the same opposition as the women who fought for the vote. There is no physical, intellectual, moral, theological or spiritual reason why women shouldn't be ordained.'

Elizabeth Dean continued to campaign for a variety of reforms through the Labour Party and also joined the Co-operative Women's Guild, which since 1883 had been fighting for women and families. Once women had the vote, there was much talk of the need to educate them to use it responsibly. The Guild held weekly talks and ran social evenings, giving many women their first opportunity to go to meetings where they would not be afraid to speak up. New organisations, like the Townswomen's Guilds and the National Association of Women Citizens, monitored council meetings and lobbied councillors on any decisions which affected women.

They also taught women about citizenship. It sounds a strangely old-fashioned word today, but at the time women were not used to taking an interest in anything outside their family circle. They had not been expected to know how local or central government worked, for that was men's business.

After 1918 feminists' energy and time reverted to the causes which had made them want the vote in the first place. As the excitement died down, women shed their suffragette image and tried to look like responsible citizens, working for numerous special interest groups, each lobbying for separate causes; for equal pay, birth control, family allowances, against the marriage bar, to extend the vote to all women. It was difficult to decide what the priority should be. Some suffragists continued as a cohesive force, renaming themselves the National Union of Societies for Equal Citizenship. In 1919 Eleanor Rathbone took over from Millicent Fawcett to become its president. During the next few years she shifted their priorities away from the old feminists' fight for equality with men towards working-class mothers and their problems. As she explained to her members in 1925, 'At last we have done with the boring business of measuring everything that women want, or that is offered them, by men's standards, to see if it is exactly up to sample. At last we can stop looking at all our problems through men's eyes and discussing them in men's phraseology. We can demand what we want for women, not because it is what men have got but because it is what women need to fulfil the potentialities of their own natures and to adjust themselves to the circumstances of their own lives.'

Eleanor Rathbone and the new feminists were concerned with women's singular needs as wives and mothers – for birth control and family allow-ances, for instance – while the old feminists wanted women to broaden their horizons and look beyond the home. Anxious that women should be able to compete on equal terms, the old feminists did not want to make much of their special difficulties. One point which feminists were agreed upon was the need to extend the vote to all women. It was obviously absurd that women under thirty were not allowed to vote when men could vote at twenty-one.

For the first time in history, women sat in the House of Commons. (They had to wait until 1958 to sit in the House of Lords.) The first women MPs were unlikely heirs to the suffragist movement. Constance Markiewicz, a Sinn Fein hardliner, had been the first woman to be elected but never actually took up her seat as she was opposed to Irish representation at Westminster. Then Nancy Astor got in at a by-election created by her husband's accession to the House of Lords. Not only was she an American but she had never campaigned for women's rights in her life. All the same, she was cheered by veteran suffragettes on her way to Westminster and presented with a suffragette brooch. She had hardly taken her seat before she was bombarded with letters from women all over the country and she

Above: November 1919. Nancy Astor becomes the first woman to take her seat at Westminster.

soon became a tough fighter on their behalf. A keen inter-war feminist remembers that 'many of us admired Lady Astor because of her stand in parliament. She was always very smartly dressed. It was very amusing, she always wore a hat. She didn't sit in parliament without her hat on and she stood up against the men. She didn't mince her words. When she realised there were no toilets or anything for females she stood up in the House and said so.'

The second woman MP, Margaret Wintringham, also replaced her husband. When the Liberal MP for Louth died in 1921 his widow was persuaded to fight the by-election. Then the National Liberal MP for Berwick-on-Tweed was banned from standing for parliament for seven years because of a technical offence committed by his agent, so his wife, Mabel Philipson, agreed to keep the seat warm for him. It began to look suspiciously as if women had won the right to stand for parliament simply to be substitutes for their husbands!

By 1923 their numbers were boosted by women who had fought constituencies in their own right, including three unmarried Labour MPs. A husband in politics was not, after all, a prerequisite for the new women MPs. They fell into two categories: they were either married with enough money to employ domestic help to look after their husbands, homes and children, or they were unmarried. There were eight of them, all working from a small room without a chair apiece. The lavatory involved a quarter of a mile walk and there was no women's bathroom despite frequent all-night sittings of the House.

It is often thought the small band of women MPs had little impact in the House of Commons. Yet sixteen Acts protecting women's interests were passed in the early 1920s, ranging from improved maternity services, pensions for widows, divorce on equal grounds to men, better maintenance terms for illegitimate children and separated wives, equal guardianship rights to children to an extraordinarily progressive Act, protecting women who could prove they were still suffering from the effects of childbirth from being accused of the crime of murder if they killed their newborn baby. These changes in the law may well have had more to do with politicians' awareness of women's voting power than the lady MPs. Certainly, Millicent Fawcett, a veteran spectator of the ways of the House of Commons, noticed a remarkable improvement in MPs' attitudes towards women after six million of them had the right to vote.

In 1929 Margaret Bondfield became the first woman privy councillor and cabinet minister. She had begun her career as a shop assistant at fourteen and made her way through the Trades Union movement to be Secretary of the National Federation of Women Workers and then Member of Parliament for Northampton. She describes the moment with touching awe in her autobiography.

Then in turn each went forward to kneel on King George V's footstool, holding

Above: Margaret Bondfield, the first woman in the Cabinet.

out the right arm. The King placed his hand upon it to be kissed. When my turn came, he broke the customary silence to say, 'I am pleased to be the one to whom has come the opportunity to receive the first woman Privy Councillor.' His smile as he spoke was cordial and sincere. My colleagues and I were very pleased that H.M. noted the precedent so amiably.

Only a tiny minority of women were making their mark in public life. In the constituencies women were having a hard time being taken at all seriously in the political parties, let alone being selected for any seats, either for local or central government. 'Men were the masters and women were left to do the soppy things,' explained Winnie Smith, a Labour Party activist who started a local women's section. 'Then I found out the women's section were just expected to do the drying-up, the washing-up, run the raffles, but they were never involved in the politics at all and they were never given the freedom so to do. They could never come out canvassing and they were not allowed to speak. Men looked down upon them as idiots or just women for the kitchen only.'

In 1928 women over twenty-one were finally given the vote. It had taken ten years for the political parties to accept that women were individuals with political allegiances as diverse as men's. There seemed no danger they would dramatically boost the power of one particular party, nor that there would ever be a Women's Party. A few voices still complained that young women were too frivolous and irresponsible to be allowed to vote and talked disparagingly about giving the vote to 'flappers'. (Before the First World War, a 'flapper' was a young girl who tied her hair back in a pigtail with a 'flapper bow' but the word had come to imply

WHO RULES THE WORLD?

Above: The cover of this Labour Party magazine reflects the attitude of all the political parties towards women between the wars.

Left: May 1929. Flappers go off to vote. For the first time, all women can vote in the general election.

flightiness as well as youth, possibly because the word came from the German slang for prostitute.)

The new law enabled Mary Stott in 1929 to cast her vote for the first time in a general election. 'I was one of the important people because I had just got on the register in time. I wasn't a leftover from 1918. I got up very, very early, soon after the polling station opened. In fact it's possible, isn't it, that I might even have been the first flapper to vote and I put on a bright red dress because I was voting Labour and I stalked off with my head high.' From that day to this, Mary Stott has never been able to vote for a woman because there has never been one standing in any constituency where she has lived.

The 1930s was not a good time for feminists. The romantic struggle for the vote had been replaced by dreary committee work. Many of the suffragist leaders had died. The movement was fragmented and younger women were not clear into which cause they should throw their energies. A growing consensus kept women tied to the home and rising poverty and international affairs tended to eclipse other issues. As the Depression deepened, women who might otherwise have been fighting for equal rights had their time cut out helping poorer women feed and clothe their children. Others were diverted to work for peace. In the years immediately before the Second World War, the Co-operative Women's Guild, for example, ran a passionate campaign warning against the perils of war and introduced the white poppy as a symbol of peace. Pacifism has always attracted women, from the peace campaigners of the First World War to the Greenham Common movement in the 1980s.

The Second World War brought women the opportunity to assert themselves once more. Joining the armed services, firewatching, driving ambulances, taking over men's jobs or looking after their families alone – often in as much danger from German bombers as the men overseas – gave them a strong sense of their own worth. Many of the social reforms feminists had been fighting for, such as family allowances and state health care for women, were incorporated in the 1942 Beveridge Plan and all the political parties were committed to its principles. Feminist attention shifted to the many remaining inequalities between men and women.

Huge numbers of women were working alongside men who were being paid a much higher rate for the job. Not surprisingly, equal pay became an issue once more. The government resisted, but women kept up pressure all through the war. In 1944 a royal commission was set up to look into equal pay. 'It was a delaying tactic, as royal commissions almost always have been,' cynically points out a civil servant, who had been called to give evidence. 'Forget not that there had been a number of other committees on equal pay over the years and nobody had ever given them equal pay.' The majority on the commission once again rejected equal pay but at least the issue was kept alive. Another optimistic attempt at feminist legislation failed during the war when enthusiasts tried to get all discrimination made illegal through the Equal Citizenship (Blanket) Bill. It did not even get as far as being introduced in the House of Commons.

However, the war years saw gathering enthusiasm for women's issues. The Women's Freedom League (originally a splinter group from Mrs Pankhurst's suffragettes) gained a new lease of life. When younger women like Amy Bush joined, the League was still run by old suffragettes proudly sporting their prison badges. Amy was involved in two successful campaigns: giving women the right to keep their nationality on marriage to a foreigner and winning the right to the same compensation for war injuries as men. If a woman was injured in a bombing raid, she was only entitled to four-fifths of the compensation of the man next door hit by the same bomb. The assumption was that disablement mattered less for a woman than for a man! Four petitions were presented to parliament urging that compensation was made the same for men and women. Amy Bush, collecting signatures, discovered to her surprise and despair that few women would sign without first asking their husbands' permission. Amy joined a deputation to the deputy prime minister, Clement Attlee. 'We went to the House of Commons and Mr Attlee was sitting there – he doodled an awful lot – but we made our point and I felt we weren't getting anywhere until the General Secretary of the Firemen's Union stood up and he said, "It's absolutely disgusting. We men are furious, the women are there sitting in the ambulances in the centre, the bombs dropping, and if anything happens to them we know very well that their compensation will only be four-fifths of ours and yet they're as much in the danger zone as we are." And Attlee looked up at this.' It appeared to be the turning point. Having established they had the men's support for their claim, they were given equal compensation.

When Amy was not busy with the League's work, she helped the National Association of Women Citizens. It was quite common for women like Amy, who had grown up in a world which frowned on married women working, to devote themselves entirely to the women's cause. They could start off the week with a meeting on Monday morning and keep going day and night with various committees and other voluntary work until the weekend. The National Association of Women Citizens was still anxious to get women into local government and Amy was encouraged to have a go. First she was warned by the more experienced MP, Edith Summerskill, to sort out her domestic affairs. 'I don't care what they say,' she told Amy, 'some men who really believe in equality may help in the domestic situation, but very few of them do and you will have an added burden, you will have the home to run, the children to look after and also your work on the council or in parliament, so get that settled.'

There was a short-lived campaign to encourage more women to stand for parliament, run by Women for Westminster, forerunner to the present

Above: Barbara Castle. In 1945 Blackburn Labour women threatened to stop making tea for the men unless they included a woman on their shortlist for their new MP. Barbara was chosen and won.

Right: Feminism was out of fashion in the 1950s. What mattered was family life.

300 Group, which trained women to speak in public and to familiarise themselves with political affairs. In 1945, a record number of women MPs reached Westminster, but after nearly thirty years, that was still disappointingly few. Barbara Castle was one of only twenty-four women in the House of Commons. Barbara had been brought up in a socialist household where the women were treated as equals and she had been active in the Labour Party for several years and a local councillor in London. 'I remember I was longing to get into the House of Commons from the word go and during the war I remember mentioning it to one of my male colleagues and he said "Well, of course, Barbara, I think you'd make a very good MP but unfortunately women won't vote for women," and that was their great alibi for years.' In fact, Barbara owed her own success to the Blackburn Labour women's section who threatened to stop making tea for the men if there was not a woman on the short list. As Barbara had just made a well-acclaimed speech at the Party Conference they invited her to put her name forward. 'That gave me my chance. The big difficulty for women is to get a chance in the first place. If they can only get a start, then they're on their own and can hold their own.'

Generally, women at this time were not pushing to get into Westminster. In the post-war years, most thought their contribution lay as mothers and housewives, rebuilding family life. Although in 1955 women teachers and women in the professional arm of the civil service finally won their long battle for equal pay, the women's movement went quiet in the 1950s. As Sheila Rowbotham, who was to become a leading feminist historian, remembers, feminists were not presented in an attractive way. 'From dim

" *This is what comes of marrying a career woman.* "

childhood memories I had a stereotype of emancipated women: frightening people in tweed suits and horn-rimmed glasses with stern buns at the back of their heads.... Feminism seemed the very antithesis of the freedom I connected with getting away from home and school.'

A new generation was growing up, unclear what they stood for, other than general dissatisfaction with their parents' way of life. Sally Alexander, with Sheila Rowbotham one of the pioneers of the new British women's movement, disagreed with her elders' views on almost everything. She had many angry confrontations with her parents and school teachers over issues such as hanging, homosexuality, and pacifism. War films were all the rage and Sally was horrified by the destruction she saw on the screen. It distanced her even further from her family. 'How could they not have been pacifists,' she wondered. All the people she admired were rebels, but they were all men. She looked in vain for women role models. She identified with Marlon Brando, with James Dean – with angry young *men*. 'Indeed even women were described after Osborne as angry young men. Iris Murdoch and Doris Lessing were described as "angry young men". I did identify with all those kind of tough, idealistic, aggressive young rebels. I think that was not just the self-confidence of the young but of the first generation to have felt that the world did owe them a living. We were the Welfare State children.' Many of them had received an excellent education at grammar school; a third of graduates were women but once they left university they found themselves in a man's world, where men were breadwinners and women were dependent wives. Educated women who did not wish to immerse themselves in domesticity were uncertain of the way forward.

Into the void came the intellectual gurus with a feminist analysis of what was wrong. First Simone de Beauvoir with *The Second Sex*. An actor, frustrated by the limited roles for women in the theatre, remembers reading it and finding it amazing. 'It said a lot of the things I had hidden at the back of my mind. It clarified things, I just had this notion there was something wrong somewhere.' In 1963 Betty Friedan's *The Feminine Mystique* and later Germaine Greer's *The Female Eunuch* had the same kind of impact. Sheila Jeffreys, who was to become one of the more controversial thinkers of the women's liberation movement and the architect of revolutionary feminism, was converted to feminism by *The Female Eunuch* and Kate Millett's *Sexual Politics*. Until she read them, she had been a fairly typical product of the swinging sixties, a bright student, with long blonde hair and a string of lovers. 'The two books together, both the personal and the political, really were convincing to me and I realised what I'd been doing to myself and I suddenly started to hear everything differently. I was listening to every programme on the radio and I was feeling all the insults that were being directed at women in everything I was hearing, reading, seeing. It was like a sort of complete new light on the world. In fact I became very suspicious of the men I knew. I was so aware now that in the whole of the culture women were regarded as inferior. I knew that I was one of those women. That meant the men I knew were probably seeing me in that way, which was a shock to me and a shock to my pride.'

Feminist books were eagerly embraced. They crystallised unformed ideas that were springing up all over the country and gave a voice to swelling frustration in an affluent and highly political decade. The 1960s was a time of excitement and optimism. Sally Alexander radiates enthusiasm when she thinks back on it. 'The relative affluence gave young people a sense of possibility that things could be changed. You weren't having to think all the time, "If I don't pass my exams, will I ever get a job?" Unemployment was a memory of the thirties. It wasn't like it is for young people now. So I think it just gave you the space to think about what you might want to change.' In those days you could drop in and out of work, travel to distant countries, throw yourself into the civil rights movement. Interest on campus focused on liberation movements: blacks in America and South Africa, Che Guevara in Bolivia and the Vietnamese War. British women deny that the women's liberation movement spread from America. 'It coincided,' says Rosalind Delmar, 'but it was indigenous. People were asking the same questions at the same time. It was as much to do with radical politics. I think that at least the part of the women's liberation movement that I knew came out of the aspirations and the disappointments of women who had felt that they'd worked hard, gone for an education and discovered that their horizons were extremely limited.' Rosalind, herself, was at a university where there were thirty-six men tutors and no women. Awarded distinction for her research, she was then taken aside and told not to apply for a job as 'ladies don't do very well here'. Excluded from the mainstream of academia, the women's movement in Britain threw up its own writers, thinkers and historians. The 1960s feminists were not prosperous, middle-aged ladies but young intellectuals. There were no Pankhursts or Fawcetts. Leaders were eschewed.

Mary Stott calls the 1960s 'the do-it-yourself decade' with British groups being born to a large extent by women contacting each other through *The Guardian*'s women's page, which Mary edited. The National Housewives' Register, Pre-School Playgroups Association and the National Association for the Welfare of Children in Hospital began in this way. Graduate housewives had the time and energy for grassroots campaigning.

By 1969 many British towns had women's groups. Some of them catapulted into being after headline-hitting events such as the Ford women's strike in 1968, which looked as if it might be the beginning of a new era of women using their industrial power to better their position. Others just evolved as women found fellow feeling with each other. The Peckham Rye Group started when two young mothers, Jan Williams and Hazel Twort, met at the local One O'Clock Club where their small children played. There they found other mothers as fed up as they were with housework and with husbands who never rolled up their sleeves and did the washing-up or found boiling an egg too difficult. They shared a common sense of frustration with domestic matters and talked of breaking free to do something other than housework. 'You felt lovely, you know, suddenly there was somebody else understanding and you weren't the only one and you weren't going mad. You weren't this peculiar sort of person who couldn't cope with this sort of life.' The day-time mothers' club inspired them to set up weekly evening meetings when, free of children, they tried to discuss their dissatisfactions objectively. Up and down the country similar groups sprang up. Nothing was formalised. No one was in the chair or taking minutes. As one woman recalls, 'We were very conscious of feeling sisterhood. It sounds a bit soft, I suppose, but because we went through our lives as girls looking for a man and a family, we were competing all the time against other women and suddenly we found we all had the same feelings. We all had the same fears. We all felt the same oppression and if we were going to change it we had to do it together.' The more they questioned the status quo, the more they pinpointed areas of underprivilege they had not previously recognised. Women who had felt isolated could now share their problems. Should they go out to work? What kind of childcare should they arrange? Why did they feel shy of speaking in public? Were they frigid? As their hidden worries surfaced, they were spurred into political action. The moment had come to mobilise the disparate elements into a national movement.

Left: Men minding the crèche at the first national meeting of the Women's Liberation Movement, 1970.

The first national meeting of the growing movement came in February 1970 at Ruskin College, Oxford. Sally Alexander, one of the organisers, explained how it came about. 'For the previous few years there had been a huge gathering of historians at Ruskin and, in one of the breaks during the discussion in 1969, a group of women had got together and decided that the next history conference at Ruskin should be a women's history conference. So Sheila Rowbotham who is a feminist historian, a very wonderful and distinguished feminist historian, went to the front of the hall and asked for papers on women's history. Whereupon the whole audience burst into laughter which made us feel very startled. But there were people from all over the country there and they came forward and gave their names and said that they were interested in a national women's conference. So that was one way that we contacted people and then, you know, the grapevine.' In Peckham Jan and Hazel heard about Ruskin and prepared a paper on housework. Others came to speak on child psychology, women's history, women's work, the debates ranged widely. Someone invoked the spirit of the suffragettes and said they, too, should be prepared to go to prison again for their beliefs. A passion, which had been dormant for sixty years, came alive.

'We wanted to change everything, absolutely everything,' remembers Sally Alexander. 'Every cultural value with which we'd been brought up, we wanted to change. We thought we could change the world and not just the relationships between women and men, but everything that flowed from that – the way we brought up our children, the kinds of people that

Right: The style may be a little different but feminist marchers in the 1970s had much in common with suffragette marchers sixty years earlier.

we would raise. That moment of complete optimism was quite shortlived, but that's what we wanted.' Their sweeping demands, such as for twenty-four hour nurseries and abortion on demand, made them appear politically naive, but the movement had a witty and original approach. Their marches and meetings attracted publicity, often hostile, but like the suffragettes before them, the new feminists made sure they were often in the news. They, too, were depicted as unattractive man-haters. The label which stuck was 'bra burners'. The bra-burning myth originated in America when feminists protested against the Atlanta City beauty contest. Shouting that such contests degraded women, they symbolically dumped bras and girdles in a 'freedom trash bucket'. Press photos were taken and imaginative reporters added flames. A legend was born.

Some of the older feminists thought they should establish contact with the new movement. Kathleen Halpin has been involved with the women's movement for over fifty years through the Fawcett Society. (With various name changes, the Society stretches right back to the early struggles for the vote in the nineteenth century and has continued its fight for legislative change ever since.) When members of the Fawcett Society approached the younger women, they 'soon discovered, after trying to co-operate, that there really wasn't any basic ground on which we could work together. It was worse than the suffragettes and the suffragists because they had a completely different view. They wanted to change society without knowing what they were going to put in its place.' The suffragettes and suffragists had fought against specific and clear injustice, such as depriving women of the vote. It was hard for the older feminists to understand that the new feminists were looking beyond equality. In talking of liberation, they were trying to get rid of the massive inferiority complex from which they believed most women suffered.

The older women were confused by the new movement's obsession with fairy stories being sexist or history being biased and many felt alienated when feminists attacked language and hit out with what seemed weird and unnecessary nitpicking, inventing words which seemed strange then but now roll off the tongue. At the time there was no vocabulary to describe what women were on about. They had to invent the jargon to explain their analysis. Identifying with the national liberation movements in the 1960s, they borrowed some of their vocabulary, using such words as male 'chauvinist', women's 'liberation'. 'Equality wasn't what women wanted in the Women's Liberation Movement at all,' explains Sally Alexander. 'I mean, equality seemed a very narrow, limited, levelling sort of demand. Whereas liberation seemed to open up possibilities of an entirely new and different relationship between the sexes.' The new Women's Liberation Movement understood that their needs were often different from men's and they confronted that fact squarely.

Special interest groups mushroomed: Women in Industry, Women in

SEXISM IN ENGLISH
LANGUAGE TEACHING

Medicine, Women in Libraries, Women and Manual Trades, Women in Publishing, Women in Media and many others. They attacked the inequalities in their own areas. Why, for example, were women thought unsuitable to read the news? Why were women in television usually stuck as researchers, while men were producers? Why were there so few women managers in industry? During the 1970s these groups ran campaigns which were largely successful. Women publishers set up Virago to give women a voice in the publishing world, re-issuing books by women writers which were out of print, publishing new books by women writers and books about women's issues. They did so well that other publishers started their own women's units. Women newsreaders became increasingly common. More attention was paid to giving girls the same opportunities at schools as boys. Second-chance education expanded. Universities began to offer courses in women's studies. At work and at home, women projected a tougher image.

In Manchester Angela Cooper and Luchia Fitzgerald threw themselves into the Movement. They went to conferences, performed in their own Northern Women's Liberation Rock Band, composing songs like 'Equal Pay Blues' and 'Male Chauvinist Oink'. Luchia had left her native Ireland at fourteen and worked in the dying cotton mills in the 1960s, but pay and conditions were so bad that she left to become a bus conductor in Salford. She and the other women conductors earned less than the men but made up the difference by fiddling the fares – rough justice in their eyes. Angela joined the Movement while she was a student at Manchester Polytechnic. In her own words she was a 'freaky rebel, into swearing, drugs, drinking and sex. We were chicks and they were guys and you were cool if you wore bell-bottom trousers.' To begin with Angela and Luchia's Manchester group met in rooms above pubs but they were jeered at by the regular customers. 'There go those bra-burning libbers,' so they looked for their own place. 'We needed a base because there were so many groups by this time, and also we wanted a point of contact with women who weren't in the groups and part of the organisation already. So we thought by opening a centre, by offering a service, if you like, in terms of infor-mation, advice, free pregnancy testing, contraception referral, that sort of thing, we would have a point of contact with women who may not have heard of our ideas or may not share them.' One thing led to another and before long they had a phone line and unofficial crisis centre for rape victims and battered wives. They had never imagined how many women would turn to them for help. With nowhere else to go, they squatted in an empty house and turned it into a refuge which eventually became semi-official with a grant from the local authority. Similar shelters in other parts of the country banded together to form the Women's Aid Federation which successfully lobbied parliament and led to legislation in 1976 to help women who were beaten up by their own husbands.

Women's liberation began to sink into the nation's consciousness. Many were sympathetic to the general message of the Movement even if they found some of their specific demands extreme. Sally Shaw, a local councillor in Manchester, initially felt irritated by the new feminists on the council, but she soon came round to their way of thinking. Until they arrived, she and the other women had always adapted to the council traditions and felt proud to be treated as honorary men. 'It had never occurred to us to challenge the fact that these meetings started at inconvenient times. These younger women were really shaking the whole foundations of our view of ourselves. I think that although we'd appeared to be emancipated, we'd still not got right down to the roots of it. We were still working in a male-dominated system for men and we were just brushing away any feeling that we had legitimate demands to make. We had to work within their system – and some of us were very successful – but it was a male system.'

The law was changing too, although often as much due to the efforts of established pressure groups, like the Fawcett Society, as to the new movement. After 1970, equal pay was brought in. From 1975, sex discrimination was banned in education, job recruitment and advertising and

© Posy Simmonds 1987

the Equal Opportunities Commission was set up to see that the new Act was observed. Legislation entitled women to have their jobs kept open for them if they stopped working temporarily to have a baby. Throughout the 1970s the number of working mothers increased. Although few women reached top management, an increasing number occupied the middle ground.

As the Movement achieved a degree of success, divisions surfaced. According to Sally Alexander, it was increasingly difficult 'to think of the Women's Liberation Movement as an entity. There were also quite severe political differences within the movement which made it more difficult to go on thinking of ourselves as a unified whole.'

Although the first annual conference of the Movement had included men, it was later decided to exclude them altogether to give women more space to work out their own demands. But by cutting off men it became tempting to exaggerate their place in the world and the easiness of their lives compared with women's. As Sally Alexander put it, 'Women live with men and they work with men and they have babies that are men. I feel critical of men but I also enjoy men and like men and want to have relationships with them and want to change the world with men.' In some sections of the Movement, this was treacherous talk.

In 1977 Sheila Jeffreys spoke at the national conference on 'the need for revolutionary feminism against the liberal takeover of the Women's Liberation Movement'. The revolutionary idea was that women should separate themselves from men. She argued that men were the enemy, asserting their power over women through sex, physical strength and the threat of violence. 'What we were trying to explain was the crucial role of violence and sexuality in the social control of women; and when you look at the whole structure and the way that men's violence affects women in every aspect of their lives, it becomes huge. Think of sexual harassment at work, of being afraid to walk out on the street, what happens to you on the tube of an evening and so on. When you actually look at the whole texture it explains such a lot about women's lives.' Men abused women sexually and their pornography degraded women. Sheila called for a 'feminist revolution, not small tinkerings with the system, not small changes in sex roles, not just trying to make men clean the toilet but actually really changing the system, pulling the plug out from male power over women'.

Many women who had originally looked to the Women's Movement for sympathy, felt under attack. The rhetoric of the revolutionary feminists was extreme: marriage was hell and sex was political. They regarded heterosexual women, married or not, as, in a sense, collaborators for sleeping with the enemy. These ideas were unacceptable to liberal-minded women like Rosalind Delmar. 'For example "all men are rapists" which is not something that I think. Then together with this tremendous illiberalism.

There was great demand for retributive punishment which I could not find acceptable.' Besides it is over-simple to blame men entirely for the way things are. Female biology determined women's role until the medical breakthroughs this century brought more choice. Today, few women see themselves only as victims with no control over their own fate.

The arguments grew more acrimonious and after 1978 there were no more national conferences. Luchia Fitzgerald believes that for some women the umbrella organisation had outgrown its usefulness. 'There was that element to it. The movement had served a lot of women, mainly the middle-class women who are now in strategic positions in the media and places like that, and a lot of working-class women were left standing there, you know, hands on hips, wanting to know where do we go from here?'

Perhaps the answer is that it is time to re-assess. There have been rapid changes during the 1970s and 1980s. Thanks to the Women's Movement, attitudes are different: the language is less patronising; women are tolerated – if not always welcomed – in places previously forbidden to them. Political parties, banks, industry now take women seriously and so do women themselves. They have become more assertive and confident. It is easy to see why an old suffragette like Elizabeth Dean feels proud of women today.

Yet it is still true that rich men have the best of all worlds and poor women the worst, and that poverty is increasingly a woman's problem. Some of the benefits women depend on, such as family allowances, have come under attack in recent years. One in eight families is looked after by women alone (compared with one in two hundred by men alone). Many women cannot take jobs as they have to look after elderly relatives. Women's schooling and domestic circumstances leave them with lower earning power than men and more limited job opportunities. Even women in high-powered jobs are held back by family responsibilities. There are few women at the top in industry or any of the professions and remarkably few in parliament. Despite the example of a woman prime minister and the best endeavours of the 300 Group to fill half the House of Commons with women, only six per cent of MPs are women.

The battle is far from over. Although the Women's Movement has lost momentum and split into various special interest groups, this is precisely what it did in the years after the vote was won. The dilemma then was whether women should be fighting for a fair field and no favour or for just treatment which recognised sexual differences. That argument still goes on today but modern women are not content merely to be allowed to fit into the male order as honorary men. They are learning that the path to equality lies in facing up to the differences between men and women and making their own special demands when they need to. Emancipation is not a once and for all achievement, but has to be re-examined and fought for – in each succeeding generation.

Bibliography

Among the many books about women or written by women over the last hundred years, I have found the following particularly useful.

ADAM, R. *A woman's place 1910–1975* Chatto & Windus, 1975.
BEAUMAN, N. *A very great profession: the woman's novel 1914–1939* Virago, 1983.
BEDDOE, D. *Discovering women's history: a practical manual* Pandora, 1983.
BLACK, C. *Married women's work* Virago, new edn., 1983.
BLACK, J. and GARLAND, M. *A history of fashion* Orbis, 2nd edn., 1980.
BRAYBON, G. *Women workers in the First World War* Croom Helm, 1981.
BRITTAIN, V. *Lady into woman: a history of women from Victoria to Elizabeth II* Dakers, 1983.
COOTE, A. and CAMPBELL, B. *Sweet freedom: the struggle for women's liberation* Blackwell, rev. edn., 1987.
DAVIDOFF, L. *The best circles: society, etiquette and the Season* Cresset, new edn., 1986.
DAVIDSON, C. *A woman's work is never done: history of housework in the British Isles, 1650–1950* Chatto, 1986.
DAVIES, M.L. *Life as we have known it* Virago, 1977.
DAVIES, M.L. *Maternity: letters from working women* Virago, 1978.

DORNER, J. *Fashion in the twenties and thirties* Allan, 1973.
DYHOUSE, C. *Girls growing up in late Victorian and Edwardian England* Routledge, 1981.
FORSTER, M. *Significant sisters: grassroots of active feminism, 1839–1939* Secker & Warburg, 1984; Penguin, 1986.
FRIEDAN, B. *The feminine mystique* Penguin, 1982.
FRIEDAN, B. *The second stage* Sphere, 1983.
GAVRON, H. *The captive wife: conflict of housebound mothers* Routledge, 1983.
GROVE, V. *The compleat woman: can she have it all?* Chatto, 1981.
HARDYMENT, C. *Dream babies: child care from Locke to Spock* Cape, 1983.
HARDYMENT, C. *From mangle to microwave: mechanization of the household* Polity Press, 1988.
HOLTBY, W. *Women, and a changing civilisation* John Lane, 1934.
JEPHCOTT, A.P. *Girls growing up* Faber, 1942.
JEPHCOTT, A.P. *Rising twenty* Faber, 1948.
JOHN, A.V. *By the sweat of their brow: women workers at Victorian coal mines* C.U.P., 1984.
KEENAN, B. *The women we wanted to look like* Macmillan, 1977.

KENNER, C. *No time for women: exploring women's health in the 1930s and today* Pandora, 1985.
LEWIS, J. *Labour and love: women's experience of home and family, 1850–1940* Blackwell, 1986.
LEWIS, J. *The politics of motherhood: child and maternal welfare in England, 1900–1939* Croom Helm, 1980.
LEWIS, J. *Women in England, 1870–1950* Wheatsheaf, 1984.
LIDDIARD, M. *The mothercraft manual* Churchill, 12th edn., 1954.
LIDDINGTON, J. and NORRIS, J. *One hand tied behind us: rise of the women's suffrage movement* Virago, 1978.
McBRIDE, T. *The domestic revolution: the modernization of household service in England and France, 1820–1920* Croom Helm, 1976.
MITCHELL, J. *Women: the longest revolution: essays on feminism, literature and psychoanalysis* Virago, 1984.
OAKLEY, A. *From here to maternity: becoming a mother* Penguin, 1981.
OAKLEY, A. *Housewife* Penguin, 1976.
OAKLEY, A. *Subject women* Martin Robertson, 1981; Fontana, new edn., 1985.

OAKLEY, A. and MITCHELL, J. *The rights and wrongs of women* Penguin, 1976.
RAIKES, E. *Dorothea Beale of Cheltenham* Constable, 1908.
REEVES, M. *Round about a pound a week* Virago, 1979.
RICE, M.S. *Working-class wives* Virago, 1981.
ROBERTS, E. *A woman's place: an oral history of working-class women, 1890–1940* Blackwell, new edn., 1986.
ROWBOTHAM, S. *Hidden from history* Pluto, 3rd rev. edn., 1977.
SHARPE, S. *Double identity: lives of working mothers* Penguin, 1984.

SHARPE, S. *Just like a girl: how girls learn to be women* Penguin, 1981.
SPENDER, D. *There's always been a women's movement in the twentieth century* Pandora, 1983.
STEEDMAN, C. *The tidy house: little girls writing* Virago, 1983.
STRACHEY, R. *The cause: a short history of the women's movement in Great Britain* Virago, new edn., 1978.
SUMMERFIELD, P. *Woman workers in the Second World War* Croom Helm, 1986.
SUMMERFIELD, P. and BRAYBON, G. *Out of the cage* Pandora, 1987.
VALLANCE, E. *Woman in the house: a study of women members of Parliament* Athlone, 1979; new edn., 1982.
WEEKS, J. *Sex, politics and society: the regulation of sexuality since 1800* (Themes in British social history) Longman, 1981.
WHITE, C. *Women's magazines, 1693–1968* M. Joseph, 1970.
WILSON, E. *Adorned in dreams: fashion and modernity* Virago, 1985.
WRIGHT, A. E. *The unexpurgated case against woman suffrage* Constable, 1913.

AUTOBIOGRAPHIES & BIOGRAPHIES

BLOOM, U. *Sixty years of home* Hurst and Blackett, 1960.
BONDFIELD, M. *A life's work* Hutchinson, 1949.
BOURNE, A. *A doctor's creed: The memoirs of a gynaecologist* Gollancz, 1962.
BRITTAIN, V. *Testament of friendship* Virago, 1980.
BRITTAIN, V. *Testament of youth: an autobiographical study of the years 1900–25* Virago, 1978.
CARTLAND, B. *We danced all night* Hutchinson, 1970.
CHEW, A. *The life and writings of a working woman* Virago, 1982.
DAYUS, K. *Her people: memories of an Edwardian childhood* Virago, 1982.

HALL, E. *Canary girls and stockpots* Luton: Workers' Educational Association, 1977.
HALL, R. *Marie Stopes: a biography* Deutsch, 1978; Virago, 1978.
INGHAM, M. *Now we are thirty: women of the breakthrough generation* Methuen, 1981.
MITCHELL, H. *The hard way up: The autobiography of Hannah Mitchell, suffragette and rebel* Virago, new edn., 1977.
MITCHINSON, N. *All change here: girlhood and marriage* Bodley Head, 1975.
ROBINSON, J. *The life and times of Francie Nichol of South Shields* Allen and Unwin, 1975.

SCANNELL, D. *Mother knew best: an East End childhood* Firecrest, new edn., 1978.
STOCKS, M. *Eleanor Rathbone: a biography* Gollancz, 1949.
STOCKS, M. *My commonplace book* Davies, 1970.
STOTT, M. *Before I go* Virago, 1985.
STOTT, M. *Forgettings no excuse* Faber, 1973.
VERNON, B. *Ellen Wilkinson: a biography* Croom Helm, new edn., 1982.
WILLMOTT, P. *A green girl* P. Owen, 1983.

Picture Credits

Pages 16 *top* Beamish Photo Library; 16 *bottom* Mrs Button; 19 Imperial War Museum; 21 Beamish Photo Library; 22 BBC Hulton Picture Library; 24, 25 Margaret Wheeler; 27 Smythe/Centre for Cartoon & Caricature, Canterbury; 28 *Red Star Weekly*; 31 Ray/*Punch*; 34 International Wages for Housework Campaign; 35 Legal & General Building Society; 36 Posy Simmonds; 40 *Strand Magazine*; 42, 43 Cheltenham Ladies' College; 44 *top* Catherine Colley; 44 *bottom* Sybil Canadine; 45 Girl Guides; 46, 48 Cheltenham Ladies' College; 50 Dorothy Marshall; 51 BBC Hulton Picture Library; 52 Cheltenham Ladies' College; 54 BBC Hulton Picture Library; 55 *bottom* Angela Holdsworth; 57 Ladybird Books; 58 Michael Heath/*Punch*; 60 The Ashton Family; 61 BBC Hulton Picture Library; 62 Jo Harvatt; 63 Salvation Army Archives and Research Centre; 67 With the approval of the Keeper of Records of Scotland; 68 Violet Pattison; 70 *bottom*, 71 Daisy Noakes; 72, 73 St Catherine's House, Register of Births, Deaths and Marriages; 76 Popperfoto; 77 Sterling Winthrop Group Records Office; 79 Vicky/Centre for Cartoon & Caricature, Canterbury; 80 Barnaby's Picture Library; 81 Viv

Quillin; 82 Bella Keyzer; 85 Monitor Syndication; 87 BBC Hulton Picture Library; 88 *The Wife's Handbook*; 89, 90, 91 BBC Hulton Picture Library; 92 Hilda Bates; 93 Beatrice Sandys; 95 BBC Hulton Picture Library; 96, 97 Mary Evans Picture Library; 98, 100 BBC Hulton Picture Library; 101 Beamish Photo Library; 102 W. J. Rendell Ltd; 103 Albert/*Punch*; 105 The Mansell Collection; 109 Dolly Scannell; 111 BBC Hulton Picture Library; 112 Salvation Army Archives and Research Centre; 113 London Borough of Camden Local History Library; 114 North Islington Welfare Centre; 115 Illustrated London News Picture Library; 117 *The Mothercraft Manual*; 120 Popperfoto; 121, 124 BBC Hulton Picture Library; 125 from *Baby & Child Care* by Dr Benjamin Spock, published by Bodley Head; 126 BBC Hulton Picture Library; 127 Sally Fraser; 128 Leon Morris; 129 Liz McCann; 130 Posy Simmonds; 131 Topham; 135 Beamish Photo Library; 136 *top* Imperial War Museum; 136 *bottom* Irene Angell; 137 Daisy Noakes; 138 Imperial War Museum; 139 Winifred Routledge; 140, 143 BBC Hulton Picture Library; 144 Patricia Elton; 145 BBC Hulton Picture Library; 146 Kathleen Atwell; 148 Popperfoto; 149

BBC Hulton Picture Library; 152 *left* Brenda Mayo; 152 *right* Rex Features Ltd; 153 Associated Newspapers; 154 *top* Sheila Jeffreys; 154 *bottom* Family Planning Association; 155 *True*; 158 Mates Healthcare Ltd; 159 The Mansell Collection; 160 BBC Hulton Picture Library; 161 *bottom* Imperial War Museum; 162 *top* BBC Hulton Picture Library; 162 *bottom* Arthur Ferrier/*Punch*; 164 *top* The *Sketch*; 165 *left* Hannah Greenwood; 165 *right* Kobal Collection; 166 BBC Hulton Picture Library; 167 O. L. D. Ghilchip/*Punch*; 168 Keystone; 169 *bottom* Popperfoto; 171 Fiona Campbell-Walter; 173 Keystone; 174 BBC Hulton Picture Library; 177 Sally & Richard Greenhill; 180 *top* Mary Evans Picture Library; 181 BBC Hulton Picture Library; 182, 183 *left* Victoria Lidiard; 183 *right* Mary Evans/The Fawcett Library; 185 BBC Hulton Picture Library; 186 The Fawcett Library; 187 *left* Low/Mail Newspapers Plc; 187 *right*, 188, 189 BBC Hulton Picture Library; 190 *top* The Labour Party; 190 *bottom*, 193 *top* BBC Hulton Picture Library; 193 *bottom Punch*; 196, 197 Sally Fraser; 198 Mary Evans/The Fawcett Library; 200 Posy Simmonds.

Index